PLACES FOR HAPPINESS

PLACES FOR HAPPINESS

Community, Self, and Performance in the Philippines

William Peterson

University of Hawai'i Press
Honolulu

Paperback edition 2018

Printed in the United States of America

23 22 21 20 19 18 6 5 4 3 2 1

Library of Congress Cataloging-in-Publication Data

Peterson, William, author.
Places for happiness : community, self, and performance in the Philippines / William Peterson.
pages cm
Includes bibliographical references and index.
ISBN 978-0-8248-5163-7 (cloth : alk. paper)
1. Street theatre—Social aspects—Philippines. 2. Street theatre—Political aspects—Philippines. 3. Folk festivals—Philippines. 4. Happiness—Philippines. I. Title.
PN2960.P6P48 2016
792.09599—dc23

2015029146

ISBN 978-0-8248-7520-6 (pbk.)

University of Hawaiʻi Press books are printed on acid-free paper and meet the guidelines for permanence and durability of the Council on Library Resources.

Composition by Westchester Publishing Services

To my parents, Rozanne and Bill,
my first and finest teachers

Contents

Acknowledgments

The first time I saw dance "from" the Philippines was when I accompanied my Filipino American boyfriend Doug Maligro on a road trip to Sacramento in 1981 with a troupe of cultural dancers performing some of the same dances I would encounter a generation later in the Philippines. Because Doug, like many dancing men living in San Francisco in the early 1980s, lived a short life, I want to start by acknowledging all of those who came before this time and who made the field I explore in this book so rich and complex. My point of entry into community-based performance in the Philippines was through Nic Tiongson and Doreen Fernandez, both of whom came to the National University of Singapore in 1992 sharing their monumental achievement, the multivolume *CCP Encyclopedia of Philippine Art.* In subsequent trips to the Philippines, both were exceedingly generous with their time, and Doreen, who moonlighted as a restaurant critic, always pointed me toward the best spots in Quezon City for food. My friend Francis Tanglao Aguas helped secure my first research gig at Ateneo de Manila University, which opened the doors to productive future relationships with Ricky Abad and Father Luis David at Ateneo, as well as another period of residence there. At the University of the Philippines (Diliman), Professor Belen Calignacion twice supported productive research attachments in the Department of Speech Communication and Theatre Arts that provided me with a base for my research during longer periods in the Philippines. I have learned much from former students at both universities, particularly MeLê Yamomo and Sir Anril Pineda-Tiatco, both of whom have made the transition from student to outstanding scholar in the time I have been privileged to have known them. Also generous with their time and knowledge on the ground in the Philippines have been Mae Paner, Marian Pastor Roces, Eli Obligacion, Danny Mandia, as well as my festival friends and celebrants, notably Peter Magturo, Merlin Espeso, and the Motus and Dela Cruz families of Kalibo. I thank the ever mobile David Schwartz for his wit, humor, and intellectual challenges, and especially my dear friend Milton Tan, who introduced me to Marinduque in 2006 and shared his loving family with me. Completing the circuit of extraordinary souls I have been blessed to have known in the Philippines is John

Joseph “Magic” Manahan Christie, whose extraordinarily vibrant but all-too-short life reminds me on a daily basis of the need to be fully present for every moment of our lives.

This book has been supported by numerous fellowships and research attachments outside the Philippines, including a Visiting Senior Research Fellowship in the Cultural Studies Cluster at the National University of Singapore's (NUS) Asia Research Institute, guided by the playful intelligence of Professor Chua Beng Huat; a stint as visiting professor in the East-West Center at the University of Hawai‘i; a fellowship at the International Institute for Asian Studies at the University of Leiden; a visiting professorship in Theatre Studies/Theaterwetenschap at the University of Amsterdam; and an Isaac Manasseh Meyer Fellowship in the Faculty of Arts and Social Sciences at NUS.

This research was initially supported by travel grants and a sabbatical from the Faculty of Arts at California State University, San Bernardino, and then from 2006 to 2014 by travel grants and two periods of study leave while employed as a senior lecturer in the Centre for Theatre and Performance at Monash University. My colleagues there all contributed in important ways to the framing of this research, and I would especially like to thank Maryrose Casey, Stuart Grant, Julian Millie, Margaret Kartomi, and David Hannan for helping to expand my intellectual horizons while I was at Monash. Also many thanks to the following PhD students I have had the honor of supervising while at Monash and whose work was frequently in productive conversation with my own: Reagan Maiquez, Tharanga Dandeniya, Marlenny Deenerwan, Alamgir Hossain, Nithya Nagarajan, Indika Ferdinando, and Arjun Raina. Finally, I would like to acknowledge my new home, the School of Humanities and Creative Arts at Flinders University, which generously offered me teaching relief and a soft landing pad in Adelaide in the last half of 2014, enabling me to complete the revisions and final edits as this book moved toward publication.

I would also like to acknowledge the journals in which aspects of this research have been developed and published over the past decade, notably *Asian Theatre Journal,* under the sensible, sound, efficient editorship of Kathy Foley, *Theatre Journal, Australasian Drama Studies Journal, About Performance, Budhi: A Journal of Ideas and Culture,* and *Harvard Asia Quarterly.* I am grateful for the detailed, thoughtful feedback from my external readers at the University of Hawai‘i Press whose input has made this a much better book than it would have been. Finally, I would like to thank Pamela Kelley, my editor at the University of Hawai‘i Press, for the care, attention, and support she has given this project as it developed into a book that possesses a shape and a clarity that it would not have had without her guidance.

Introduction

"It's More Fun in the Philippines"

"It's more fun in the Philippines!" So proclaimed the Department of Tourism in 2012 with its new slogan in an effort to rebrand the country, replacing the earlier "Wow Philippines!" and the ill-fated *Pilipinas, Kay Ganda!* (The Philippines, How Beautiful!).[1] The promise of fun builds on the expectations and the stereotypes of the Philippines as a country full of fun-loving happy people. Internally, this promise of "more fun" provoked much debate and more than a bit of derision, with pronouncements such as "Graft is more fun in the Philippines" or "Poverty is more fun in the Philippines" circulating online in public and private postings. Public intellectuals, like Conrado de Quiros, who writes for the investigative daily, the *Inquirer,* preferred the earlier slogan, with its promise that the country held untold and unexpected richness that would evoke wonder and a sense of discovery, provoking an extended, "Wow!" (de Quiros 2012). For some of us who move back and forth between the Philippines and other countries, however, "wow" felt as if it were responding to negative expectations, suggesting that the Philippines will not be nearly as bad as you might expect it to be. With its grinding poverty, famous corruption, warlord crony capitalism, and crumbling infrastructure, to convince the outside world that the Philippines rates a "wow!" was always going to be a hard sell. Fun, on the other hand, is a natural. The stereotype of the friendly Filipino is widely circulated internationally, and although the slogan may well provoke a cringe from an educated, middle-class domestic audience or those with a social conscience who cannot imagine how the oppressed can be having much fun, it suggests a country that a generic tourist from anywhere might want to visit. Who, after all, does not want to have fun? And given a choice, wouldn't one want to vacation in a country where the promise of "more fun" would seem a supportable claim, one backed up by the traveler's bible, the *Lonely Planet,* which opines, "despite the poverty that afflicts much of the nation, the Filipinos themselves are among the most ebullient and easygoing people anywhere" (Lonely Planet 2012).

The connection between "fun," performance, and human happiness in a Filipino context hit home on a Philippine Airlines Fiesta Class flight from my home in Melbourne to Manila in 2009, when, in the minutes prior to leaving the gate,

I heard children playing in the seats ahead of me. Looking up, I saw two children improvising an energetic, two-character shadow play with their hands onto the screen along the bulkhead, backlit by an overhead projector displaying the message, "Thank you for flying Philippine Airlines." Those of us sitting near the screen broke up with laughter, which encouraged the children to become increasingly animated with their hand puppetry. A man in the seat behind me uttered with a tinge of pride, "Only in the Philippines," as if by being inside the thin metal cocoon of the airplane while on the Melbourne airport tarmac, we were already transported to another land, where public and private space, where the individual and the collective are experienced differently than they are in individualistic Australia. Anyone who has spent significant periods of time in the Philippines has heard the phrase "only in the Philippines" used in response to everything from the extrajudicial killings that cast a shadow over the election season to excessive and joyous street dancing at festival time. But in this instance I felt that my fellow passenger was referring to this sense of uninhibited fun through performance, one that captivated the attention of those in the adjacent seats, and for a brief moment before the flight crew interrupted with emergency instructions brought us together as a community of viewers taking pleasure from an improvised performance. Fun was its own reason for being, and from that we took pleasure that contributed to our individual and collective happiness. Indeed, the flight was already "more fun," even though we were not yet in the Philippines!

How an individual Filipino's need for happiness is met through involvement in localized performance practices that link them to a community and that in turn provide a shared, foundational identity for both the individual and community are the twinned, connected core concerns of this book. The ways in which these socially and culturally embedded performance practices are distinctively local in expression, and as a collectivity, distinctively Filipino are equally important. Thus this book will seek to identify frames that shape and contain the individual, that locate them in time and place, and in the specifics of a local culture and local imaginary, while inquiring into what defines and activates the collective and in turn how what is local expands its expressive home by engaging in a dialogue with regional, national, and even diasporic Filipino imaginaries. Throughout, the inquiry will start and often return to the ways in which community-based performance in its expression responds to and fulfills basic human needs. By bringing forth the internal, phenomenological, and embodied aspects of a range of community-based performance practices that contribute to human happiness, what is inside the body will be plotted out through the coordinates of culture. While I seek out what participation in an event means and what it feels like to experience, in the chapters that follow I also offer a framework that moves through cultural coordinates that variously interweave individual experience with the collective. Ultimately this book seeks out "places" for happiness that are not merely physical and cultural locations but are also resident inside the human organism.

Happiness, Ritual, Celebration, and Performance

Though happiness as a subject of philosophical inquiry has a long history going back to Plato and Aristotle, who linked it to virtue and actions,[2] it was famously the U.S. Declaration of Independence that enshrined "the pursuit of happiness" as an inalienable right, one that could be fostered by good governance. Yet only in the past few decades have governments around the world increasingly taken stock of the metrics measuring happiness and considered the types of interventions that might increase the happiness of their citizenry. This contemporary interest in happiness largely dates from 1999, when Bhutan's young monarch, Jigme Khesar Namgyel Wangchuck, set out to measure "gross national happiness" as a matter of official government policy (Witcher 2010), offering a counter to the indices of gross national product and gross domestic product, which have driven government policies in the developed and developing world for over half a century. Bhutan's formula identifies seventy-two indicators of happiness, which are further divided into categories such as physical well-being, education, and good governance (Chi Viet Giang 2010). Speaking at a United Nations summit on Millennium Development Goals (MDGs) in 2010, Bhutan's prime minister, Jigmi Thinley, argued for including happiness as the "ninth MDG" (Witcher 2010), and indeed in recent years there has been an explosion of happiness polls from a range of corporations, intergovernmental organizations, and nongovernmental organizations.

Perhaps the most comprehensive and reliable transnational poll of human happiness is conducted by the Gallup organization using a list of questions that focus on the positive emotions experienced by individuals. Carried out each year since 2006 and based on data from 1,000 individuals in 143 countries, it asks questions such as: Did you feel well-rested yesterday? Were you treated with respect all day yesterday? Did you smile or laugh a lot yesterday? (Clifton 2012). Using these measures, which track cross-culturally more reliably than simply asking whether one felt happy yesterday, the Philippines in 2012 was ranked eighth internationally when it came to the percentage of adults reporting the highest range of positive emotions (ibid.). Significantly, the Philippines was in the top-ranked position in Asia, whereas when it came to experiencing emotions of all sorts, both negative and positive, in 2011 Gallup placed the Philippines in the top spot globally (Clifton 2012), a result that prompted one prominent Filipino news Web site to proclaim: "OMG, Philippines is the world's most 'emotional' country!" (Aquino 2012). Given the poverty that numerous Filipinos face, the fact that so many live for much of their lives far from their loved ones while earning wages that allow those who remain behind to survive, and the political landscape, which remains closer to a klepto-oligarchy than a functioning democracy, it seems nothing short of impossible that the Philippines should be anywhere except at or near the very bottom of all or most international happiness rankings. Yet it is not. Happiness, following from the Gallup organization's set of questions, is socially constituted, formed through interactions with others in communities bounded by care and mutual respect. One might well dismiss the Gallup framework as too social, insofar as it is clearly unable to measure happiness obtained through asceticism or in pursuit of a solitary, meditative life, but here I would counter that the social bias of the poll reflects Filipino core values, where the self only truly exists in relation to the other. And in this socially constituted basis for happiness, I will argue that performance through celebration and ritual is the key productive, purposeful activity that links the individual to the collective in ways that contribute to happiness in the Philippines.

The impulse toward celebration and the scale of celebration itself is one of the outstanding features that those looking in from the outside have historically recognized as differentiating many of the individual cultures contained within the Philippine archipelago from cultures they had previously encountered. The earliest chroniclers of life in the archipelago going back to Magellan's chronicler Antonio Pigafetta along with centuries of observations by Jesuits, Dominicans, Augustinians, and Spanish suggest that even compared with the cultures of central America, the amount of labor, care, and attention devoted to community-based celebrations was extraordinary.[3] Although one can point to innumerable examples where the drive toward celebration and spectacle was so great that it ultimately led cultures and peoples into decline or extinction,[4] what is significant about the Philippines is that this impulse was present in the absence of strong, unified centers from which political, military, and economic control were exercised. Throughout the archipelago, the human energy going into acts of community celebration reflecting localized cultural practices has long been impressive in scale. Lucy Mae San Pablo Burns recalls the performative extravagance imbedded in a phrase she frequently heard as a child growing up in Olongopo City: *"Puro arte lang iyan,"* which turns the Spanish phrase "puro arte" (literally "pure art") into something that comes closer to the meaning of "She's just putting on a show" (San Pablo Burns 2013, 1). *Puro arte* in a Filipino context, she argues, "performs a much more ironic function, gesturing rather to the labor of overacting, histrionics, playfulness, and purely over-the-top dramatics" (2). Excessive labor and, indeed, excesses of all kinds characterize virtually all of the performance work around which this book is organized and it has been in large measure what initially drew me to these forms.

This book brings together more than a decade of research on community-based performance in the Philippines, focusing on theatre, dance, and ritual activities that are created and presented outside the context of theatre venues, much of it taking place in the streets. Shortly after I initiated fieldwork in the Philippines in 2001, I found myself drawn to mass-participation performance events oriented around the Church calendar, initially those associated with Holy Week, the week between Palm Sunday and Easter. My earliest encounters with passion plays or *sinakulos* and the street masquerades of the famous *morions*[5] on the island of Marinduque accord with San Pablo Burns' observations: because of the excessive theatricality of what I experienced both on the stage and in the streets and because the events of the week fused play and fun with religiosity, I wanted to understand and experience more than just what the rituals signified in terms of their religious meaning. As Adam Seligman and Robert Weller observe, "Ritual concentrates on the performative nature of the act, rather than on its denotative meaning. In its purely formal aspect, ritual puts questions of belief or truth aside in favour of the shared world that its action creates and requires" (Seligman and Weller 2012, 94). When local informants are asked why they carry out penitential acts in these often richly theatricalized modes, they unanimously respond that they are carrying out a *panata,* or religious vow. Had I taken what was being said at face value, my larger inquiry might have gone no further. I might well have assumed that because a sacred vow was the motivating force, there was nothing to write about beyond the ways in which their actions responded to the fulfillment of that vow and restored balance in their world. But instead, as Seligman and Weller have noted, I found that at this and other field sites, "performance simply and elegantly side-tracks the problem of shared meaning by allowing participants to express acceptance of an order without requiring a full understanding of it" (95). It became clear early on that the important thing was what was being brought into being through the act of performance and how the experience of participation affected human bodies and lives while preparing for the event, during the event, and in its aftermath.

When my fieldwork later extended into what is known in the Philippines as "street dancing," or what might be labelled as "folk-inflected line-dancing" for the non-Filipino reader, my concern with what participation means for individuals and communities of dancers deepened. How does participation express and enact the relationship of the individual to a community that is variously local, regional, and sometimes also appropriated by a larger imaginary of Filipino culture that extends even beyond the boundaries of the nation-state? Instead of seeing these dances merely as *panata,* or as social dramas that heal some kind of breach (Turner 1982), I came to understand that "ritual action creates a new world, in self-conscious tension with an unritualized world" (Seligman et al. 2008, 21). Following from Seligman et al., the ritual component of these performances is "subjunctive—the creation of an order *as if* it were truly the case . . . an order that is self-consciously distinct from other possible social worlds" (20). These "as if" worlds, deeply grounded in the particulars of place, profoundly social in their creative manufacturing, and so expressly and excessively theatrical in their expression are what initially drew me in and what I sought to understand.

This book relies on three interlocking analytic frames extending from concepts that are well-known to Filipino anthropologists and sociologists, but have not previously been placed into productive conversation with one another through the lens of performance, while also considering how in their collective functioning they contribute to human happiness. I also draw from phenomenology and psychology as I seek to map out the internal landscape of participating in durational, highly codified performance activities. These frames include (1) the internal, experiential mode within the body of the participant, borrowing from the work of psychologist Mihaly Csikszentmihalyi; (2) the relationship between "self" and "other," drawing from the Filipino linguistic and cultural concepts of *sarili* (self) and *loób* (interiority), which will contribute to an understanding of the social dimensions of participation and how the communal functions; and (3) the overarching frame of *bayan,* which is sometimes misleadingly translated as "nation," but can signify the land, the relationship of a group of individuals to a particular place and its modes of cultural expression, the appropriation of such modes of expression by the nation, as well as the larger cultural imaginary of what it means to be Filipino. Each frame will be set out below and will provide a spine that is woven throughout the book.

Three Frames

I have turned to the early work of psychologist Mihaly Csikszentmihalyi to gain insights into the internal dynamics of "flow" as it supports the conditions that maximize the felt state of happiness for participants in many of the performance activities documented in this book. Csikszentmihalyi famously argued that individuals most commonly describe an optimal experience as having the following features:

> [A] sense that one's skills are adequate to cope with the challenges at hand, in a goal-directed, rule-bound action system that provides clear clues as

> to how well one is performing. Concentration is so intense that there is no attention left over to think about anything irrelevant, or to worry about problems. Self-consciousness disappears, and the sense of time becomes distorted. An activity that produces such experiences is so gratifying that people are willing to do it for its own sake, with little concern for what they will get out of it, even when it is difficult, or dangerous. (Csikszentmihalyi 1992, 71)

Virtually all of the performance activities analyzed in this book adhere to a specific "rule-bound action system," and many feature a competitive component in which participating groups are judged according to fixed criteria. Community-based performance, whether it is enacting a role in a passion play, dancing in a competitive event, or seeking a one-to-one correspondence with the sufferings of Christ by opening one's body to actual physical pain, always involves the condition of "intense" concentration, so much so that "time becomes distorted." One of the features of the performance work described in this book that marks it as different from other forms of performance is precisely this final aspect in Csikszentmihalyi's definition of the internal state of flow, namely, that it is done for its own sake, even when "difficult, or dangerous." This sense that the activity is so gratifying as to cancel out any or all other productive activities during the time in which preparations are being made for performance or while the performance is taking place has been the starting point for me at every field site I have visited. I have found it useful to start with the question, "What rewards are so great as to make the participants in this event give up weeks or even months of productive labor and place this activity as the most important or central one in their lives every year?" Here the internal dynamics of the flow assist in mapping out at least a partial answer to this question.

Csikszentmihalyi notes what he terms *flow activities* "have as their primary function the provision of enjoyable experiences," citing "play, art, pageantry, ritual and sports" as some examples (Csikszentmihalyi 1992, 72). Many of the forms described in this book combine all of those categories, and fit more broadly into what in French would be called "jeu," but in English is translated somewhat more narrowly as "game." Csikszentmihalyi cites the work of French psychological anthropologist Roger Caillois whose four categories of games he summarizes as follows:

> *Agon* includes games that have competition as their main feature, such as most sports and athletic events; *alea* is the class that includes all games of chance, from dice to bingo; *ilinx*, or vertigo, is the name he gives to activities that alter consciousness by scrambling ordinary perception, such

> as riding a merry-go-round or skydiving; and *mimicry* is the group of activities in which alternative realities are created, such as dance, theatre, and the arts in general. (Csikszentmihalyi 1992, 72)

This framework, incorporating *jeu* in its multiple forms of expression, is reflected in all of the performance activities described in this book. There is an *agonistic* dimension to many of these events, as noted previously, which provides a focal point for the individual and the group as they seek to win the top prizes, and in the case of many festivals in the Philippines, these include cash prizes. Events are often *aleatory* in that they incorporate ritual practices that invoke divine intercession although the nature of the response cannot be determined by the penitent/actor. Similarly, the extreme physical conditions of heat, hunger, or exhaustion present during an event may produce vertigo, and chanting, dancing, and singing may put the participant and the spectator into an altered state of consciousness, sometimes distorting time. And finally, at the center of all of these practices is mimicry, a carefully regulated and controlled process of imitation that creates something new in which "we are more than what we actually are through fantasy, pretence, and disguise" (Csikszentmihalyi 1992, 73). Yet within Csikszentmihalyi's framework, one that emerged from a vast cross-cultural data-collection exercise over many years, lies both its strength and its limitation. Although it maps out an inner experience for activities that provide focused concentration where the individual enters into a state distinct from the quotidian, one that Eugenio Barba (1991) characterizes as "extra-daily," it does not fully consider the self in relation to others while engaged in such an experience, nor does it take into account how the social and cultural construction of self may contribute to happiness.

Thus the second frame supporting this study considers the self in relation to others, drawing from concepts advanced by Filipino sociologists, anthropologists, psychologists, and theologians whose work rarely circulates in scholarship outside the Philippines. Any understanding of the individual and social dimensions of "inside" and "outside" in the Philippines necessarily requires engaging with the concepts of interiority and exteriority that circulate in psychology and sociology and that have informed a generation of scholarship in Philippine Studies. Particularly useful here is work of the psychologist, Virgilio Enriquez, the sociologist, F. Landa Jocano, and the theologian, Father Dionisio Miranda, who collectively provide an internal mapping of the Filipino "self" rooted in concepts that find expression in the Filipino language,[6] culture, and religion. Enriquez sought to indigenize Filipino psychology by starting from the premise that "Instead of lifting a Filipino concept from a network of concepts to which it belongs, it is far preferable to make full use of the language as the main resource" (Enriquez 1986,

9). He critiqued the cherry-picking of cultural concepts, such as *hiya, utang na loób,* and *pakikisama,*[7] that were studied "as separate values in isolation to all others," adding that when recycled by popular writers outside the Philippines these values are situated "at the very seat of the Filipino's personality; the absence of which they deemed fatal to the former's ethnicity" (Enriquez 1989, 49).

The concept for which Enriquez is best known is his explication of the superordinate term *kapwa,* "which embraces both the categories of 'outsider' *(ibang-tao)* and 'one of us' *(hindi ibang-tao)*" (Enriquez 1986, 11), the literal meaning of which is "not an outsider."

> [W]hen asked for the closest English equivalent of *kapwa,* one word that generally comes to mind is the English word "others." In meaning, the Filipino word *kapwa* is very different from this: *kapwa* is the unity of the "self" and "others". In English the word "others" is actually used in opposition to the "self", and implies the recognition of the self as a separate identity. In contrast, *kapwa* is a recognition of shared identity. (Enriquez 1986, 11)

This has important implications for behavior inasmuch as a "person starts having a *kapwa* not so much because of a recognition of status given him by others but more so because of his awareness of shared identity" (Enriquez 1986, 12). Similarly, Miranda observes:

> Filipino dictionaries render *kapwa* with "both" or "fellow-being," underlining an understanding of shared identity that the word and concept "other" as used in the West practically excludes, inasmuch as it stresses separateness of identity. *Kapwa* is thus a concept that embraces both myself as well as the other. It is a concept that truly equalizes both partners by focusing on the dignity and being of both. Unless that be given, *kapwa* applies neither to myself nor to the other. (Miranda 1989, 50–51)

Indeed, the porousness of this boundary between self and others and the necessity of its codependence and cooperation is essential to the functioning of all of the ritual and performance work examined in this book.

Jocano extends Enriquez's formulation with a complex sociological and psychological internal mapping of the Filipino "self" that is briefly summarized here. His starting point is the observation that "[t]here is no direct Filipino word for the English term 'self'" (Jocano 2001, 97), and that the closest term, *sarili,* refers rather to "the subject of his/her own consciousness" with respect to his or her: "(1) physical body, (2) emotional well-being, and (3) mental state" (ibid.). To understand self, he argues, one must look to the concept of *kaloóban,* derived from the root word *loób,* which means "inside," or more accurately, "interiority." *Kaloóban* "refers to the inner dimensions of personal consciousness that combines the perceptions, the mental state, and the emotional well-being of a person vis-à-vis the situation or condition within which interaction is carried out or about to take place" (ibid.). Thus self is not a divided consciousness in the Cartesian sense, but rather a unified one that perceives, thinks, and feels, while also existing within a social setting or context in which the self interacts with the other. The self, in other words, is defined internally and simultaneously by his external social actions. Indeed, there is no dichotomy between the self and the external. Jocano notes that in his fieldwork respondents routinely used the word *loób* to characterize "almost anything they feel and do as individuals in relation to others, to the things around them, or to the events they are involved in or are responding to" (ibid.). States are described as coming from or experienced within, *sa loób,* rather than being activated by an external force. Thus feeling bad, he notes, is *"masamâ ang loób* (bad inside)" (ibid.).[8]

If *kaloóban* encompasses the inner disposition, the internal dimensions of consciousness, it is expressed to the outside world, according to Jocano, chiefly through *malay* (consciousness, which includes thought, reason, and judgment), *dama* (perception through intuitive feel), and *ugalì* (the sum of a person's qualities) (Jocano 2001, 102–108). It is the concept of *dama* that is particularly significant for this study, insofar as it suggests that the self experiences the world and is understood and judged as a person by the external manifestations of what in other systems might be seen as internal, emotional qualities. *Dama,* argues Jocano, is further divided into *kahulugán* ("the intended meaning or significance we attach to objects, ideas, events, or actions"), *habág* ("sympathy, a deep feeling of compassion for someone in trouble or in need"), and *damay,* which he asserts "represents the surface level of feelings. It is the action part of *dama.* It is to show in actual practice the act of compassion" (106). This has important implications, particularly in a largely Christian country, and one in which much public performance is linked to actively taking on the suffering and pain of Christ, as is commonly done during Holy Week. Though participants in a performance, festival, or ritual event may be motivated by *panata,* participation may touch on other internal receptors that generate the feeling of happiness. Further, *panata* is not limited to taking on the sufferings of Christ directly, but can even include excessive dancing when that activity is being offered for devotional purposes, as we will see in chapter 5. The need of the individual to integrate *sa loób* (inside) with *sa labas* (outside) through one's physical actions and external presentation is a current that runs through this book, in that it is present in every instance of embodied behavior through performance.

Because the third framework, *bayan,* has its roots in place, in a physical location in this world, I find it useful to plant this part of the field within the phenomenology of place. Edward Casey (1996) argues that perception cannot be separated from either the body of the perceiver or the place in which the act of perception occurs. Casey's perceptual framework, which builds on Merleau-Ponty's view of the primacy of "place" over "space," rests on "the dialectic of perception and place," one that "is as intricate as it is profound, and it is never-ending" (Casey 1996, 19):

> Given that we are never without perception, the existence of this dialectic means that we are never without emplaced experiences. It signifies as well that we are not only *in* places but *of* them. Human beings—along with other entities on earth—are ineluctably place-bound. More even than earthlings, we are placelings, and our very perceptual apparatus, our sensing body, reflects the kinds of places we inhabit. (Casey 1996, 19)

I borrow from Casey here in introducing the Filipino concept of *bayan* because fundamentally, *bayan* is bounded by place, by the place to which one feels a strong attachment. The country's most well-known patriotic song, "Bayan Ko" (usually translated as "My Country"), which became a powerful anti-Marcos anthem in the 1970s and early 1980s, links one's feelings about the nation of the Philippines with the features of the land, which are in turn personified and form the basis of the narrative contained within the song's lyrics. The first stanza, which sets up this relationship, is as follows:

> *Ang bayan kong Pilipinas,*
> *Lupain ng ginto't bulaklak.*
> *Pag-ibig na sa kanyang palad,*
> *Nag-alay ng ganda't dilag.*
>
> My country [or *bayan* as land, place, nation], the Philippines,
> Land of gold and flowers.
> With love in the palm of her hands,
> She offered beauty and splendor.

Perception is impossible without place, and as human beings we are always and forever emplaced. When we experience happiness, it is in the world in which our bodies are located. Thus this inquiry, which examines communities that come together through performance, is bounded not just by what people do and how they distinguish themselves from other groups, but in how the sedimented layer of culture, history, and the land itself constitutes places of and for happiness. *Bayan,* as we shall see, is central to this formulation.

Though community can be linked to place, it is also defined by how one feels in relation to others—expressed through the expandable meaning of the word *bayan,* which can signify virtually every possible grouping from *barangay* (barrio or neighborhood) to region to nation.[9] *Bayan* may also transcend geographic place; thus *Bayan Pilipinas* or the "Filipino people" are not contained by national boundaries in that one can both feel a part of and even constitute *bayan* even while living outside the Philippines. It is not that the meaning of *bayan* is imprecise, but rather that it is created and continually reconstituted and realigned based on how one feels in relationship to the group, built on the set of allegiances one has to others who are connected to a particular place, whether it is geographically small (e.g., *barangay* level) or large (the Filipino *bayan* in the global diaspora). Here I build on Damon Woods' understanding of *bayan,* He asserts that rather than corresponding to "people" or "citizens," when we think of *bayan,* "we should think in sets of definable loyalties that could be mobilized for common enterprises" (Woods 2005, 7). Woods offers a persuasive critique of the ways in which earlier scholars (Phelan 1959; Scott 1994a), in their efforts to reconstruct the preconquest Filipino self, too often relied on Spanish sources that placed their own imagined equivalences on top of what they observed in the Philippines (e.g., a *datu* was equivalent to a king, a *barangay* was the local word for barrio), and failed to recognize the shifting nature of allegiances and identifications behind these constructs and that culture and power were differently constructed in this archipelagic environment. Therefore, *bayan* is relational in this respect, thus linking the way it is understood and constituted to the previous frame of self in relation to other.

Referring back to Phelan and Scott in particular, Woods suggests that "in the project of rewriting Philippine history *baranggay* is representative of the problem and *bayan* the solution; *baranggay* as an imposed view—based on a report from an outsider,[10] and *bayan* as a fluid and evolving basis of Tagalog identity—found in Tagalog sources" (Woods 2005, 1–2). Filipinos, asserts Woods, identify themselves by relationships based on family ties, age, and shared experience (11), and it is through those experiences in place that one forms attachments that generate the collectivity of *bayan.* Engaging in a deep excavation of early Tagalog-language sources to provide the foundation for his argument, Woods asserts that whereas the notion of *bayan* and *barangay* as fixed entities suited the Spanish colonizers' project of political and social consolidation, the reality was that "*bayan* would come to express aspects of both location and relationships" (12). Instead of focusing on *barangay* as the beginning and end of communal identifications, it is more apt, I would assert, following from Woods' framework, to see *bayan* as the flexible mechanism to which identity is most firmly attached. And because *bayan* is an imagined place—one that may extend from the local to the national to the extraterritorial, and that is situated in place, in the body, and in the soul—it is elastic. Thus those who make claims to lead and define the identity of *bayan* at any level must do so in ways that speak to a shared set of values and loyalties. O. W. Wolters (1999) and Tony Day (2002), both writing more broadly about how power was constituted historically within Southeast Asia, have, like Woods, sought to consider the cultural aspects that make political and social power structures in the Philippines different in terms of how they function and set forth claims for legitimacy. Woods observes that historically "Southeast Asians identified themselves in terms of place and relationships" (Woods 2005, 7). What this means for politics and the ways in which it can attach itself to local expressions of performance identified with a particular place is significant.

At the same time, communities of individuals unite and define themselves around ritual and celebratory acts through performance—from the *barangay*-based passion play or *sinakulo* to regional celebrations that assert independence and cultural identity—these events contain within their very structure the capacity to divide and even conquer those communities themselves. This is perhaps the sad irony of much of the performance examined in this book; what brings individuals together into a community united around a common purpose, goal, or in recognition of a shared culture or set of values can also serve to pull them apart. In the Philippines, "comprador capitalism" and a corrupt political system built on the power of a largely mestizo-identified oligarchy that emerged at the end of the nineteenth century effectively minimize the power of the individual to effect political or economic change. For most Filipinos the only reliable unit is first the family, and second, the local *barangay,* which may extend only to the immediate neighborhood of adjoining homes in the case of those living in a densely populated urban shantytown. The large force that sits above it all is the political and economic class of the oligarchs who own the nation's productive capacity and who take credit for providing the individual or the community with everything of value in the political, economic, or social sphere. Thus, until recently, bridges, major construction projects, and even benches in public parks were "brought to you" by the local elite, typically the elected official at the time of the undertaking. It is their name that remains on the bridge, building, or object, reminding citizens daily of their indebtedness to the patron. So too is much community-based performance either financed by or presented under a framework created or controlled by the local or national ruling elite. Every performance event is thus to some extent a political act, just as the position of the rich and powerful is always potentially enhanced or diminished through every act of community-based performance.

Thus it is my proposition that because the socioeconomic and political self is necessarily divided, often against itself in the sense of having to actively support those opposed to their own class interests, all performance events I examine here have the potential to simultaneously bring communities together and to separate them from one another.

Entering "The Field"

My point of entry into performance in the Philippines took place more than twenty years ago, when while lecturing in theatre at the National University of Singapore, two distinguished scholars of Filipino theatre, Doreen Fernandez and Nicanor Tiongson, came to present at a seminar. What I remember from that encounter is the feeling that I was in the company of old friends or family members, that there was something familiar and comforting in both their communication style and emotional makeup. Nearly a decade later when I initiated fieldwork in the Philippines, I soon came to realize that my instinctive pull toward religious and community-based performance was not just that I had been a child preacher with a penchant for performance, but that the ways in which Filipinos socialized, both within families and with those from the outside who were admitted into communities of families and friends, had many similarities with the world in which I was raised in the upper U.S. Midwest in the 1960s and 1970s. As the eldest child on both sides of the family, born to young parents who were part of a large, extended family descended from Scandinavian immigrants, my childhood involved celebrating every birthday and holiday with a house full of family members, often while keeping an eye out on the younger kids. My identity, as is the case in many Filipino families, was linked not just to my nuclear family, but to an extended family of grandparents, aunts, uncles, cousins, and those who had married into the family. My father, like many Filipinos I have met, trusted his initial instincts about people and if he recognized some shared quality in them, they were invited into our home and our lives. We played together, partied together, and faced adversity together. Although like many families we had challenges such as alcoholism, mental illness, and the loss of loved ones, we faced these challenges together. Our lives were not singular but plural and interconnected with a vast web of family members and friends who were also family.

My other way into the field was spiritual and embodied. While I was making preparations in Manila to undertake fieldwork on the island Marinduque for the iconic Moriones Festival, my father died suddenly of a heart attack. I quickly flew home to the United States to eulogize him and see him interred in the frozen earth of the Fort Snelling National Cemetery to a twenty-one-gun salute during a Minnesota snowstorm. A few days later, my mother, with a house full of relatives to support her, told me that my father would have wanted me to return to the Philippines for Easter. So I flew back, setting out for Marinduque on a boat so overcrowded that the food supply had been exhausted and there was no room to sit. Pressed up against other bodies of those returning home to Marinduque for Holy Week on the airless back deck of the ship, exhausted and hungry, I felt instinctively that there must be some really good reasons that so many were headed to the same place. Once there, though I sought out participants and organizers with whom to speak, my primary goal was simply to see as much as possible of the big, sprawling event, one that took in street masquerades, religious processions, a multiple-evening passion play, a costume competition, a trade fair, the Sunday Mass, and a "Battle of the Bands" on the evening of Easter Sunday. I felt relatively unengaged with the spiritual dimensions of the event, especially because there was so much to take in. But it was the predawn *salubong* in which the veil of mourning is lifted from an effigy of Mother Mary that unexpectedly left its mark on me. In its enactment in the streets, a child dressed as an angel was lowered from the center point of a makeshift bamboo scaffolding to the level of the head of a veiled statue of Mary that otherwise resides in the local cathedral. That year, after the child angel reached out and grasped the veil, a brass band struck up a series of tunes well-known to me from my childhood, including marches by John Philip Sousa and the early 1960s pop song "I Will Follow Him" repopularized by Whoopi Goldberg in the movie *Sister Act*. We processed through the streets behind a series of lit wagons or *karos* that drew carved, wooden effigies of the saints through the streets, winding our way through the darkened streets toward the cathedral in the predawn hours. At the precise moment when I turned the corner and faced the narrow street that ascended to the cathedral on the hill, the church bells started pealing and I felt my father's hand on my shoulder. As I came to understand when I interviewed informants at other field sites around the country, these events are marked by experiences that are set off from the rest of our lives, and this is also why we are compelled to return each year. Thus in my first encounter with a complex, sprawling durational event, I had myself experienced something that was bracketed outside of the rest of my daily life, and I too felt the physical and spiritual pull that made me wish to repeat the experience.

It is impossible to stay on the sidelines while engaged in fieldwork on performance at festivals in the Philippines. Clifford Geertz (2000), borrowing from another anthropologist, famously used the term "deep hanging out" to describe what needs to happen at such sites. In order to make contact and to establish credibility, what is necessary, first and foremost, is presence. One has to physically be there, witnessing, not staying in fancy hotels and traveling with an entourage or a local guide, but rather arriving on local transport and hanging out with the locals in coffee shops, bars, and public spaces. The second requirement is duration. Although there have been times when economic necessity and lack of research leave have made "parachute anthropology" trips necessary, for the most part, I not only show up, but I stay on well past the party. In the small cities and poor barrios of the big cities of the Philippines I quickly learned that one gains credibility locally by being present before, during, and after the "main event." The longer one stays, the more curious people are, and the greater the likelihood that they will approach you to talk. More often than not, advance contact with potential informants is not possible, even in a country like the Philippines where virtually everyone has a mobile phone and where speed in text messaging is a competitive sport. Although an academic dean at a large university or the producer of a stage spectacle may require advance contact, most contact is done by signaling one's interest in the performance event by being present and watching until one is recognized.

A wise Filipina friend characterizes her compatriots as having a natural and well-developed capacity for practicing what she calls "natural selection." By this she means nothing Darwinian, but rather the inclination to trust one's impressions about strangers, to make an immediate assessment based on feelings, on what is perceived through external expression to be *sa loób* (on the inside) and to create openings for friendship and intimacy without hesitation based on a kind of recognition of qualities that one has in common with the other. Thus it is not so much, as the stereotype holds, that Filipinos would give you the shirt off their backs, but rather, that through the process of this kind of social "natural selection," they will trust that what they perceive from the other is real when they have reason to, when their inner voice confirms that the inner and outer are one and the same. This is what I experienced at one field site after another, and indeed it was through my friend's own process of "naturally selecting" me that I came to be adopted into a family that comes together every year to participate in the Ati-atihan Festival, the subject of a later chapter.

With respect to fieldwork from which I have obviously gained so much in ways that sustain me, one might rightly ask what locals gain from my participation. What has been clear to me from the beginning of my fieldwork is that locals are interested in knowing why an individual physically marked as a foreigner stays in town after the celebrations end, and why he would choose to hang out in a rural or urban barrio with people who have little in terms of material wealth or comforts, rather than sunning himself on the famous white sand beaches of Borocay, for instance. Whereas those in positions of privilege and power in local communities are willing to speak to a foreign academic in the hope of being positively represented or benefiting indirectly or directly from publicity in future publications, informants and locals who strike up conversations with me routinely express gratitude for my presence and my interest in their local traditions. Because the context in which many of the forms about which I write in this book is often highly circumscribed and occasionally compromised by powerful local elites, to simply be present at street level, interested in and available to everyone who walks the streets, has meant that on many occasions I have been welcomed into local communities as a kindred spirit, as one who stands with them rather than with the local power brokers. Indeed, at many key points in my research I have had to actively distance myself from local elites who have sought to co-opt me or who expected more in return than I was prepared to give. At the local level, it clearly means much to working-class and poor people in urban and provincial barrios that what they spent so much productive labor on is recognized and valued by an outsider.

As noted earlier, the work of many Filipino sociologists, historians, linguists, and anthropologists receives little circulation outside the Philippines. The most notable exception is Rey Ileto, whose pioneering 1979 study linked the Tagalog *pasyon*[11] with the revolutionary struggle against Spanish and later American colonization in the late nineteenth and early twentieth centuries, and provided a foundation for much of the scholarship on religion and performance in the Philippines since that time. Apart from Ileto, when I encounter the rapidly expanding and sophisticated scholarship produced by Filipino immigrants and first-generation Fil-Am scholars in the United States, I rarely see the names of my "homies" invoked. Rather than referencing Resil Mojares, Vicente Rafael, F. Landa Jocano, Benigno Beltran, J. Neil Garcia, Epifanio San Juan Jr., Raul Pertierra, Virgilio Enriquez, William Henry Scott, or Walden Bello, many are more likely to place their work against the backdrop of a wider Asian-Americanness, North American "identity politics," or queer studies. Although this is certainly understandable, especially given the problematic and complex cultural position of Fil-Ams historically as colonized subjects and then as neocolonized subjects within the matrices of Asian-Americanness and the American framework of multiculturalism, such writing exists at considerable remove from the cultural frameworks used by Filipinos living in the Philippines to make sense of their lives. Especially influential for pursuing this research is the detailed and rigorous work of those countering this trend, particularly Epifanio San Juan Jr. (1970, 1996, 2000, 2001), Martin Manalansan (2003), Neferti Xina Tadiar (2004), Lucy Mae San Pablo Burns (2013), Alicia Arrizón (2006), and Theodore Gonzalves (2010), all of whom consistently ground the multiplicity of diasporic Filipino experiences in North America using frameworks that are deeply rooted in the Philippines. More squarely situated in theatre is the work of the late Doreen Fernandez (1995a, 1995b, 1996), who published virtually all of the articles on Filipino theatre that appeared in internationally refereed journals during the period 1984–2000, and Nicanor Tiongson, with his towering achievement, the ten-volume Cultural Center of the Philippines work, *CCP Encyclopedia of Philippine Art* (1994a), which he oversaw while serving as head of the CCP, and his set of foundational writings on the performance forms of *sinakulo* (1999b) and *komedya* (1999a). The provocations set out in the next section and the arguments developed in this book would not have been possible without their work.

Structure of the Book

Given the archipelagic nature of the Philippines and its vast array of individuated cultures, it may seem arrogant to make a claim that this book has anything to say about the Philippines or Filipinos as a whole. Most of my field sites are in the Tagalog-speaking region, my strongest embodied experiences with dance are in the Visayas, and there is no ethnographic data from the vast south of the country. Yet by focusing on the two categories of performance with the widest currency across the entire archipelago—Holy Week performance and dance associated with local fiestas—meaningful patterns that cut across regions do emerge. Because this book examines performance activities that are practiced most enthusiastically and in greatest numbers by the vast poor and struggling middle classes of the country, they offer up a richer ground for examining shared cultural values than any other communal activity. The nature of this inquiry is such that it must necessarily be grounded in data and experiences that are obtained locally, thus making a completely comprehensive picture of all practices within these two categories impossible in a single, book-length study. My hope is that those engaged in detailed studies of practices in other regions can find use-value in the models that emerge from this research.

The first three chapters are devoted to Holy Week performance, and the following three focus on "folk" and "folk-inflected" dance as well as on what has become known as "street dancing" in the context of regional and national festivals. Because there are many categories of performance that could be said to be community-based and that might well be offered up for examination,[12] including much of the earlier work of the politically and socially conscious theatre company People's Educational Theatre Association (PETA),[13] it seemed prudent to limit the scope of this book to the two overarching categories of performance that mobilize the largest numbers of participants and spectators across the nation and that take up more time and labor than any other collective activity apart from work.

Key cultural and linguistic concepts as well as the larger political and historical forces that influence a local practice will be set out using the three frames discussed earlier, supplemented by detailed descriptions of performance events whenever relevant, drawn from many years of fieldwork. The conclusion, chapter 7, considers how performance and politics have recently come together on the national stage in ways that may point to the possibility of a more progressive and hopeful future for the country.

Because the premiere week of the year that mobilizes the greatest numbers of individuals as actors, audience members, and participants for theatre and performance is Holy Week, the week between Palm Sunday and Easter, much of my attention over the years has focused on the many variants of the *sinakulo,* or passion play, staged during that time. Thus chapter 1 maps out the features of *sinakulo* traditions at three contrasting field sites—two in Metro Manila, and one in Marinduque—using a framework borrowed from Diana Taylor (2003), which I find useful for laying out the larger context for the inscription of these events. Also established here are the characteristic features of what I term the "traditional *sinakulo,*" the "civic-based *sinakulo,*" and the "activist *sinakulo.*"

Chapter 2 seeks to move inside the experiential dimensions of the *sinakulo* and related Good Friday performances and processions by grounding it in a consideration of the relationship between the individual and Christ, particularly as it is understood and experienced in the Tagalog-speaking parts of the country. The ways in which Christ is represented and experienced by the actor will be placed into active conversation with how this Christ reflects local values and understandings of what it means to be a complete person, one who is capable of harmonizing the inner *(sa loób)* with the outer *(sa labas).*

Chapter 3 examines the Moriones Festival in Boac, the provincial capital of Marinduque. This massive, lumbering event, which culminates in the mock-beheading of the Roman soldier Longinus on Black Saturday, has a long history, but one ultimately clouded by the mists and myths of time. A consideration of the activities undertaken by the so-called *morions,* a largely male practice of dressing as Roman soldiers and participating in a range of events over the course of Holy Week, brings to the fore the ways in which local communities can fragment and also create new practices and traditions. At this site, local and provincial politics play an important role in shaping and containing the events of the week, though ultimately some individuals and groups find ways to successfully circumvent external controls.

Chapters 4 through 6 focus on folk-inflected dance, particularly street dancing, and move from the complex outer frames created by history, politics, modes of social organization, and activated by shared community values, to those internal states that dance emplaces in the body, those places of joy, happiness, and contentment that extend out into the world and with which many participants seem eager to reengage year after year. In order to make sense of how and why dance circulates so widely in the Philippines, one must inevitably start with a consideration of how it emerged from folk and indigenous dance traditions and was shaped by the pioneering fieldwork of Francisca Reyes-Aquino earlier in the twentieth century, at a time in which nationalist forces within the country were seeking to assert themselves as culturally Filipino in ways that distanced them from American cultural hegemony. Thus chapter 4 sets out a genealogy of dance that demonstrates both how Reyes' work fed into creation of the core Bayanihan repertory of five foundational dance suites as well as how dance came to be codified and embedded in the national physical education curriculum as a compulsory subject. The perception that all Filipinos can dance reflects the fact that virtually everyone with even a primary school education possesses basic competency in or familiarity with dances rooted in their own region as well as with dances from elsewhere in the country. This is a complex and fascinating story that owes as much to politics as it does to dance research, but without some understanding of how dance came to mean so much to the nationalist project and how it circulates back into the regions from which individual dances are derived, one might well uncritically accept the stereotype that Filipinos come out of the womb dancing. The chapter also considers in some detail the features of two key "suites" in the Bayanihan repertory, the "Cordillera Suite" and the "Muslim Suite."

Chapter 5 considers how dance functions in the context of the Ati-atihan Festival in the town of Kalibo in the Visayan region, and maps out a phenomenologically grounded anthropology of perception that extends from what the body experiences at an event of such a long duration. Devoted to the veneration of the Santo Niño, or Holy Child, this festival, which celebrated its eight-hundredth anniversary in 2012, fuses a pre-Christian quasi-mythic story about a thirteenth-century encounter between the dark-skinned indigenous Ati people and the lighter-skinned settlers from modern-day Borneo, onto a celebration of mass conversion of natives in the sixteenth century by a Spanish priest. Chapter 6 considers the phenomenon of street dancing, a quasi-folkloric dance form with a wide range of regional expressions, the single performance form in which the greatest number of Filipinos have experience as active participants over their lifetimes. Taught in schools and offered up as a key element in festivals where it is competitively judged and prizes are awarded, it has a significant position in the cultural landscape because it is also used as a marker for regional ethnic identities. An analysis of the features of a winning dance routine at the 2013 Aliwan Fiesta, the national street dancing competition, reveals the ways in which folk traditions have been turned into massive theatricalized expressions of the local, contained within an increasingly homogenized and national form. Examples drawn from folk, ritual, and folk-inflected dance at various sites both domestically and among Filipinos in the diaspora provide the core data around which I articulate an interactive model for *bayan*-in-action, and offer a series of frameworks demonstrating that dance is the most significant and widespread mode in which Filipinos perform their relationship to place and *bayan*.

Finally, chapter 7 focuses on the performance of politics by considering the public advocacy work of Juana Change, the fictional name given to a character created by Mae Paner and her writing partner, Rody Vera, both of whom were actively involved with PETA. Perhaps unsurprisingly, in the years following the People Power Revolution of 1986 that ousted Ferdinand Marcos, theatre and street performance eventually lost much of the vitality and urgency they had during the dark days of martial law. By the time I arrived in the Philippines for fieldwork in 2001, it was clear to me and others I interviewed that PETA's most influential work was largely in the past; thus rather than viewing community-based performance as a form created in the PETA mold, where largely middle-class, educated activists sought to activate the masses by exploring issues that they hoped would resonate with them, I opened up my field of research to accommodate the performance practices that were embraced by the largest number—those that were arguably the most community-based in their local expressions and embeddedness. At the time of my 2010 residency at the University of the Philippines, which coincided with the campaign and election of Benigno "Noynoy" Aquino, I came to see how performance was again being used to agitate for political change in a way that followed from the original activist spirit of PETA but used vastly different tactics. I also came to believe that it was perhaps performance rather than bloodshed that could offer hope for real political and economic change in the Philippines. Chapter 7 thus pulls out an important strand woven into every chapter of the book, by considering the ways in which the personal has long been the political in the Philippines, showing how through the work of Juana Change performance is being used as a spark to reignite the masses, and offering a possible pathway for lasting structural change in which happiness may in the future be less constrained by the power of the country's ruling elite over its citizens.

CHAPTER 1

Three Tagalog Sinakulos

The Repertoire and the Scenario

No category of activities brings more people across the nation together at the same time each year than the performance events associated with Holy Week, the week between Palm Sunday and Easter. This is the most performance-rich season of the year, when the country's vast, struggling middle-class and working poor devote extraordinary individual and collective energy toward creating, staging, and participating in performance activities that reflect their belief in the efficacy of these religious practices while strengthening their common bonds and demonstrating how they differ from other communities of believers.[1] Even more than at Christmas, during Easter—particularly in the days between Palm Sunday and Good Friday—the power of the Church is most fully woven into the daily lives of the 80 percent of the population that identifies as Roman Catholic.[2] During this time, featured activities, events, performances, and rituals range from the all-night readings of the passion of Christ in metered verse before makeshift altars in urban and rural barrios,[3] to the staging of vast biblical pageants extending back to creation. It is also both a communal and intensely personal time, when publicly undertaking a *panata* or vow, or standing in solidarity with those who are willing to take on a more extreme enactment of such a *panata* through corporal punishment, is at the core of a practice that links the individual to the sufferings of Christ.

In many communities throughout the Philippines, the locally produced *sinakulo* is the most significant mass-participation event of Holy Week, one that physically and spiritually brings together virtually all residents of a small *barangay* or a provincial town to witness and participate in the story of salvation through the dramatic reenactment of the *pasyon* (passion), a story that may extend back to creation. The first widely circulated *pasyon* was Gaspar Aquino de Belen's text, *Ang Mahal na Pasión ni Jesu Christong Panginoon Natin na Tola (The Sacred Passion of Our Lord Jesus Christ as a Poem),* which appeared in 1704. Nineteenth-century Filipinos' understanding of Christianity was largely based not on the Spanish-language Bible, but rather on a later version of the passion, the *Pasyon Genesis,* also known as the *Pasyon Pilapil,* named after Father Mariano Pilapil (1756–1818), who is credited with combining a number of sources to create a

Tagalog-language story of the entire history of salvation going back to the creation. Written in rhyming couplets with five lines of verse per stanza and eight syllables per line, this *pasyon* remains a key text in the Filipino Catholic tradition. Thus the passion of Christ, which in most faiths' traditions would extend only in the period from the Last Supper through to Christ's betrayal and the Crucifixion and Resurrection, in the Philippines may go back to the creation or the story of Adam and Eve in many tellings of the story and dramatic representations during Holy Week. The centrality of the *Pasyon Pilapil* in Filipino Catholic culture cannot be understated. It is read to the dying and over bodies during wakes, and it is intoned nonstop in front of small shrines in homes and in parish churches throughout Holy Week, recited in a style that is closer to chant than ordinary speech. This tradition of using elaborate language for the dead is probably pre-Christian in origin. As Franciscan chronicler Juan Francisco de San Antonio observed in 1738: "In their lamentations they insert a melancholy song with innumerable extravagant things in praise of the dead," adding that in their use of poetry, "he who would understand it must be very learned in their language, even among his own compatriots" (San Juan 1970, 184). Thus the contemporary *sinakulo* poeticizes and dramatizes the passion story, most likely building on an earlier practice in which complex, poetic language was recited in lamenting the dead.

Yet the *pasyon* in its dramatic enactment as *sinakulo* also reflects another tradition, one that interprets the Christ story as a parable for social and political activism and transfers the drama and its dramatis personae into both the soil of the Philippines and the consciousness of Filipinos. As Reynaldo Ileto demonstrated in his foundational work on the ubiquity of the *pasyon,* "The masses' experience of Holy Week fundamentally shaped the style of peasant brotherhood and uprisings during the Spanish and early American colonial periods" (Ileto 1979, 15). Revolutionary leaders were seen to embody the sufferings of Christ, whereas followers functioned as disciples and were expected to leave behind all personal considerations and be willing to sacrifice their lives if necessary. Ileto asserts that "In a society without freedom of speech and legitimate channels of protest, the *pasyon* made available a language for venting ill feelings against oppressive friars, *principales,*[4] and agents of the state" (21). At a time when those running the instruments of Church and state control were remote from the lives of ordinary Filipinos, the *pasyon* showed "that social status based on wealth and education has no real value" (19). Ileto asserts that for Filipinos the *pasyon* constitutes a "universal history, the beginning and end of time, rather than a simple gospel story" (18). Thus the social and religious values embedded in the *pasyon* were ingrained in the consciousness of Filipinos by the nineteenth century as they organized the world and helped create a framework for social justice that endures to this day.

This chapter considers the practices that connect believers and penitents, both personally and within their respective communities, to the story of the *pasyon*, through an examination of the *sinakulo* at three field sites in the Tagalog-speaking region of the country. Two sites are in Metro Manila, one is outside the capital, and data are drawn from two or more periods of fieldwork undertaken between 2005 and 2013. Each site reflects one of three general categories of *sinakulo* also found elsewhere in the country during Holy Week: (1) the "traditional *sinakulo*," a community-based folk tradition that is largely unchanged from year to year and adheres quite rigorously to a plan or script believed to follow an originary practice; (2) the "civic-based *sinakulo*," performed before a wider audience, often funded and shaped by the political and economic elite of a community, but based on earlier practices that often differed radically from contemporary expressions of the tradition; and (3) the "activist *sinakulo*," featuring hybrid performance practices that are community-based, but also played out on a wider civic scale in an urban context, and that infuse the *sinakulo* with contemporary social and economic relevance. These categories are not intended to be exhaustive, as it is beyond the scope of this book to attempt to map out the genealogies of the many practices throughout the country—or even within the Tagalog region—that fall within these frames. It would not be possible even over the course of the professional careers of a team of researchers to engage in detailed fieldwork at all of the thousands of sites in the Philippines where Holy Week practices involve the staging of a *sinakulo* in a particular city, town, municipality, or *barangay*.[5]

In mapping out the complexities of how these *sinakulo* function at each of these sites, I will draw from Diana Taylor's (2003) formulation, which she used in examining similarly complex hybridized forms in her native Mexico. Taylor's concern with both the construction and constructedness of the past in the present, as reflected in a range of grassroots and populist performance modes and "traditions," has clear application to a similar part of the field in the Philippines where the focus is on performance forms that are known within specific communities to an incredible level of detail, yet are largely unknown to and undocumented for the outside world. Because these performance practices are situated in the body, in communities, and in places at particular times, much like the forms Taylor writes about in Mexico, they exist as "repertoire" rather than "archive," and, as such, they are best examined through the multivalent lens of what she terms "scenario" rather than as a set of singular or interlocking narratives or "texts." Taylor sets out six analytical frames for "scenario" that are useful in organizing the data from three field sites for the *sinakulo*. She suggests that at the outset, "to recall, recount, or reactivate a scenario we need to conjure up the physical location" (Taylor 2003, 29). In a *sinakulo* context this includes the physical environment and the overarching meanings that extend from the *sinakulo*'s situatedness in its home province, *barangay*, as well as the specific built or natural features present at the site of the staged enactment. Echoing Edward Casey, who argued "there is no knowing or sensing a place except by being in that place" (Casey 1996, 18), Taylor sees place as primary, observing that "The place allows us to think about the possibilities of the action" (Taylor 2003, 29).

The second element, "the embodiment of the social actors," "requires us to wrestle with the social construction of bodies in particular contexts" (ibid.). Casey similarly observed that, "The primacy of perception is ultimately a primacy of the lived body—a body that . . . is a creature of habitual cultural and social processes" (Casey 1996, 19). Third, Taylor notes that "scenarios, by encapsulating both the setup and the action/behaviors, are formulaic structures that predispose certain outcomes and yet allow for reversal, parody, and change" (Taylor 2003, 31). The fourth frame relates to the "multifaceted systems at work in the scenario itself" (ibid.), and points to the multiple modes through which the scenario is expressed, replicated, and passed along. "Fifth, the scenario forces us to situate ourselves in relationship to it, as participants, spectators, or witnesses, we need to 'be there,' part of the act of transfer" (32).

Taylor's sixth and final element relates to ways in which mimesis may function in performance. She observes that "a scenario is not necessarily, or even primarily, mimetic" (ibid.). Mimesis is especially important to consider with respect to Filipino performance forms, given the cultural stereotype that Filipinos have a particular gift for imitation. This notion of Filipinos as imitators goes back to the mission of American colonization, the terms of which were set forth by William Howard Taft, the first governor-general of the Philippines and future U.S. president: "[The Filipinos] are merely in a state of Christian pupilage. They are imitative. They are glad to be educated, glad to study some languages other than their own, glad to follow European and American ideals" (cited in Rafael 2000, 34–35). Today, more than a century later, their "excellence" in the global marketplace has come to be associated with a particular talent for mimicry, a construct that essentially erases any distinctive cultural elements that cannot be readily identified with the legacy of Spanish or American colonization. Yet mimicry is never fully successful inasmuch as to the outsider, as Homi Bhabha observes, it is situated in the postcolonial category of, "almost the same but not quite" (1994, 86). Because the *sinakulo* is the mass performance form most likely to be seen as "like" or "imitative" of passion plays found elsewhere in the Catholic world, particularly in Spain, Portugal, or their former colonies, it is especially important to consider the ways in which mimesis is subverted and imitation serves to create a practice that means something different or new when differently emplaced. It is, I argue, the genius that Filipinos have in integrating external influences into their spiritual, psychological, linguistic, emotional, and cultural frameworks that turns mimesis back on itself, making it distinctively Pinoy.

Thus my analysis follows six analytical frames, where each seeks to:

1. Conjure up the physical location, the site for the emplacement of human bodies
2. Identify the embodied, social actors and consider their social construction
3. Demonstrate how scenarios can playfully allow for reversal, parody, and change
4. Consider the modes through which the scenario is expressed and the systems at work within the scenario
5. Situate ourselves in the scenario as participants, spectators, witnesses
6. Determine how the scenario is not necessarily mimetic and how it may cite, conjure, and even disrupt the past

Because these frames often overlap, I will not attempt to enumerate them separately while moving through each field site. Nevertheless, by the end of the chapter, my aim is to have provided a reasonably complete analysis based on these criteria.

The "Traditional *Sinakulo*"

Our starting point, the "traditional *sinakulo*," is in many respects frequently no more "traditional" than any other *sinakulo* form, but rather is marked as such by those who participate and who consider its claim to authenticity as the defining feature of the form. This form can be situated more squarely into a folk performance tradition, which resides in a particular community of people with shared values and long-standing traditions, where it is essential not to alter the tradition, but rather to preserve it much as has been done "traditionally" in order to ensure its spiritual efficacy. Participants in this form typically enact *panata* through their active involvement in these events, and to alter them is not only to change their meaning but also to possibly deprive the participant of the benefits of divine grace and mercy that come from performing those acts. One of the ironies is that some of these traditions do not have particularly long histories in their originary practice, sometimes dating back only a few generations in their current form. Organizers and participants are often deeply invested personally in the unchanging nature of the "tradition" inasmuch as performing in a *sinakulo* that uses the same conventions of staging and speech links them to friends and relatives who played these roles before them, as well as those who will succeed them in future generations.

My field site for this practice is the urban *barangay* of Barangka Ibaba in Mandaluyong City, part of Metro Manila. Bordering on the Pasig River to the south, and with an official population of 8,943,[6] which is most certainly vastly undercounted, this cramped, densely populated *barangay* is reachable by moving through a maze of narrow streets heading down toward the river from the main thoroughfare of Boni Avenue. Boni Avenue connects the famed EDSA Boulevard, site of the People Power (or EDSA) Revolution that brought down the Marcos regime, with the center of Mandaluyong City. Accessible largely on foot or via motorized tricycle, on reaching this *barangay,* one has the feeling of being at the end of the line, perhaps because one travels downhill to reach it and it is so tightly bound in by other neighborhoods. The *barangay* has a cozy, well-tended feel, despite its lack of material wealth, suggesting internal cohesion—that residents are largely born into this neighborhood and that the transient population is probably small. The *barangay* captain serves as a key figure in terms of the social organization of the neighborhood, and whereas he or she is generally a local business owner or highly respected member of the community, this person is unlikely to be from a social or economic class that differs vastly from other residents in a small urban *barangay* such as this.

The *sinakulo* is staged in an open area in front of the *barangay* captain's home (Jesus C. "Jesse" Cruz), where two roads come together; known as the Barangka Ibaba Plaza, the narrow space accommodates a temporary, raised staged, and the audience sits on plastic chairs extending back into the street facing it. A local auto repair shop, adjacent to the backstage area, serves as the "greenroom" where actors put on their costumes and makeup and wait for their next appearance onstage. Using an established text staged in a manner that has remained fundamentally unchanged since it was first performed in 1965, local community members who participate as actors and support staff routinely point out that the sacrifice of time and labor connected with staging this eighteen- to twenty-hour extravaganza constitutes *panata.* Weekend rehearsals for this six-night enactment of the life of Christ begin three months earlier (Angeles 2010), when the fifty or so participating actors begin working with directors Arnold Teodoro and Boyet Reyes (Duran-Seco 2009; Mandaluyong City n.d.). According to Nolan Angeles (2010), a city employee who is the de facto producer of the event, "Once the role is given to you it seems that only death can separate you from the role. Not even old age can separate you." All participants come from either the immediate *barangay* or a neighboring one, and many actors are related to one another. The name of the religious organization that stages the play, the San Roque Senakulista ng Barangka, points to its specificity and brings together three levels of associations; they are the *sinakulistas*—or those who perform the *sinakulo*—from the *barangay* of Barangka in the parish of Saint Roch.

The text, preserved in its "original" form as a thick photocopy of a typed manuscript that dates from the mid-1960s, tells the story of salvation from Adam and Eve over six nights, starting on Holy Monday and continuing through Black Saturday. Credited to Rading de Guzman, the text incorporates content from the Old Testament, the Gospels, and the Tagalog text, *Martir sa Golgota* (Martyrdom at Golgotha[7]), whereas the foundational text is based on an older *sinakulo* that probably came from a *sinakulo* group in nearby Pasig (Angeles 2010). The key text contributing to the storyline, *Martir sa Golgota,* is most likely a translation of *El Martir del Golgota,* a novelized account of the last days of Christ by Spanish playwright and novelist Pérez Escrich (1829–1897), a popular religious text widely circulated in the Philippines from the late nineteenth century. The ways in which claims to textual authority are made seem to have no connection with verifiability or the actual, physical existence of texts or urtexts. As Fenella Cannell observed when trying to map the genealogy of source texts contributing to the *pasyon* used in the Bicol region, "the conclusion to draw from this proliferation of texts and virtual texts is that it was not only the content of a particular text which defined its arcane power, but also the context in which the translation was made and the book used" (Cannell 2006, 158). The original source texts from which the "traditional" text used in Mandaluyong City was derived cannot be physically located, a fact that does not seem to trouble anyone involved with the production; rather the imprecision of its origins contributes to the sense that it constitutes a unique, sacred text that cannot be altered, passed through a lineage from Rading de Guzman that has power because it is not fully known. Some of the language used in the performance text is archaic, complex, and highly poetic, with specific phrases that are regarded as "tongue twisters" (Angeles 2010). The dramatic text is not fully memorized by participants, and much of the spoken dialogue is prompted to the actors by one of the directors from a position either behind the stage curtains or on the side of the stage. With up to three hours of dialogue over six nights, the memorization of a twenty-four-hour-long performance text for those in leading roles would be a herculean task, particularly for an amateur actor. Nevertheless, in some sections in performance the dialogue flows freely and it appears that actors have fully committed the text to memory.

The open-air proscenium arch stage, constructed almost entirely from bamboo supports, plywood, and woven mats, rests on a metal support structure and is erected every year in the Barangka Ibaba Plaza a few days before the first installment of the *sinakulo* on Holy Monday. Production costs, estimated at between

200,000 and 250,000 pesos in 2010, are met by the city of Mandaluyong and include the costs of storing and moving the massive stage, hiring a band that plays live music underscoring the action, and feeding the cast and crew while the show is in production. Possibly the largest budget items, the elaborate, layered, eye-catching costumes, are provided by the performers themselves, who either make them or rely on family or other community members to design and construct them. Apart from the costumes, the show's most prominent visual features are the fifteen or so large backdrops with key, generic locations painted onto sheets of traditional coco cloth. A "gift" from a local congressman in the mid-1980s, the backdrops reputedly took six months to execute and are painted in a style that resembles that used in *komedya,* the indigenized version of the popular Spanish theatre form *comedia,* where stock scenes, painted in perspective on a flat surface, can reappear many times over the course of a single evening.

A press release describes the 2010 *sinakulo* as being given a "melodramatic rendering" (Click the City n.d.) and indeed the style of the production would appear to owe much to the great melodramatic form of *komedya,* popular in the Philippines in the late nineteenth and early twentieth centuries. The Filipino *komedya* usually contained plots of intrigue and love where the non-Christian Moros—or Muslims from the south of the country—were ultimately subdued by the virtuous Christians, typically after one of the young love interests converted to Christianity and renounced his or her former faith. In the Philippines, their local Muslims became stand-ins for the Moors of Spain and North Africa in the Spanish *comedia* (thus Moors become "Moros"), which, when represented visually onstage, creates a kind of double-distancing from any "real" historical source and becomes a fantasy twice removed from reality. Traditional Filipino *komedya,* still staged by devoted amateur societies in many provincial towns, relies on a number of fixed conventions in acting and movement that are reflected in the "traditional" *sinakulo.* As in *komedya* and nineteenth-century Western melodrama, music underscores the action, highlighting key dramatic moments and cuing the audience to offer up a particular reaction. The musical score of this *sinakulo,* which dates largely from the same period as the script, relies on Spanish-inflected music in the musical modes of Filipino *komedya,* although in the lighter, less dramatic moments it also incorporates songs that were popular in the mid-1960s.[8]

The bad guys in the *sinakulo* are the clamourous and extravagantly attired Roman soldiers dressed in fanciful (and one might also say fancy) neo-Roman garb. Their boisterous, noisy, scene-stealing onstage antics provoke the loudest, most exuberant responses from the audience each night. These roles, collectively referred to as the *hudyos*[9] (or Jews by virtue of being the collective tormentors of Christ), also include actors in the key roles of Judas, Herod, and Pilate. Oddly,

Roman soldiers can also constitute the "Jews," and it would appear that this category of "bad guys" dates back to the period when to the Spanish the *Judios* were the persecuted enemy; to the colonized Filipino, they were no doubt an abstract category. The "*hudyo* Roman soldiers" together with Herod take manic delight in inflicting pain on the innocent, while the soldiers, played by young men in the community, are given extra star turns in front of the curtain during the *sinakulo*'s frequent scene changes as they prance across the stage to the beat of a *paso doble* march played by the live band. The marching style that corresponds to the *paso doble* is a feature of the *komedya* and serves a similar function here:

> The marching conveys the idea of distance, of a long grand entry, associated with triumphal processions and the royalty's dignified and important comings and goings. It is also a posturing, a show demonstrative of flair and skill; a good "marcher" gives the viewer the kind of thrill associated with toreadors entering a bull-ring. While the bravura is a non-verbal declamation, it is also the opening or closing move in a game, since the entrance or exit always marks the beginning or the end of a scene. (Fernandez 1995a, 65)

Wearing colorful capes and glittering armor, the young men in these roles march across the stage during the entr'actes, their posing interrupted by the spontaneous clapping and catcalls of appreciative—and mostly youthful—fans, many of whom are clearly peers or classmates.

Over the course of the last three nights of the *sinakulo* particularly, these bravura displays come fast and frequently, with added drama after Christ is arrested in the Garden of Gethsemane because from then on their march also incorporates the soldiers' beating of Christ as he moves across the narrow lip of the stage. When Christ falters and almost falls off the stage and into the audience after being pushed by a soldier, a sequence that occurs repeatedly on Friday and Saturday nights, the audience erupts with wild shouts and screams. Though in its predictability this bit of stage business might in other circumstances become less effective over time, here it seems to become more satisfying for the audience each time it is repeated. Having witnessed this spectacle many times, it feels as though the response is heightened precisely because it is so clearly set up by the action that precedes it. This, coupled with the fact that it invites the collective response of the audience, makes it "work" theatrically as a convention every time it is repeated; as in nineteenth-century melodrama where the audience participated as respondents in key moments cued by visuals and/or sound, here the active community of spectators participates in the generation of a shared moment of heightened theatricality.

Figure 1. Christ being abused by Roman soldiers, *San Roque Senakulista ng Barangka,* Mandaluyong City, Metro Manila. Photo by author.

Similarly, the repeated onstage moments of bravado by the soldier-boys and our collective response to their antics constitute a "rule-bound action system" (Csikszentmihalyi 1992, 71), fusing two categories of games identified by Roger Caillois, *agon* and *mimicry.* As the young men display themselves like bullfighters entering a ring—indeed the *paso doble* is also used for such purposes—it becomes a competitive game between the young men of the community, recalling Caillois' observation that *agon* is "always a question of rivalry which hinges on a single quality" (Caillois 1961, 14), here judged by the wild applause of assembled fans. It is also playfully mimetic inasmuch as "All play presupposes the temporary acceptance, if not of an illusion (indeed this last word means nothing less than beginning a game: *in-lusio*), then at least of a closed, conventional, and, in certain respects, imaginary universe" (19). Thus the competitive game of display and audience judgment sits within a complex mimetic universe that situates the contemporary moment within a richly layered historical and cultural form.

The most consistently interactive moments across all six nights take place in those scenes where the soldiers behave badly by decapitating or killing children or display themselves to the audience in the *paso doble* star turns. Indeed, Hamlet's famous "advice to the Players," in which he instructs them not to try to "out-Herod Herod," points to the popularity of the star villains in the religious drama popular in earlier centuries, and without the flamboyant "bad guys," nearly twenty-four hours of religious drama spread out over six nights would probably not be palatable to the audience. As Nicanor Tiongson observes, in acting terms the *hudyos* are in stark contrast to those who play the holy figures:

> As in the *komedya,* there are two distinct camps in the *sinakulo.* All the holy people *(banal),* led by Christ and the Virgin, chant their lines in a lachrymose manner, walk to the beat of funeral march, and move and gesture with anemic meekness, responding to injustice with submissive tears. All the bad people *(hudyos),* on the other hand, practically spit out their lines in a crisp and harsh chant, march pompously into and out of the scene to a double-step march, and saw the air with numerous gestures that are vigorous as they are obnoxious. (Tiongson 1983, 12–13)

What matters is not so much what Christ says—indeed his words are largely inaudible to the audience in the San Roque *sinakulo*—but rather how the act of staging and watching the spectacle provides the basis for bringing the community together. As organizer Angeles observes, "let's face the fact, people do not watch the *sinakulo* because they want to hear the language. . . . That's why . . . we have extravagant and colourful costumes that are very pleasing to the eyes. It's not important to understand the lines" (Angeles 2010). Nevertheless the issue of the voiceless, passive Christ is an important one, and the criticism leveled by some, such as Tiongson (1983), at the traditional *sinakulo* for its representation of Christ will be taken up in the next chapter. What is important here, however, is that the expressive range of *komedya,* with its melodramatic acting, "shtick" antics, fanciful costumes, Spanish marches, good guys and *hudyos,* all underscored by a live band that guides the active response from the audience, is what underpins the expressive universe of this *sinakulo* and that these features are largely present in other "traditional *sinakulos*" as well.

Over six nights the most inherently dramatic stories from the history of salvation are represented onstage, heightened for melodramatic effect and enhanced by stage spectacle. Early in the cycle, the story of Cain and Abel is given considerable dramatic space as Cain cruelly beats his extraordinarily passive younger brother. Cain becomes the traditional villain of melodrama, taking visible pleasure from the pain he inflicts, pummeling his brother with increasing intensity as Abel pitifully pleads for his life. He finishes his brother off while he lies face-down on the stage, laughing maniacally after delivering the fatal blow, his sadism becoming the chief feature of the actor's performance of the role. As was the case when the *hudyos* beat Christ, here Cain's extreme badness provokes the youthful audience sitting nearest the stage to punctuate the fight with their shouts, actively participating in the action. In a similar manner, the biblical story of the massacre of the innocents, King Herod the Great's attempt to eliminate the threat of the infant Christ by ordering the killing of all infant males under two years of age in Bethlehem, is infused with melodrama. As with the actor playing Cain who delights in being evil, young men portraying Roman soldiers gleefully rip the heads off of distinctly non-Filipino baby dolls, raising them aloft and throwing them across the stage, while they snarl, smirk, and smile at the heartbreak of weeping mothers huddled together onstage. The massacre is followed by a lengthy domestic scene between King Herod and his wife as they mourn the death of their own child, a story not found in the Bible. Their pain and anguish is milked for all of its melodramatic value, and as Herod's wife hurls abuse at her husband, he pleads with her, clutching his broken heart with one hand and reaching out to her with the other as a deeply languorous tune underscores the action. Though the Roman soldiers seem to be largely motivated by pure evil, as in melodrama, even the bad guys possess a conscience that can be touched; and as they suffer heartbreak and torment over their moral failings, the audience is presumably meant to profit by their negative example. This is the case with the chief *hudyo,* Judas (Hudas), when after his betrayal of Christ, he is overcome by grief and regrets his actions as he comes to realize that he has sold his soul for a bag of money. His suicide by hanging is staged spectacularly, and as his lifeless body sways on the stage, the audience erupts with appreciative shouts. On the final Saturday night of the *sinakulo,* not only is the Resurrection staged, but the literal end of time is depicted as we witness Christ and Mother Mary ascending into the eternal realm, presided over by God the Father in an elaborate final tableau. This final dramatic ascension, which incorporates child-angels, is done with great fanfare and scenic spectacle, and accompanied by the lighting of bottle rockets from the front of the stage.

One of the distinctive features of this *sinakulo* is the preponderance of young children watching, and indeed the prime seating directly in front of the stage is reserved for them, with seating strictly policed by a virtual army of "aunties," or respected elder women. According to Angeles, this focus on reaching the children is not only because of the educative function of the *sinakulo* but also because of its communitarian ethos:

> I'd like the kids to watch this. They might not understand it but what is important for me is that they know that the tradition goes on and that sooner or later they will be the ones handling it because we will be passing

> on the torch to them. What is important . . . is for them to realize that their fathers, their brothers and sisters were all part of the *sinakulo* . . . and when the time comes, that it will be their time to pass on the tradition. (Angeles 2010)

Doreen Fernandez's observations about the eschatological framework for *komedya* apply to this *sinakulo* as well: "Each *komedya* is part of a continuum, reminiscent of *komedyas* past, predictive of *komedyas* to come" (Fernandez 1995a, 67). The *sinakulo* is done to connect intergenerationally not only with the living but also with the dead who once enacted the roles just as they are being enacted today, while also pointing toward a future where the youth in the audience will someday bequeath the tradition to the next generation. The copresence of the dead was acknowledged on the first night of the 2010 *sinakulo* when the recently deceased Delfin Deocura, the "original" Christ in this presentation, was publicly honored by the organizers in a formal presentation to his widow. In this tradition especially, continuity in terms of staging and acting practices not only ensures the efficacy of the *panata* but also serves to connect past, present, and future generations, extending the bounds of community across time even as it remains deeply emplaced.

The "Civic-Based *Sinakulo*"

Situated one hundred miles southwest of Manila on the island of Marinduque and within the Tagalog-speaking region, the *sinakulo* in the provincial capital of Boac begins with the story of Adam and Eve on Wednesday night and ends with the martyrdom by beheading of the Roman soldier Longinus on Black Saturday. The *sinakulo* is situated within the context of an overarching festival centered around a penitential practice in which men don full face masks and dress up as Roman centurions, parade through the streets, and are integrated into the four-part stage version of the *sinakulo*. The related events featuring these masked men, known locally as *morions*, also linked to the leader of the centurions, the Roman soldier Longinus, believed by many to be the first Roman convert to Christianity as well as the first martyr, will be the focus of chapter 3. The *sinakulo* was developed and presented by the Marinduque provincial government, largely under the direction of the governor, Carmencita Reyes, whose office provides the funds to produce the event. For many years, the *sinakulo*'s director as well as actors in leading roles such as Longinus, Pontius Pilate, and his wife Claudia, have been employees of the provincial government.

Staged in the Boac Morion Park on Wednesday, Thursday, and Saturday nights, the space consists of terraced, poured-concrete seating constituting two sides of the park's rectangular shape looking out over a massive central platform that accommodates a standing, mobile audience, which consists largely of younger people. An elaborate, permanent structure resembling a Roman temple occupies the far end of the park, and adjacent to it and across from the seated audience is a raised area where outdoor scenes from the life of Christ are depicted. There is a small pond for the baptism scene with Saint John the Baptist, a cave on the hillside that will serve as a tomb, and an elevated area for the three crosses for the Crucifixion at Calvary. The forestage in front of the classically inspired *scaenae frons* of the temple serves as a backdrop for all city street scenes, and the area under and immediately in front of the "temple" roof accommodates indoor scenes. Dominating the raised stage is a large throne used by Pontius Pilate. From it flows a massive red carpet spilling down the temple steps. In its simultaneous depiction of multiple locations, the staging recalls that of the European passion plays associated with the Corpus Christi Festival in the sixteenth century.[10]

One of the peculiarities of Boac's *sinakulo* is that the entire Tagalog soundtrack is prerecorded. The current version was set down after the 1986 EDSA Revolution by radio drama actors at the behest of Reyes—then Marinduque's representative in the House of Representatives—who developed the script with well-known writers Celso Carunungan and Aura Mijares (Lilles 2005; Mandia 2005).[11] Until a generation ago, radio drama was a popular form in the Philippines, especially among the older generation and in remote provinces where television reception was limited. The style in these radio dramas was melodramatic and full of rapid changes in vocal inflection, as if the absence of the actor's body required an excess of emotion through the only remaining expressive tool, the voice. The disembodied voices in the *sinakulo* were created by actors, many of them now deceased, and are mimed by living actors using highly dramatic gestures, in the style of Hollywood epic films. In the Boac *sinakulo,* all characters seem to be speaking in the manner of the narrator in the 1956 biblical blockbuster *The Ten Commandments,* as if each word is meant to be etched into stone tablets for eternity. Christ's voice is carefully modulated to reflect his humility and resignation to his fate; God the Father's is deep and resonant with power[12]; and Longinus' booming pronouncements positively spew testosterone. The influence of Hollywood epic films of the late 1950s and early 1960s on the form has been remarked on by locals (Malitao 2007; Mandia 2005), and although at this point it is largely vestigial rather than direct, the relationship between Hollywood versions of the story of Christ and its representation in the Philippines is an important one that will be taken up further in the next two chapters.

Since none of the actors speak, the acting style is similar to that of silent movies. *Sinakulo* director, Rufinio "J. R." Malitao Jr., follows the basic directing patterns set down in the mid-1980s by Ed Alcantara (Malitao 2007; Mandia 2005), whose voice is still heard as both God and Longinus. This may well be the only theatrical event where the show's original director is quite literally the "voice of God." The actor playing Longinus delivers his pronouncements with grand, sweeping gestures, but in moments of extreme turmoil he flails about the stage in a mechanical dance. The contrast between the gestural patterns of Longinus and the more life-like movements of Christ are perhaps as differently conceived as any in the cast, and there are occasions when such contrasting acting styles on the same stage takes on an almost comic tone. Indeed, some of Longinus' most overwrought moments evoke unrestrained laughter from the standing pit, suggesting that not everyone is won over by the Roman's declamatory vocal style and overly energetic performance. Many of the canned music tracks are lifted from *The Ten Commandments,* and music functions much as it did in these mid-century Hollywood epics, underscoring the play's action and heightening dramatic tension. At times, the swelling symphonic track overpowers the prerecorded dialogue track. The nearly sixty-year-old score seems to support the overblown acting style, as if the *sinakulo* were itself an adaptation of an old Hollywood movie. For those without knowledge of the source of the music used, which might well constitute most of the audience today, this is simply the "traditional" music used for the local *sinakulo.*

The archaic and anachronistic music and acting styles invite openings for vastly different receptions to the *sinakulo.* Many locals clearly come to support friends and family members, or simply because it is the biggest civic event of the year, one that also has a strong spiritual dimension, but not all audience members are impressed with the *sinakulo.* Indeed, many from outside Marinduque who have traveled there to see the show have told me they found the show incredibly boring, and they failed to return on subsequent nights to see the epic unfold. Further, many locals privately state that they would like to see the *sinakulo* updated, although to publicly assert such a view can be difficult or even dangerous given that the powerful local ruling clan, the Reyes family, is associated with the work in its current form.

Because most actors perform in the *sinakulo* year after year and all are unpaid, rehearsals are not extensive, with preparations beginning about a month before the event for newcomers. Arriving for the final week of rehearsals are the performers returning to enact the major roles. These are typically employees of the provincial government. Glenn Arevalo, a mining engineer who works for the provincial government, has played Longinus for many years, and appeared again as recently as 2013. Most of the approximately fifty actors in supporting roles already know how and where to move around the fixed playing area before rehearsals begin, and newcomers are quickly brought into the process with the help of returning participants. The scale of the crowd scenes is impressive, and given that actors are often moving in the dark on steep hillsides awash with vegetation, the sure-footedness and precision of these amateur actors reflects their collective discipline.

When asked why they participate in the *sinakulo,* the first reason cited by informants is always *panata,* typically undertaken over a number of years during Holy Week for one of the following reasons: to ensure future blessings; to give thanks for prayers answered; to seek the restoration of health either for themselves or their loved ones; or to expiate one's sins. Of the four, the last is least likely to be articulated because a *panata* is fundamentally a ritual action designed to elicit concrete, positive future outcomes, even though it may appear to be a penitential act. Of the many current and former *sinakulo* participants-actors interviewed, Marian Cunanan, who held a senior provincial government post under Reyes in 2007, offered perhaps the most comprehensive list of additional benefits that accrue to participants: (1) being in the company of friends and enjoying the sense of community that extends from working together; (2) taking pleasure from being watched while wearing extravagant costumes; and (3) being recognized for one's work in the production. Cunanan, who had played Pilate's wife Claudia twice when I interviewed her (2007), observes that this final recognition comes "after [Holy Week] when you walk on the streets and they call you Claudia." Indeed, it is common for individuals to become identified with the roles they play (Tiongson 2005); thus Mary is expected to be an exemplary and deeply moral young woman, and the actor playing Jesus has a complex relationship with the role, the audience, and the wider community, as we shall see in the next chapter. Cunanan's observations speak to the past, present, and future of playing the role, and when combined with *panata,* these elements form a complete circuit. Starting with the spiritual foundation provided by *panata,* the individual takes pleasure from the communal bonds created and strengthened through participation; they enjoy the act of performing and the attention received while onstage in their finery; and then, long after Holy Week, they take pride in being recognized and associated with a particular role.

On all three nights of the evening *sinakulo* (Wednesday, Thursday, and Saturday), each actor in a prominent role is individually introduced, which takes up a full fifteen minutes at the start of the show and reflects the importance of public recognition of one's participation. The preshow spectacle resembles Resil Mojares' (1985) description of the formal introductions that preceded the popular *komedya* in early twentieth-century Cebu in its practice of recognizing performers with appropriate pomp.[13] Mojares notes that in Cebu, a speech by local dignitaries and an invocation *(alabacion)* to God or the local patron saint was followed by "a long-winded formal presentation *(presentacion)* of players when performers or groups of performers stiffly march on stage to the sound of band music" (Mojares 1985, 76). By the end of the lengthy introduction to the Boac *sinakulo,* the large temple stage features in excess of fifty named performers, joined by an equal or slightly larger number of *morion.* Costuming, colorful and lively, relies heavily on a 1950s Hollywood ideal of Roman style, with little attention paid to historical authenticity. Whereas all Roman soldiers are enacted by masked *morions,* the remaining actors appear without masks.

Highlights from the Old Testament are presented in truncated form in the Wednesday *sinakulo.* The first segment, an evocation of the creation expressed through dance, is followed by Adam and Eve in the Garden of Eden and proceeds quickly to the events connected with the prophesizing of Christ and his birth. Thursday's *sinakulo* covers the major events in the life of Christ, beginning with his baptism by John the Baptist and continuing through key scenes such as Christ's temptation by Lucifer, miracles such as the turning of water into wine, his driving of the moneychangers from the temple, the recruitment of the disciples, his prayer in the Garden of Gethsemane, the Last Supper, and his betrayal and arrest. The conclusion of Thursday's *sinakulo* is not Christ's arrest, but rather the death of Judas. In the final scene that night, following his betrayal of Christ, Judas staggers around the vast outdoor acting area, sobbing uncontrollably, climbing up a tree and tying a rope around his neck. Then, in a dramatic moment, he flings himself from the tree and swings wildly from side to side as he appears to die of strangulation, though a closer inspection in the dim light reveals that he is wearing a body harness. The effect is so lifelike that, as in the "traditional *sinakulo,*" every year it elicits applause and wild cheers, particularly from the young people who crowd the area nearest to the tree in anticipation of this grisly scene. This impulse to take vengeance on the body of Judas is a highlight of other Holy Week activities elsewhere in the country as well, evoking a similarly spirited response from the audience.[14] As the audience reaction to Judas' death demonstrates, the standing, mobile segment of the audience quickly becomes embedded in both the spectacle and the action of the *sinakulo* as they shift about to secure the best positions from which to view key scenes along the long raised verge. On Good Friday the *sinakulo* literally bursts off the stage and onto the streets and all residents can become "spect-actors," to borrow Augusto Boal's (1993) term,[15] actively witnessing the suffering of Christ or, as some do, carrying out penitential practices.[16] Because this practice is not formally part of the Boac *sinakulo,* and is reflective of the widespread Good Friday tradition of enacting the Stations of the Cross in the streets, it will be considered in some detail in the next chapter.

On Saturday night the *morions* spill into the park from the city streets for the final *sinakulo,* and the entire cast is again formally introduced. The action begins where it ended on Good Friday, as lights come up on the crucified Christ on the hill, flanked by the other two men on crosses. The Roman soldier Longinus, blind in one eye, repeats the scene from the previous afternoon in which he pierces Christ's side with his lance and his blindness is miraculously cured by the blood that spurts from the wound. From this moment he becomes the principal dramatic focus of the final *sinakulo,* as his conversion and subsequent proselytizing, followed by his capture and execution, enable the soldier to essentially steal the show from Christ and the Marys on the eve of Easter. The soldier fuels a domestic conflict between Pilate and his wife, who pleads with her husband for Longinus' life, leaving the Resurrection of Christ behind as a kind of dramatic footnote by the end of the evening. Because the Saturday night *sinakulo* departs the most radically from the standard *pasyon,* it merits further elaboration.

Following the restoration of Longinus' sight, the action continues in the palace of Pontius Pilate, who is depicted as enslaved to passion, suggesting not so much Pilate as Herod Antipas.[17] Underscored by canned music, performers who appear to be women, all wearing highly revealing diaphanous gowns, dance for Pilate, while their fabric-draped arms suggest not so much sensuality as the movements of a strange, flightless bird. Pilate is set up as a generic, depraved Arab sultan with many concubines, paralleling the depiction of Moors in *komedya,* while the women dance for the pleasure of the enthroned man. When the dance ends, girlish laughter fills the soundscape, suggesting that the women are happy to serve the master's needs. One informant, conflating the construction of the Filipino *bakla*—fundamentally a woman in a man's body—with the Western category "gay,"[18] observed that "the Pontius Pilate dancers are gays," adding that "they're the only ones with the guts to wear sexy costumes" that "no lady" would wear. The decadent stage show is interrupted by news of the potential challenge posed by the proselytizing Longinus, and Pilate seeks counsel from his priests, one of whom in 2005 appeared to be inexplicably costumed like a scholar in Chinese *jingju.* In the next scene, Longinus testifies in the streets about the miracle of Christ's mercy, moving jerkily from stranger to stranger along the length of the outdoor stage, appearing positively drunk with enthusiasm as he gesticulates wildly.

As Longinus' proselytizing reaches a fever pitch, a blinding light darts outward from inside Christ's tomb and grand orchestral music builds to a crescendo, while on the adjacent side of the playing area, strobe lights simulate an earthquake in Pilate's palace as Romans flee the scene in a panic. Suddenly the boulder blocking the tomb's entrance is "miraculously" pushed aside and Christ emerges. It is as if the Resurrection were cued by Longinus' testimony. With his shroud decorously draped across his semi-nude form, Christ moves slowly and wordlessly through the outdoor landscape to the ever-swelling strains of triumphal orchestral music, his hand raised up to bless the assembled multitudes, before ascending a partially hidden forklift into heaven. Throughout the drama of Christ's resurrection, the Marys are mere props, never uttering a word and disappearing into darkness.

Pilate's wife Claudia, the only female role with significant dialogue, drives the subplot that moves the rest of the evening's events along,[19] and after dreaming that Jesus was a "just man," she urges her husband to spare Longinus.[20] She has a private meeting with Longinus outside the palace, and the suggestion seems to be that she may be harboring an unrequited romantic interest in the soldier. In spite of being plagued by dreams in which he is overtaken by pesky onstage devils, Pilate rejects her advice and condemns the soldier to death. In the play's concluding scene, Longinus is brought to a chopping block at the center of the outdoor stage and beheaded most spectacularly by his fellow *morion* who stand in as Roman soldiers. The lights flash off, a loud crack is heard, and the lights flash back on as his distinctive, one-eyed *morion* head rolls down the hill toward a screaming, youthful standing audience that has prepositioned itself in the best viewing spot. Longinus' body is then taken away in semidarkness as the music again swells, marking the sacrifice of the first Roman martyred for his Christian beliefs.

Though the director, J. R. Malitao, replicates the stage blocking of the *sinakulo*'s original director, he also observes, "I've seen it in the movies," again referring to the Hollywood biblical epics of the late 1950s and early 1960s. In this genre, which included box office hits such as *Sodom and Gomorrah* (1962), *David and Goliath* (1960), and *Solomon and Sheba* (1959), as well as films that focused on the life of Christ, notably *King of Kings* (1961) and *The Greatest Story Ever Told* (1965), great effort was made and no expense spared in making each scene adhere to prevailing visual codes that governed representations as the "real" or "authentic" biblical environment. Shot on locations in the United States, Egypt, Italy, and Spain, these largely Old Testament epics featured elaborate and often massive constructed sets, costumes consistent with the iconographic images of contemporary Jews and Egyptians, and emplaced in environments that looked similar to those circulated in the Sunday school primers of the era; this collective visual representation offered a "real" image of the Holy Land, along with the remarkably white people who inhabited it. Much of this iconographic style appears to have been fixed by the late nineteenth century, and it bears noting that the famed Cyclorama of Jerusalem in Montreal, created in 1895 by French panoramist Paul Philippoteaux, with its great cinematic magnificence, concretizes popular culture

Figure 2. Longinus meeting secretly with Claudia, Saturday night *sinakulo,* Boac Morion Park, Marinduque. Photo by author.

fantasies of the way Jerusalem and its inhabitants "really" looked, using a visual style that anticipates the great biblical epic films. Though films such as *The Ten Commandments* may be seen by some as dated fantasies reflecting the visual style of a bygone era, at Boac and other sites, the images from these films continue to provide the foundation for an iconography regarded as authentic. In his compelling book *Visual Piety,* David Morgan considers what Christians say about their relationship to religious images and how they display and use them in their daily lives, demonstrating how "the act of looking itself contributes to religious formation and, indeed, constitutes a powerful practice of belief" (Morgan 1999, 3). I have observed a similar kind of "visual piety" with respect to the circulation, use, and provenance of imagery in dramatic representations and performance associated with Holy Week. What is "real" and "authentic" thus becomes what has been absorbed from the movies and reinforced through popular religious iconography. For those watching the Boac *sinakulo,* the experience is primarily an act of looking, one where the visual style reflects a filmic view of the Holy Land and the people in it.

"The Activist *Sinakulo*"

The final category, the "activist *sinakulo,*" has a relatively recent history, emplacing a dynamic, charismatic Christ at the center of the dramatic representation and using the story of the *pasyon* as a platform for drawing attention to contemporary social and economic injustice. Largely confined to the Metro Manila area, these productions have also had a strong community-outreach component, sometimes bringing in nonactors from relatively impoverished or underresourced communities into a framework of social activism determined by an organization or well-known director. One notable example of such a work was *Kalbaryo ng Maralitang Tagalungsod (Calvary of the Urban Poor),* a *sinakulo* staged from 1988 to 1992 by Al Santos, which incorporated the residents of the "Smokey Mountain" garbage dump in Tondo, Manila (Rodel 2002, 155), where tens of thousands of residents once eked out a tenuous existence in a massive, famously polluted site. Santos' work was noted for recuperating agency in a tradition that some, most notably Tiongson (1983, 14) and Eugene van Erven, have elsewhere critiqued for glorifying a passive Christ,[21] essentially reinforcing the message of the old Spanish colonial masters by teaching "Filipinos to resign themselves to their earthly poverty and oppression as a trial of God for which they would reap their rewards in the Hereafter" (van Erven 1992, 32). Tiongson, responsible for most of the scholarship on the traditional *sinakulo,* has also expressed concerns about *sinakulos* that "propagate values of passivity and blind obedience by making Christ the model of subservience" (Tiongson 1992, 32), though he is equally critical of the reconfigured contemporary *pasyon* where the story of Christ becomes the raw material on which the director might impose his personal stamp:

> Actually I'm not happy about the way the Christ story has been stolen by people who do not believe in it and how it has been used for political ends. . . . I have a very uneasy feeling that it's just riding on the popularity of the Christ story . . . I guess from my perspective because I grew up with the *sinakulo* that meant a lot to the people who appeared in it. . . . The people who participated in it appeared in it for life. . . . It governed their lives. There were things you did not do, especially if you were known as the virgin in the *sinakulo*. . . . It affected your personal morals, your personal relationships. . . . The very act of appearing in a *sinakulo* was a kind of prayer. . . . I think it's the intrusion of people from the outside who are coming from basically a secular point of view that can sometimes be anti-religion who come in and see the *sinakulo* as a chance to promote their own political agenda. (Tiongson 2005)

Tiongson's comments also point to a tricky double bind that operates when working with and speaking for the urban and rural poor, which has played itself out in the long history of the People's Educational Theatre Association (PETA). As van Erven discovered while traveling with the company and observing their work in 1986, PETA company members themselves admitted that as social activists from comfortable middle-class backgrounds in Manila, they were not always able to successfully reach out to and gain the confidence of the working poor (van Erven 1992, 63). Further, those from such backgrounds are also unlikely to have much personal experience with the kind of traditional *sinakulo* to which Tiongson refers. Thus his criticism of the ways in which an established artist might adapt it to suit personal needs has merit. Yet, as Ileto (1979) demonstrated, there is a long tradition of one-to-one identification with the places of the *pasyon* with sites in the Philippines, and a further identification of Christ and his disciples as models for revolutionary societies that were created to fight Spanish and later American colonizers. Thus one can argue that the activist Christ is deeply emplaced in the Filipino consciousness and merits continuous restaging and rediscovery. The example that follows suggests that it is possible to infuse the *sinakulo* with contemporary relevance without detaching it from its cultural or spiritual moorings.

Between the two extremes of the rewritten *sinakulo* set in the slums of contemporary Manila and the "traditional *sinakulo*" is the Manila Mobile Theatre's production of the *Martir sa Golgota*, the longest-running *sinakulo* in this category, and one that has reached a large audience over time. Under the artistic direction of veteran theatre, film, and television actor and local politician Lou Veloso, since 1989 this group has staged the life of Christ, taking the show from its home in the city of Santa Ana in Metro Manila, and restaging it in various locations elsewhere in the area, including Tondo, one of the city's most notoriously impoverished areas. The *sinakulo* is essentially an extension of a community arts project based in the modest Santa Ana Arts Center, a small indoor rehearsal and performance space that anchors one end of a public square in the heart of one of Manila's oldest neighborhoods. Unlike the traditional *sinakulo* that may dramatize the entire history of salvation, moving on to the story of the adult Christ only by the second or third evening's enactment, Veloso's Easter pageant, as the play's title suggests, relies on the Filipino version of the martyrdom of Christ, though it starts with his earliest miracles and the recruitment of his disciples. Veloso's *sinakulo* melds music, song, dance, extravagant costumes, and professional production values to present what he calls a "fighting Christ, an activist Christ" (Veloso 2010), supported by a cast of film and television actors in the leading roles who have given up their time to participate without remuneration. In style of presentation, the *sinakulo* is closer to musical theatre than the traditional *sinakulo,* with songs composed by Veloso expertly rendered by professional actors in the main roles, many with strong singing voices. As many as seventy actors, the majority of whom are drawn from the ranks of the community-based group, Tanghalang Santa Ana, fill the stage in the key crowd scenes, some of which also feature large choral numbers. Rehearsals with this group start a month before the production, and run for seven to ten hours every day (ibid.), a time commitment that is daunting but that results in a show so tight in its direction and choreography that it is often difficult to tell the difference between the amateur actors and the professional ones. As with participation in *sinakulo* and Holy Week performances elsewhere, actors involved in this production cite *panata* as their primary reason for participation.

Unlike the epic, multiple-evening *sinakulo* staged by the San Roque *Senakulistas,* Veloso's relatively abbreviated passion is staged over a single evening, lasting just over two hours. While deceptively simple in its staging, in that it requires little more than a raised stage and lighting rig, its complexity is in its choreography, the detailed and sometimes sumptuous costumes worn by the actors, and the inventive use of props. It tours with a sophisticated sound system, which uses original, prerecorded music, and a professional portable lighting rig. The annual *sinakulo* typically starts with a satirical skit on a topical story that invites the audience to consider the moral dilemmas confronted by Filipinos today, indirectly linking the Christ story to contemporary social and political activism. The 2009 show took the famously corrupt former president Gloria Macapagal-Arroyo to task, while the 2010 production commenced with a sketch comedy scene in which candidates in the upcoming presidential election jostled for position on a fictional television show. Veloso is very much a theatre person, and this *sinakulo* reflects a deep understanding of how to shape and structure a theatrical event to maximize its dramatic effectiveness.

As a piece of musical theatre featuring actors from outside the community in which it is created, the *Martir sa Golgota* has a double appeal; those who see the show in Santa Ana witness friends and family sharing the stage with well-known actors, whereas audiences both in Santa Ana and elsewhere when on tour, particularly those living in the poorest neighborhoods—those identified as "Class C and D municipalities"—where it is also staged, are unlikely to have ever witnessed a professional theatrical production, much less one featuring good-looking actors known from television. Offered free to the public, in 2013 the production was staged not only at its home in Santa Ana but also in Tondo, San Andres, Luneta Park in central Manila, and in Pagsanjan, Laguna. Two additional shows were staged that year at the Cultural Center of the Philippines (CCP) on the Friday and

Saturday prior to Holy Week, providing a middle-class and well-heeled audience with the chance to pay to see a show that has been staged for free to poorer residents of the city for the past twenty-four years.[22]

Veloso's work with the group continues throughout the year and has also included an activist take on the *panunuluyan,* the enactment of Mary and Joseph's search for an inn, staged in the streets before Christmas with actors from the community. Following the mode of community-based performance developed by and most associated with PETA, Veloso has also created original work with local Santa Ana residents dealing with topics such as drug abuse, family life, and environmental concerns (CPC News 2008). As Veloso observes, "We've had more than a hundred members from all walks of life. We have had drivers, teachers, mothers, out-of-school youth as members" (Philippine Entertainment Portal 2009). As a local counselor with a significant reputation as an award-winning film and television artist, Veloso has been able to access funding to support this group as a community-based arts project, and also to pay for the costs associated with hiring equipment and touring the show. All who participate do so without being paid. Echoing the comments of actors interviewed, Veloso observed that "for us working in this play, this serves as our annual religious offering" (Philippine Entertainment Portal 2009).

The start of the *sinakulo* proper is heralded by music lifted from the sound track of *The Ten Commandments,* as Christ appears in the first scene as a grown man being baptized by John the Baptist. Tuneful and sometimes highly emotional songs are placed at regular intervals throughout the play, underscoring key dramatic moments. In one such song early in the play, Jesus recruits his disciples as they cast their nets for fish, and another musical number is delivered by an angel as Christ prays for guidance in the Garden of Gethsemane. A good deal of the first part of the *sinakulo* is taken up with scenes featuring exchanges between the Jewish priests, and then between the priests and Pilate as they prevail upon Pilate to have Jesus arrested and crucified. As in the two prior *sinakulos,* Judas has a prominent role in three key scenes: In the first, he accepts the iconic red bag of coins from the priests in return for betraying Christ, and in the second, he attempts to give back the money to ease his guilty conscience. His third and most dramatic scene is given over to a musical number in which he sings through his deep remorse, and the scene ends in his suicide by hanging. A more nuanced *hudyo,* Pilate, resplendent in a white cape and elaborate finery, carries a number of key scenes, including one that turns into a domestic conflict with his wife Claudia, who plants misgivings in his mind about the wisdom of crucifying Christ. A reluctant Pilate gives the final verdict as Jesus is brought onto the stage by Roman soldiers.

In 2010, the second night of the *sinakulo* was staged in an outdoor public theatre space in San Juan, a city bordering on Santa Ana and also part of Metro Manila. Unlike the portrayal in the previous night's show, the scourging of Christ took place offstage as a retinue of Roman soldiers spilled into the streets behind the theatre space to pursue the Savior, stopping at preset locations marked by lit candles and makeshift shrines. At each station, Christ stumbled and they beat him, enacting a kind of compressed *Via Cruces,* or Stations of the Cross, a foundational Good Friday practice that will be examined in some detail in the next chapter. Leading Christ back onto the stage after the chase through the streets, the soldiers formed a line across the lip of the stage with their bodies and shields, blocking the audience's view of the upstage area while Christ was raised on the cross. Although Migui Moreno, the actor playing Christ that night, appeared to be more exhausted than bloodied by this point, the actors playing the roles of Gestas and Dismas,[23] the two criminals crucified along with Christ, had rivers of stage blood running down their faces and chests. The Marys then came out for the obligatory scene at the foot of the cross, while an angel in white appeared and started singing the popular nationalistic song, "Pinakamamahal Kong Bayan" (My Beloved Country), the lyrics of which fuse the sufferings of the nation with a prayer to God. This was a sweeping, highly emotional number in which a resurrected Jesus lovingly embraced a flag held in place by Pontius Pilate. By this point, although the stage was filling with the remaining cast in preparation for the curtain call, there is nevertheless something odd about Church and state coming together in the form of Pilate and Christ, especially inasmuch as the emotional, highly charged lyrics of the song and its sweeping melody make clear that *bayan* represents the Filipino people collectively. As if to dispel any doubt about who "we the people" are, a giant flag was unfurled, covering the entire width of the stage and forming a backdrop behind Christ, Pilate, the Priests, and all of the actors. This was an impressive spectacle, though the celebratory quality of the ending that literally wraps Christ in the Filipino flag seemed out of step with the short playlet that preceded the 2009 *sinakulo,* which dealt with political corruption, and in 2010 ridiculed presidential hopefuls. The suggestion seems to be that by trusting in Christ, the nation and its people will come together and triumph, that any obstacle can be overcome through Christ, including a corrupt state. Indeed, in the final image before the curtain call, the cast members are on their knees, arms aloft as in supplication as they look up and off in the distance with the national flag behind them. It is a vision of a unified nation that exists in the future, not the present, insofar as what is visually expressed seems a hope for a better future, and is not a reflection of any contemporary reality. It is a melodramatic ending in many respects, and not altogether at odds with the ending of the traditional *sinakulo*

Figure 3. Finale of *Martir sa Golgota,* Migui Moreno as Christ (left) with Don Umali as Pontius Pilate, Manila Mobile Theatre, directed by Lou Velosa. Photo by author.

where we look toward a future through salvation, one marked by eschatological time. In this final respect at least, Veloso's *sinakulo,* though nationalistic and proudly Filipino, is also uncannily consistent with the older *sinakulo* tradition.

The Scenario and Mimesis in the *Sinakulo*

In spite of their differences in form, structure, modes of representation, and degree and type of audience engagement, all three *sinakulo* might well be considered "traditional" inasmuch as they all follow a formula devised at least a generation ago, which builds on and adapts an even older and vaster range of cultural and religious performance texts. Similarly, the texts that form the basis for these *sinakulo* are derived from foundational texts that in many cases are difficult or impossible to locate, one might even say shrouded in mystery. For the *Martir sa Golgota,* what is the relationship of the Tagalog text, circulated informally by Indio priests in the late nineteenth and early twentieth centuries, to the Spanish text, *El Martir del Golgata,* by Pérez Escrich? And who created the adaptation of this text that forms the basis of the San Roque *sinakulo?* Possibly someone living in the city of Pasay sometime in the early to mid-twentieth century, though the text is credited to a local, Rading de Guzman. As Fenella Cannell's (2006) experience attempting to trace out these kinds of genealogies in Cebu suggests, authoritatively setting out lineages through textual traditions is a potentially fruitless and pointless exercise. What matters more is how these texts, adapted and living on in repertory, function in the lives of the communities of believers who support, stage, and participate in them. Their power is to some extent enhanced by maintaining a degree of mystery about their precise origins.

Whereas the social actors on the stage of these *sinakulos* may reflect class positions and relationships that differ from the local and regional power structures and the ruling elite, who are known to and recognized by local audiences, all who participate do so as a form of *panata*. These practices take up vast amounts of time and energy, and it is no accident that they are often strongest and most widely taken up as community-based events in areas where many are unemployed or underemployed. All make demands on the physical body, particularly in a durational performance event such as the six-night San Roque *sinakulo* or the multiple nights of *sinakulos* in different locations by the Manila Mobile Theatre. Those at the top of the social and economic heap may even shape and control the form of the *sinakulo* itself, as we have seen in Marinduque, where the provincial governor contributed in ways that are widely acknowledged, but not altogether transparent. The unseen actors are the political entities that sponsor these events, and through their apparent inaction or action they gain political capital through their support; this is clearly the case for the *barangay* captain of Barangka Ibaba and the local government of Mandaluyong City, a representative of which introduces the play each night. Although they are not shaping the script, their presence every night reminds those present that they are responsible for bringing it to the audience.

As we have seen, these three *sinakulo* scenarios, as Taylor observes of work that exists as repertoire, are not mimetic in any straightforward sense. They all cite performances and social and religious constructs originating elsewhere and conjure the past, actively re-creating that relationship over time. Thus for the young men in the Barangka Ibaba who parade across the stage to the *paso doble* in their finery, hand sewn by the mothers, grandmothers, and aunts of the *barangay,* they are undertaking a *panata;* they are Spanish soldiers fighting the Moors linked to colonized Filipinos fighting their own Moors, the Muslims of the South; they are actors, dancers, show-offs, members of a community of working class people in a crowded *barangay* in Metro Manila, kids having fun playing dress-up for friends and family members; and finally and most fundamentally through their sacrifice of time, commitment, and energy they are expressing their Christian faith and their unending, depthless gratitude for Christ's enormous sacrifice. Given the manifold layers (re)presented in the body of a single actor in a single *sinakulo* in just one of the three categories, it is clear that representation cannot be mimetic in any straightforward sense. The Boac *sinakulo,* far from merely mimicking old Hollywood movies, when analyzed dynamically as a complex religious and social scenario achieves something closer to what Michael Taussig calls "mimetic excess . . . a form of human capacity potentiated by post-coloniality . . . [that] . . . provides a welcome opportunity to live subjectively as neither subject nor object of history but as both, at one and the same time" (Taussig 1993, 255). Though one can identify ways in which each form described here bears similarities to and is drawn directly or indirectly from the forms disseminated by old colonial masters, the Spanish and the Americans, it is in how Filipinos use these influences and what they mean within their respective localized cultural, religious, and psychological frameworks that places them beyond imitation, into the category of "mimetic excess." Similarly, as Homi Bhabha observes, "In order to be effective, mimicry must continually produce its slippage, its excess, its difference" (Bhabha 1994, 86). It is in its "excess" and its "slippage," where what might seem at first glance to be simple mimicry, that the *sinakulo* thrives and lives on. In this fissure created by culture, history, religion, colonization, and understandings of the self in relation to the other, the *sinakulo* continues as it has for the better part of two centuries to provide an original, dynamic experiential pathway into the passion of Christ. And it is to Christ's role in all of this that we turn in the next chapter.

CHAPTER 2

The Body of Christ

Those looking into the Philippines through the lens of the Western media might well have the impression that on Good Friday the entire country is one massive, grisly Crucifixion scene with penitents being nailed to crosses at every turn. One of the most startling and lurid headlines reinforcing this stereotype appeared in the *Sydney Morning Herald* on Easter Sunday 2010, proclaiming, "Filipinos mark Easter with whippings" (Malakunas 2010). By contrast, that same day the corresponding story in the Manila-based *Philippines Inquirer* (2010) appeared under the caption, "RP [Republic of the Philippines] marks Good Friday with tradition, rituals." Perhaps no clearer contrast between the views of outside and inside can be found than through these two headlines framing two radically divergent views of what happens during Holy Week in the Philippines. Sydney's Easter Sunday article, drawn from Agence France Press and reprinted in daily newspapers throughout the world,[1] focused exclusively and most spectacularly on the Holy Week penitential practice for which the country is best known internationally, namely, what Tiatco and Bonifacio-Ramolete (2008) have termed "the performance of pain and suffering," famously enacted in the *barangay* of Cutud, outside the city of San Fernando in Pampanga province, north of Manila. Here twenty or more penitents have their hands and feet pierced with nails on a raised cross as part of a range of performance events that include a *sinakulo* and an enactment of the Stations of the Cross on the streets of Cutud. This crucifixion is a relatively contemporary practice, dating from 1962, when faith healer Tatang Temyong, who had played Christ in the local *sinakulo,* sought "to do a deeper *panata*" that went beyond "being tied on the cross for fifteen minutes" (Tiatco and Bonifacio-Ramolete 2008, 63). The experience was eventually opened up to outside participants (67), and by the mid-1990s it had become an internationalized spectacle that was covered by major media sources worldwide, and thus the dominant practice associated with the whole of the country by much of the rest of the world at Easter.

Another site where actual crucifixions take place is in the *barangay* of Kapitangan in Paombong, Bulacan province.[2] In 2009, Australian documentarian and comedy writer John Safran sought out this alternative site to personally experience crucifixion. Safran, who was raised in Melbourne as an orthodox Jew, convinced local residents that he was a Catholic student named John Michael who wished to undertake a *panata* for his mother who was dying of cancer. Later that year his "performance of pain and suffering" was the highlight of the final episode of an eight-part comic documentary series shown on Australian public television titled "Race Relations." In the promotional clip for the final episode, Safran proclaimed that his act of being nailed to the cross was to be "the ultimate renouncement of my ethnic heritage, the ultimate Jewish obliteration" (ABC Television 2009). Safran, who has a history of approaching difficult subjects from oblique or comic angles with a near forensic attention to detail, departed from past practice and used subterfuge to gain the trust of others to enter into and be accepted as part of a community of believers who were undertaking this exceptional and painful identification with the sufferings of Christ. At the village level, people felt betrayed and disrespected by Safran's act and the way in which it held this tradition up to mockery before a television audience in a wealthy, Western country. On discovering the deception, his local host, who was crucified along with Safran, sought his signature on an affidavit indicating that the footage would not be used for comic purposes (Sta. Maria 2009; Symons 2009). It is clear that Safran was trusted, that families and indeed an entire community had opened up their hearts and minds to him, and accepted him as a kindred spirit. From a Filipino *barangay* or village perspective, he not only betrayed that trust, but did so quite spectacularly, essentially pretending to take on the ultimate *panata* that connects the individual on an experiential, corporal level with the sufferings of Christ. By not engaging honestly with his host community and by taking on the "performance of pain and suffering" as a theatrical exercise for television, Safran, like the screaming newspaper headlines that focus on "whippings" in the Philippines, cut himself off from a meaningful engagement with what Christ might mean to Filipinos.[3]

Safran's crucifixion and its dissemination through an Australian television documentary bring into sharp focus two guiding principles that underscore the inquiry in this chapter: first, that the performance of actual pain and suffering is just one element on a very long continuum of practices involving *panata* that link Filipinos personally with the sufferings of Christ; and second, that all Holy Week performance activities, and particularly those associated with the suffering of Christ, must be considered within the particulars of their community-based context to make sense. Most Filipinos do not get nailed to crosses and those few who do, do it to fulfill a vow, not because they see themselves as sinners who need to be scourged so they do not continue to sin in the future. This chapter considers why, particularly during Holy Week, so many individuals seek out some kind of experiential connection with the sufferings of Christ. What do Filipinos want from

Christ and how is it expressed through performance? What are the qualities of Christ that attract them? Even more fundamentally, in what ways might we identify features of a Christ who has been Filipinized (or at least Tagalized, given that this is not an exhaustive, national study)? And finally, how do those yearnings for a particular relationship with Christ play themselves out in communities of faith?

This chapter maps out the relationship between the body of Christ and the bodies of those who *stand in for him* as well as the larger majority of Catholics who *stand with him* during Holy Week by moving through four interlocking frames that start with the internal, spiritual, and psychological dimensions of that relationship and also take in external, representational considerations. These frames consider (1) the emotional, psychological, and spiritual needs that are met by seeking out an experiential connection with the sufferings of Christ; (2) the actual practice of walking with Christ through the Stations of the Cross on Good Friday, which is prevalent in many urban and rural *barangay* in the Philippines; (3) the performing body of the actor Christ in the *sinakulo,* with special reference to the contrast between what I term the "Suffering Christ" and the "*Kaibigan* (or Best Friend) Christ"; and (4) the representation of what is believed to be the real or "authentic" Christ in the *sinakulo,* particularly as it has been influenced by Mel Gibson's 2004 movie, *The Passion of the Christ.* These frames move from those that are internal, *sa loób,* the human organism, and conclude with those external representational elements that serve to define and reinforce the connection the individual has to Christ. Thus the chapter will necessarily be as much about the experience of enacting Christ as it is about how that enactment creates a range of openings for individuals to relate to the suffering that the actorly Christ enacts on their behalf.

Connecting with the Suffering of Christ

More than the promise of the Resurrection, the vast majority of the human and emotional energy during Holy Week is focused on generating an empathetic response to the sufferings of Christ, which for many individuals requires taking on some measure of sacrifice, discomfort, or even pain. According to Father Benigno Beltran (1987), in Filipino Folk Catholicism,[4] the dominant practice outside of the middle-class enclaves of Manila and other big cities, Holy Week ritual activities are the active, experiential expressions of divine grace. Beltran, who for many years served as resident priest at the infamous Smokey Mountain slum, argues that the Filipino experience of being Catholic "is characterized by a thaumaturgical thrust—the desire of the people to experience the extraordinary effects of the supernatural in their lives," in contrast to the relatively doctrine-driven

Roman Catholicism emanating from the Vatican that "is oriented toward the cognitive dimension of the faith" (Beltran 1987, 6). Beltran, who argues convincingly that "Folk Catholicism" best reflects the actual faith practice of the greatest number of Filipino Catholics,[5] delineates the field as follows:

> Folk Catholicism is a sort of "Catholic underworld" with its own self-consistency, its own logic and rationality and its own frame of reference. It is a coherent and integrated though largely unarticulated conception of a general order of existence which orients the life of the masses, maintains their sense of personal communitarian identity, and provides practical solutions to the problems of everyday life and immediate personal concerns. (Beltran 1987, 5)

"Folk Catholicism" acknowledges and has room for the vast range of adaptations carried out by local clergy as they built upon prior belief systems and understandings of heaven, hell, and the afterlife and sought to indigenize the teachings of the Catholic Church using local frameworks for understanding and expressing their faith. Though the propagation of faith by the Catholic Church has a long history of cross-cultural adaptation, in the Philippines Spanish friars went beyond the practices that had proved successful in making converts in Central and Latin America. There the spread of the faith was largely through the Latin Mass, with clergy speaking Spanish or Portuguese, but in the Philippines the priests, dispatched from Mexico, were expected to learn the local language and use it to disseminate the teachings of the Church. When native "Indio" priests started to replace Spanish friars in the nineteenth century, the practice of indigenization using local languages and understandings of Christ and key concepts in the Bible became even more localized and dispersed, even as Manila became the center of the formal Church hierarchy.

Today as throughout history, "folk" practices are tolerated because they are successful in mobilizing the faithful. Whereas in some cases folk practices are actively supported by the Church, in other instances, particularly where there is bloodletting, the official protests of the Church are ignored and local clergy turn a blind eye. Even the regular denunciation of the extreme penitential practices found in Cutud by the Catholic Bishops' Conference of the Philippines has not stopped anyone from engaging in them (*Philippine Daily Inquirer* 2013). Beltran's survey of nearly ten thousand practicing Catholics found that 36.3 percent of the men had at some point inflicted pain on themselves for religious reasons (Beltran 1987, 62), a figure that has probably remained relatively constant over the past generation. Those who self-flagellate and who endure crucifixion believe that their actions have efficacy and for many, their annual *panata* is the experiential cornerstone of their faith, proof that belief in God and in the power of Jesus Christ can ensure future blessings on those they love. The spiritual use-value of these practices becomes clearer when they are placed into frameworks identified by Filipino scholars across the fields of sociology, anthropology, sociolinguistics, psychology, and Philippine Studies. Drawing from these fields and placing them into active conversation with one another, the following analysis maps out the thaumaturgical dimensions of faith through the connection of the active spectator and the actor with the sufferings of Christ.

Father Beltran, who actively participated in the 1986 EDSA (People Power) Revolution that brought down the Marcos regime, suggests that political and economic oppression fuels the identification most Filipinos have with the sufferings of Christ:

> In a country where poverty, deprivation, and oppression are the common lot of the masses, it is not surprising that the image of the crucified one, head bowed, mouth agape in excruciating agony, provides consolation and an outlet for pent-up emotions of sympathy and tragedy for the ignorant and the heavy-laden. (Beltran 1987, 123)

Yet poverty, deprivation, and oppression alone explain neither the rapid acceptance of the Catholic faith in Tagalog-speaking regions of the Philippines in the colonial period nor the need so many Filipinos have for an experiential connection with the sufferings of Christ. Beltran observes that "the idea of corporal mortification as a penance for sins was foreign to ancient Filipinos," and instead it was Christ's suffering and sacrifice that had resonance in that it tapped into the Filipino construct of *damay,* a kind of "supra-empathy" that makes a merely empathetic response to the suffering of others inadequate. Beltran notes that the practice of corporeal mortification

> became more prevalent . . . especially when it was connected with one's *damay,* sympathy with or suffering with Jesus. In popular religious movements, belief in the need to participate in Jesus' sufferings through pity and empathy is particularly stressed. The focus on the victim-Christ in folk Catholicism reinforces the desire to personally relate oneself to the Passion though ascetic practices. (Beltran 1987, 115)

F. Landa Jocano places *damay* in a Tagalog linguistic and social context, drawing on extensive fieldwork and interviews through a vast network of informants, extending Beltran's analysis of religion into the Filipino sociology of the self. His inquiry, using concepts rooted in culture and language, seeks to describe how the world is constituted through feeling for the Filipino. *Damay,* observes Jocano, is the last and final of three components of selfhood known collectively as *damá,* which constitutes how Filipinos organize the way they feel about the world. The overarching *damá* consists of a chain that starts with *kahulugán* (the meaning attached to events, people, and objects) and proceeds to *habág* (sympathy for people in need), ending (potentially at least) with *damay,* which "is to show in actual practice the act of compassion" (Jocano 2001, 106). Thus an initial understanding that produces meaning may lead to sympathy for others, whereas a more fully evolved individual is willing and able to respond to the needs of others "in actual practice." Or to put it another way, in order to complete the circuit of a feeling person, one has to be willing to undertake compassionate acts in support of one's fellow man, acts that may even involve taking on the physical sufferings of others.

Vicente Rafael suggests that one of the factors that may explain massive and rapid conversions in the Tagalog-speaking regions historically is the sense of indebtedness to Christ, a debt that cannot be paid fully, aligning it with the cultural concept of *utang na loób,* often translated as "debt of gratitude." He observes: "To say that 'Christ died for you' is to say that you are perpetually indebted to God insofar as you have become a recipient of a gift so enormous as to defy equal return," adding that "such a gift can never be fully repaid" (Rafael 1998, 96). Thus the scale of the debt owed to Christ, combined with the culturally driven tendency to engage in active acts of compassion, may account for the pervasiveness of Holy Week activities involving a *panata* that actively takes on some form of suffering, whether it is in the form of sleep-deprivation through all-night readings of the *pasyon,* participation in street processions under the weight of bulky and heat-inducing costumes and masks, or practices that involve mortifications of the flesh.

The overused concept of *utang na loób* as debt is inadequate on its own when seeking to understand the cultural and spiritual necessity for such a complete identification with the sufferings of Christ.[6] The Filipino concept of *kapwa,* often misleadingly translated as "self," may offer further insights. Virgilio Enriquez, who mapped out a Filipino *sikologi* (psychology) using concepts embedded in the Filipino language, observed that *kapwa,* which is what it means to be a person, fuses the categories of "outsider" *(ibang-tao)* and "one of us" *(hindi ibang-tao)* (Enriquez 1986, 11). *Ibang* literally means "other," thus making *ibang-tao* the designation for "other person." What in English might be called an "insider" is expressed as *hindi ibang-tao,* or literally "not a/the person" (i.e. not "other"). *Kapwa,* he argues, is the "unity of the "self" and "others," not an "other" as separate from self, but rather an assertion of a "shared identity" (Enriquez 1986, 11). Thus, an individual becomes fully human only insofar as he lives by and for the other in a way that recalls Levinas' famous formulation of "being for the Other" that does not mean "the negation of the I" (Levinas 1969, 304), but is rather a requirement for the I to exist.

Beltran provides yet another reason that the suffering of Christ on Good Friday seems to eclipse the importance of the Resurrection on Easter Sunday in the practice of Folk Catholicism (Beltran 1987, 138). This emphasis on death and suffering, he argues, has deep cultural roots:

> It has been said, for example, that the early Filipino's veneration of the dead coincided with the distinguishing marks of Spanish popular faith, which was characterized by a profound sense of tragedy, a terrible dread of death, and a religious fervor that dwelt morbidly on the wounds and agony of Christ. The empathy with suffering and death, sometimes bordering on gruesome fascination, is a part of everyday life in the Philippines. (Beltran 1987, 138)

In the Philippines it is not unusual for loved ones to pose for a photograph with the dead as they lie in their coffins at a public viewing, a practice that would be considered disrespectful or aberrant in many other cultures. Considerable meaning is attached to the expression on the face of the deceased because it is meant to provide clues as to their spiritual state at the time of their death (Cannell 1999, 142). The concept of the afterlife in Tagalog culture prior to the arrival of Catholicism was murky at best, in that it was regarded not as a celestial place of angels and rejoicing, but as a kind of netherworld that overlapped with the world of the living, thus making necessary the continual appeasing of the spirits of the dead (Rafael 1998). Indeed the promise of a clearly defined afterlife was seen by many as one of the reasons that much of the archipelago embraced Christianity so quickly. Thus the practices that might cause one to conclude that Filipinos have a "gruesome fascination with death" may instead reflect the pre-Christian belief that there is little to separate life from death; therefore, death must necessarily be incorporated back into life.

Stations of the Cross

The fourteen Stations of the Cross, only some of which are set out in the Gospels,[7] are meant to represent the physical locations in which key moments in Christ's final journey to Calvary are reenacted. By the late sixteenth century it had become a common practice in European towns to set up reproductions of these holy sites on the streets, providing penitents with the opportunity to pause and reflect on the sufferings of Christ at each stop. This practice, in turn, was brought inside the physical structure of Catholic churches in the seventeenth century, and the execution of such shrines was and still is largely the province of the Franciscan order (Catholic Encyclopedia 2015b). Significantly, the Franciscan order was one of the two most influential orders (the other being the Augustinians) in the Tagalog-speaking region and they were responsible for setting up the practice in Boac, Marinduque, where, as in other cities and towns, the action corresponding to each "station" takes place at preset locations on the city streets. Though the Boac version of the Stations of the Cross is more theatrically inflected than most, with moments of high drama designed to elicit strong, vocal responses from the locals who move with the procession through the streets on Good Friday, it reflects a practice found throughout the country where individuals walk with Christ, while some penitents enact varying degrees of suffering and mortification to complete their identification with their savior. For the faithful, following Christ on the arduous path toward Calvary activates and physicalizes the *damay* one has for his sufferings and his sacrifice. The fourteen stations are:

1) Christ condemned to death;
2) the cross is laid upon him;
3) His first fall;
4) He meets His Blessed Mother;
5) Simon of Cyrene is made to bear the cross;
6) Christ's face is wiped by Veronica;
7) His second fall;
8) He meets the women of Jerusalem;
9) His third fall;
10) He is stripped of His garments;
11) His crucifixion;
12) His death on the cross;
13) His body is taken down from the cross; and
14) laid in the tomb.

(Catholic Encyclopedia, "Way of the Cross," 2015b)

By bringing the Stations of the Cross to a particular town, the streets are effectively transformed into a *Via Crucis* (Way of the Cross) or *Via Dolorosa* (Way of Sorrow). In Boac, the first two stations are staged inside the Morion Park, where on the permanent raised stage Pilate condemns Jesus, who exits the park for the city streets carrying his cross. Once outside the park, stops are made at stations typically marked with a cross and candle and it is here where Christ meets his mother (Station 4), Simon helps him carry his cross (Station 5), or Veronica wipes his face (Station 6). The actor playing Christ in the *sinakulo* on the two previous nights undertakes the role, insofar as it is essentially a continuation of the Thursday night presentation that ended with him being condemned by Pilate. Here, as in many other towns, the drama of the *Via Crucis* begins after noon and ends with the mock Crucifixion at 3:00 p.m., the time at which Christ is believed to have died. In the Boac version, Christ is accompanied by two other penitents, local men enacting the roles of Gestas and Dismas, the two criminals who were crucified alongside Christ. Also undertaking these roles as *panata,* the men sweat and strain under the burden of their crosses while, like Christ, they are relentlessly pursued by *morions* clad as Roman soldiers who beat them with whips made of hemp. The violence does not approach the level of bloodletting found in other parts of the country, notably the Cutud site, and perhaps for this reason Boac is not the object of attention from foreign media. Nevertheless, welts are raised on the skin of the three and abrasions and cuts result in some bleeding. Whereas physical violence is kept to a minimum, given the midday heat and the fact that all three are carrying crosses, there is no doubt that this ordeal exacts a significant physical toll.

This mixture of performance and ritual violence links the presentation to forms where performers gain transcendence in the eyes of the group through enduring punishment which could not normally be condoned, while those who are watching or running alongside the charging *morions* and the struggling Christ become active participants themselves as they are implicated in the drama. In 2005, as I ran through the streets with the raucous procession, struggling to take a photo of these men as they were scourged by *morions,* I was blindly following some ethnographic impulse to capture the event visually in order to re-create it. Years later, at another *Via Crucis,* as I dashed blindly through the dark narrow streets and alleyways of the Manila city of San Juan, risking falling into open holes of crumbling concrete while keeping up with Christ as he was pursued by Roman soldiers, I felt fearless, superhuman, almost floating outside my own body while being connected physically to the pack of men and boys running with me. At one point as we ran through a long, pitch-black tunnel under a road as the shouts of the soldiers and runners bounced sharply off the walls, it felt as if time had stopped, that we would be trapped in this state of hyperawareness and extreme sensory overload forever. Years later, I can reinhabit this state through its body-memory, which leads me to suspect that for many, the experiential connection is not just with the sufferings of Christ, but with the mass of people with whom one shares that experience as a collective entity. Such sensations leave a deep imprint on the body and are pleasurable and memorable because they are so far outside the experience of daily life; thus the body may compel one to return to the same site year after year, in the hope of repeating the experience where one exists suspended in time, connected with others as a single moving, heaving, breathing conscious mass. Such segmented activities, woven into the experience of Holy Week, combine *ilinx* (or vertigo) with a mimetic activity, increasing its intensity, while coming close to or even bringing the participant inside a "flow state" similar to those described by Csikszentmihalyi's informants.

After Christ falls for the third time (Station 9), the Boac procession moves back into the Morion Park for the final five stations. Calvary is physicalized by the highest point in the outdoor staging area and it is here where Christ and his two companions are tied to their respective crosses and raised. Unlike penitents in Cutud, the hands of these men are not pierced with nails, though all three bear light wounds on their bodies. As the canned music from the sound system swells to a crescendo, the men are raised up to form an impressive iconographic tableau. The only dialogue occurs as Longinus pierces Christ's side, is cured of his blindness, and then enthusiastically proclaims the miracle, becoming the first Roman Christian, preparing us for the sequel on Saturday night that ends with his beheading. As Christ is taken down from the cross, the three Marys are there to receive him for the requisite tableau,[8] and his battered body is brought to the nearby tomb. Though the formal action ends with his entombment, in 2005 many spectators climbed onto the raised stage and waited outside the tomb until the actor playing Christ reappeared from behind the enormous wire and papier-mâché boulder that covered the tomb's opening. Bearing the marks of his beatings and appearing exhausted and dazed, Christ, played by Allen Madrigal, permitted himself to be photographed again by a seemingly endless procession of people, mostly in group portraits. Smiling and posing with friends and family, their expressions starkly contrasted with those of the penitent/actor Christ, who appeared to inhabit another dimension. Here the resurrected Christ appeared from his tomb not for ascension into heaven, but to pose for photos, mirroring the practice of family members posing with their dead loved ones. Thus, we now turn to the dynamic exchange between the actor/penitent Christ and those who interact with or are touched by him.

The "Suffering Christ" and the "Best Friend Christ"

One of the Good Friday preshow activities I witnessed in Boac in 2005 was a series of photo opportunities with the Roman centurion *morions* and *sinakulo* actors featured in the brief playlet in which Christ is condemned to death preceding the *Via Crucis*. Although posing with Longinus was popular, as was being photographed with the large *morion* in the heavily muscled breastplate and the mask that looked like a very white and pretty Michael Jackson after too many nose jobs, the star was clearly Allen Madrigal as Christ, who already appeared battered even prior to the public scourging through the streets. Madrigal possessed an ascetic, palpably detached quality, one of quiet resignation, as if he were totally prepared for anything that might await him. There seemed to be no separation between Allen the man, the actor playing Christ, and Christ the man. Yet there was a further element worthy of note. Madrigal was the first in a series of what I would later come to call a "hot Christ," one that corresponded to the popular iconic representation of Christ while also being in remarkable accordance with Filipino ideals of physical beauty, which is to say mestizo-looking, taller than average, and light-skinned, with a narrow, pronounced nose bridge.[9] I later learned that Madrigal, who played Christ in the *sinakulo* for six of eight years through 2005, had been personally recruited for the role by Carmencita Reyes, accepting it only after being told that Governor Reyes would be calling him directly if he refused a third time (Madrigal 2005). Given Reyes' many years of work in theatricalizing the *sinakulo,* it seems reasonable to assume that Madrigal's looks played a part in the recruitment process. When I later queued up with other fans for my photo with Madrigal after the crucifixion, it struck me that many people posing with him must have been stirred by the physical beauty of this attractive young man playing Christ. Yet Madrigal projected the internal qualities of resignation and sublime asceticism that rendered him unavailable, thwarting any kind of exchange as desire was returned to the viewer/experiencer, potentially transformed into a kind of sadness over such a loss, one magnified by virtue of the sheer physical beauty of the man created in the image of God.[10]

Madrigal's availability for photo opportunities, bruised and bloodied after emerging from his tomb, offers up a stand-in for Christ, one who is there for you, present for the believer to be with, in an encounter to be recorded through digital media. Never for an instant did Madrigal break his connection with this inner-Christ. In a subsequent interview, he made it clear that *panata* required this level of deep commitment. His suffering as Christ, he feels, "is sacrifice," and is done so that others realize that is how "Jesus experienced these things" (Madrigal 2005). Madrigal's Christ was available to take on the sufferings meted out to him, and although they were not as extreme as those undertaken by some in Cutud, from his first appearance when he was condemned to death in the Good Friday staging in Boac, and as he was scourged and beaten in the streets of town, he remained in a vulnerable state. This Christ stands next to us but also stands in for us, taking on pain for us, and showing that pain both internally and externally. When one stands with Madrigal/Christ for a photo op, one feels that he has taken on pain

Figure 4. Allen Madrigal as Christ, posing for photos after the Good Friday crucifixion, Boac Morion Park, Marinduque. Photo by author.

and suffering; he exudes it from his body, and one cannot fail to be moved or touched in some way by this experience.

In contrast to Madrigal and other "Suffering Christs" I have witnessed is the "Best Friend Christ," the charismatic, kind, and wise Christ, the kind of person one would naturally want to follow. These two relatively stable categories will be examined in further detail, drawing from two of the *sinakulo* traditions analyzed in the previous chapter, namely, the "traditional" and "activist" *sinakulo.* Although the "Suffering Christ" is frequently at the dramatic and spiritual center of the *sinakulo,* the charismatic, inspirational "Best Friend Christ" is also attractive in a Tagalog cultural context, opening up yet another framework for the self in relation to the other. While the Boac *sinakulo* and Good Friday activities provide a model for one way of being and experiencing Christ, the urban *sinakulos* staged by the Manila Mobile Theatre and the San Roque *Senakulista*s place their respective Christs before very different kinds of audiences, as we have seen. Whereas the San Roque actors literally inherit their roles and the *sinakulo* follows a staging practice and recitation tradition virtually unchanged since 1965, the Manila Mobile Theatre production relies on contemporary speech and song, travels to multiple sites, and uses professional actors in key dramatic roles. And whereas the Christ in the "traditional" *sinakulo* sings his lines using an archaic form of Tagalog recitation, the heartthrob professional actor playing Christ in Lou Veloso's *Martir sa Golgota* speaks his lines earnestly and convincingly in ordinary prose, seducing both his followers and the audience. Veloso's "Best Friend Christ" is a genuine good guy, one exuding both charisma and charm, enhanced by the classic mestizo good looks anyone undertaking this part in his traveling show typically possesses. The "Suffering Christ" in the *barangay* of Barangka Ibaba, by contrast, appears as a cipher for Christ, an iconic representation that even while moving onstage, appears static and painterly. The interiority of the traditional Christ's portrayal exudes holiness and otherworldliness, whereas the contemporary Christ in Veloso's production is of this world.

The Christ in the Barangka Ibaba *sinakulo,* Ferdinand "Ferdie" Santos, has been playing the role for twenty years and will presumably continue playing it for as long as he is physically able. When informants in the community speak of Santos, they consistently foreground his past as a former drug addict; his relationship to the role enacts the classic, old-school *panata,* where one takes on an intense identification with the sufferings of Christ over a lengthy period in fulfillment of a vow or as a way of offering thanks for the lifesaving intervention of the power of the living Christ. In the enactment of Christ over six nights, it is Christ's resignation and detachment from life that is most strongly expressed through Santos' physical embodiment of the Savior. Santos' Christ is set apart from the rest of the cast through his speech, a form of chanted recitation known as *tagulaylay,* which has a kind of singsong quality that makes the content of his long speeches difficult for even the most attentive audience member to discern. Tradition dictates the style, but it has the effect of disconnecting Christ from any semblance of onstage reality, placing him at considerable remove from his disciples. Whereas the other actors declaim lines in prose using a style of delivery similar to the *komedya* form, Christ's recitation is closer to that of the traditional Tagalog *pasyon* or *pabasa* that is chanted before small makeshift altars in barrios and villages throughout the country. As with the traditional *pabasa,* what is important is not so much that the chant is understood or even that it has an audience, but that it is done for its own sake and its own efficacy. Like the women reciting the chanted *pasyon,* Christ in the barrio *sinakulo* presents much of his text in a singsong delivery, with the reedy-thin voice of the actor unable to render comprehensible the archaic and poetic text to the audience, even with the amplification of a body microphone.

For locals, what matters is not so much what Christ says, but how the act of staging and watching the spectacle provides the basis for inculcating communitarian values. Because both adults and children already know the story, an iconic representation of Christ is all that is necessary. In this context, the silent, long-suffering Christ, enacted by a local man undertaking a *panata,* links him directly to past Christs in the community. As noted earlier, the 2010 *sinakulo* was preceded by a tribute to Delfin Deocura, who originated the role of Christ and passed away just a week earlier, and who was one of just three to have played the role since the *sinakulo* began in its current form in 1965. Christ serves as a cipher for extremes of suffering and pain from the moment he is arrested by the Roman soldiers in the Garden of Gethsemane near the midpoint in the six nights of performances. On Good Friday and Holy Saturday he joins the centurion-clad *hudyos* in the *paso doble* along the edge of the stage in front of the lowered curtain as they process, seemingly endlessly, toward Calvary. Wearing an iconic red robe—a donation from filmmaker Brillante Mendoza[11]—Christ nearly collapses under the weight of his heavy cross, while on each pass across the stage, he is furiously beaten by snarling centurions until he stumbles across the footlights, appearing as if he is about to fall into a screaming audience as the soldiers pull him back in the nick of time. By submitting repeatedly to this humiliation, Christ's passivity is emphasized. Referring to the classic Spanish Christ, Miguel de Unamuno's description characterizes the Christ of this *sinakulo:* "Christ stands before us as a Tragic Victim . . . bruised and bloodless, a horizontal Christ who has succumbed to death—the embodiment of unrelieved tragedy" (cited in Aligan 2001, 50). Yet for all of Santos' projection of suffering, the fact that he is widely known as a former drug addict adds another dimension to his reception by a local audience in a tight-knit, densely populated, compact urban neighborhood: His annual reenactment of Christ is a reminder of the intercession of divine grace that community members believe enables him to live a drug-free life.

The criticism some have leveled at the traditional *sinakulo* reflects the lack of agency embodied in this kind of representation of Christ. Nicanor Tiongson, the country's most prominent scholar of the *sinakulo,* has long suggested that such an enactment imposes a kind of passivity on the audience, reinforcing their position as colonized subjects. His public comments at a 1983 theatre festival express this position quite forcefully:

> If the *komedya* gave the native his colonial mind, the *sinakulo* furnished him with a colonial will. In telling the "Indio" to be like Christ, the friars had given the native his model of a good colonial. For, as the native looked at the image of Christ in Church and in the *sinakulo,* he saw a Christ whose

> main virtue was the ability to shed tears and the complete acceptance of all the sufferings dealt him by his oppressors. To be Christ-like, then, was to accept all the sufferings in this life—mainly those dealt to him by the friars and the Spaniards—and to hope in the reward that all those who suffer in this earth are to receive in the kingdom of heaven. (Tiongson 1983, 14)

Just as the *komedya* inculcated colonial values by transposing the conflict between the Spanish and the Moors onto a local conflict between the colonized Christians and the Muslims in the south of the archipelago, the traditional *sinakulo* can be seen as naturalizing the values of passivity in the face of an overwhelming external force, embodied by the power of the friars and supported by the military, economic, and political power of the Spanish colonial administration. I would argue, however, that some agency on the part of the spectators is always present, in that the entire event serves as a vehicle for the community to celebrate itself and reinforce its internal bonds. And as we have seen, these bonds travel between generations and extend into the past as well as the future. Further, in Barangka Ibaba, Santos is enacting his position in that community, reminding everyone in it that faith can overcome even the most extreme challenges, including drug addiction. Nevertheless, the fact remains that in presentation this Christ is undeniably passive, and projects a detached quality even while recruiting his disciples, a far cry from the model of an active Christ capable of engaging his disciples, which Ileto argued provided a model for the revolutionary Katipunan movement.

If the long-suffering Christ is the one with which the greatest number of Catholic Filipinos identify, then the most personally appealing is surely the charismatic and friendly Christ, the one who serves as your personal or intimate friend *(kaibigan, katoto)* and who offers eternal salvation to those who follow him. It is no accident that this flip side to the suffering Christ appears in the *sinakulo* that tours Manila and its environs, and where the actors in the key roles are not local residents enacting and presenting their socially determined and personal spiritual relationships with Christ. Embodying this dimension of Christ are the many actors—largely recruited from film and television—who have played the role in the Manila Mobile Theatre's productions of the *Martir sa Golgota,* creating what director Lou Veloso calls a "socially activist Christ." The three actors who alternated in the role of Christ in 2010, television and film actor Miguel "Migui" Moreno, Jojo Riguerra, and Al Gatmaitan, were given the brief to approach the role using a naturalistic acting framework, one in which Christ is enacted as "an ordinary human being," in the words of Russel Sorillo, who played the role for eleven years. Veloso asserts that "we do it as a fighting Christ, an activist Christ," adding that "we don't have to imitate Christ" (Sorillo 2010), suggesting that to stage a narrow culturally encoded construct of Christ is to diminish him.

According to Migui Moreno, who undertook the role for the second time in 2010, "last year [I] did Jesus more as a holy one, this year as a normal guy" (Moreno 2010). He repeated Veloso's characterization of theirs as an "activist Christ," adding that in 2010 Veloso directed him to undertake the role in a "natural way, just like a normal person, not like Jesus Christ as a god, [but] as a normal person doing those kind of chores, running errands." Reversing the famous question, "What would Jesus do?" Moreno instead describes an approach to the role that starts with the question, "What would I do if I were a guy who was Jesus?" He imagines his Christ as "a regular guy" who "can be hurt," who "cries," and who "does the stuff that normal people do." Moreno's observations about his internal state while undertaking the role recall classic method acting in the American-inflected iteration of the Stanislavski tradition: "I just try to imagine things in my own way. So it is this experience that helps me out. . . . So I imagine if I am Jesus Christ what do I do, if I'm home, if I'm with my mom, if I'm with this guy, if I'm with this person." His description mirrors the famous "what if" formulation at the heart of method acting, whereby an actor uses the memories and feelings of personal lived experience and infuses them into the inner emotional life of the character he enacts, giving the actor the ability to reproduce a rich, inner emotional life reliably and on cue. Indeed there is nothing in Moreno's approach to the role that adds a layer of "holiness" to his onstage character; instead of being a man who comes to terms with being the son of God, this is someone who at times reluctantly steps into the sacrificial role that is demanded of him. He displays the fullest range of emotions, including surprise, annoyance, and confusion, coming across as a guy who just happens to be Christ.

Moreno's internal process would appear to be the opposite of Santos' or the Christs I have observed in traditional *sinakulo* where they seem to retreat into an interiorized, trance-like state in which they are open to pain and suffering, while removed from their worldly bodies, so much so that what the spectator sees is the iconic image of the suffering Christ fused with the personal, individual embodiment of a human being taking on a physically demanding *panata*. Yet for all the actorly-ness of the Veloso/Moreno Christ, there is still a point at which the human being—Migui Moreno as penitent—can speak of entering into an internal felt state that connects him personally with the sufferings of Christ, much as the Suffering Christ. Moreno spoke of how in 2009 "some of the centurions hit me with a whip and gave me some marks" and how immediately after this experience, he "had to go backstage, because that's the first time that I felt . . . so that's what Jesus Christ did for me so that's what I'm doing for him." In the context of our conversation, "going backstage" was Moreno's way of indicating that he required a private moment away from the scrutiny of other actors or the audience, where he could come to terms in a personal rather than an actorly way with his emotional response to the correspondence between Christ's sufferings and his own enactment of a *panata*. As Moreno observed, at that moment it is clear that, "You're doing it for him."

The comments of Veloso as well as the two Christs I interviewed (Sorillo and Moreno) reflect a deep and abiding concern with creating an experience for the audience that invites a personal connection with Christ that goes beyond suffering. Their repeated invocations of an "activist Christ" were reflected onstage by a Christ who is fully human, persuasive, and charismatic. Moreno's Christ was in fact extremely charismatic, not only because of his movie-star looks, but because his enthusiasm for his message was infectious. Whether preaching, curing the blind, or assembling his team of disciples, Moreno's friendly, easygoing manner as Christ made him a figure almost anyone would naturally want to follow.[12] The contrast to the Suffering Christ is especially marked here; whereas the Suffering Christ as enacted in the traditional *sinakulo* cannot extend his presence out into the world through any means other than suffering, the "activist Christ" of Veloso and embodied by his actors is the kind of man you can imagine the historical Christ must have been; surely his success at winning adherents to the point where he was seen as a danger to both organized religion and the state must have been to some extent based on his personal charisma and the message he was preaching, not the inevitability of his tragic death. It is hard to believe that we have changed so much as a species in two thousand years that our predecessors were any less affected by the presence of a charismatic, dynamic human being in their midst than we are.

Moreno's further comments reveal the larger goal behind the enactment of an "activist Christ." Speaking of his approach to the "Sermon on the Mount" scene, he remembers being counseled by Veloso to "do this to change lives, to touch those hearts, to tell people to attend to [this]." Indeed, both Moreno and fellow actor Gatmaitan played that scene with such passion and fervor that they would credibly command followers. For Moreno, connecting with audience members on a personal and individual level is supremely important:

> So our main goal is to touch those people's hearts. If we have one thousand in the audience . . . and if we touch at least one or two persons a night that's enough for me. I mean that's an achievement. So that's our goal. So I think that maybe when I'm doing that sermon our goal is to touch one or two persons, to touch their hearts.

Although conversion or religious renewal is the implied goal, it is noteworthy that Moreno speaks not of "saving souls," but rather of "touching the hearts" of audience members. It is in fact the semblance of real human emotions in the acting that distinguishes his Christ from the "suffering Christ." Moreno's Christ communicates directly with his disciples, warmly projecting himself and displaying a full range of emotions, while his acting style is closer to what one would find in television drama, heighted for the stage, and punctuated with segments in which songs are delivered to the audience in a more presentational mode, as in musical theatre.

Veloso and Moreno's conception of Christ is not as "Tragic Victim," but rather as a humanized Christ, one whose historical existence in the Philippines no doubt dates from well before the first Tagalog-language version of the passion by Aquino de Belen appeared in 1704. Filipino *pasyon* scholar Rodel Aligan asserts that, "Aquino de Belen made Christ acceptable to the people because He is human.[13] De Belen has made Him one with the natives endowing Him with characteristic Filipino traits, thus, making Him identifiable and approachable to the level of the folk" (Aligan 2001, 50). While de Belen is probably more likely to have penned a humanized Christ with Filipino traits, which already existed in the popular imagination of the time, the essential point made by Aligan that the Christ of his *pasyon* behaves as if he were a Tagalog-speaking, close personal friend is worth setting out:

> The Tagalog *Pasyon* presents a very human Christ without denying His divinity. He is pictured as the Faithful *catoto*[14] (friend) who, in spite of rejection and suffering unjustly imposed by His enemies, remains the open-hearted Shepherd to whom everybody can turn to for merciful forgiveness. This very human portrayal of Christ makes Him accessible and approachable to anyone who wished to follow Him. It is also an invitation to listeners and readers to personally commit themselves to Him. In other words, through this human image, Christ is brought close to the experience and heart of the Tagalog audience. (Aligan 2001, 52)

Aligan's observations about the enculturated Christ in the classic Tagalog *pasyon* text also apply to Veloso's *Martir sa Golgata,* where both the enactment of Christ and the actor Christ's relationship to the audience rely on "this very human portrayal of Christ." As Aligan observes, the *pasyon* functions not merely as "religious and catechetical literature," but perhaps more significantly as "the promoter of Christian and Filipino values" (Aligan 2001, 61). Sitting within the larger universe of Catholic cross-cultural evangelization, this tradition of the *pasyon* in the Philippines, not only in its existence as text but also in its physical, embodied expression as performance, is consistent with Pope Paul VI's *Evangelii Nuntiandi,* which set down the principles for Vatican II by calling for "the intimate transformation of authentic cultural values through their integration in Christianity in the various human cultures" (66). The *pasyon* in the Philippines is thus an example of the early success of this approach to proselytizing, one that seeks to change values by deeply embedding Christianity into local cultures until they become so enmeshed that it is virtually impossible to separate them from one another.

Yet for all of the layers of acting and theatre professionalism that are placed on the passion story in the *Martir sa Golgata,* at its heart is the highly personal and emotional exchange between the felt states of the individual and the sufferings and sacrifice of Christ. This exchange is what is distinctive about the scale and ubiquity of the Tagalog undertaking of *panata,* while also deeply bound up with Tagalog ways of being in the world that require not just sympathy, but *damay,* and the obligations extending from *utang na loób.* As we have seen, *na loób* means "from the inside," suggesting that what is constituted by *utang* (debt) resides deep within the human organism, that it possesses a visceral, embodied quality. Thus the capacity for *damay* requires the individual to tap into resources that are literally within—*sa loób*—the body (see Jocano 2001, 97–110). Whether one is encountering the "Best Friend Christ" or the "Suffering Christ," for both actors and participants in the passion, that obligation to reciprocate will always require a deeply personal and embodied expression of faith that seeks to link the deeply felt internal experience with its external manifestations.

Finding the "Real" Passion of Christ

The final framework shaping the encounter between Christ and his "audience" in the *sinakulo* and in the streets on Good Friday is set by Christ's iconographic and dramatic representation. As we have seen in the case of the *sinakulo,* it is not just the iconographic representation of Christ, but the entire visual field identified with the Holy Land and its inhabitants that owes much to its representation in the Hollywood biblical epics of the 1950s and 1960s. This was and remains especially true of the Boac *sinakulo.* More recently, the representation of Christ in the Tagalog *sinakulo* has been influenced by Mel Gibson's *The Passion of the Christ.* The desire of many Filipinos to connect on an experiential level with the sufferings of Christ has no doubt contributed to the popularity and influence of the movie in the Philippines, where it circulates widely, primarily as a pirated DVD. Its grittiness and "authenticity" is enhanced by the use of ancient Aramaic rather than English or contemporary Hebrew,[15] and a further attraction is no doubt Gibson's casting of Jim Caviezel as Christ, an actor listed as one of the world's most beautiful people by *People* magazine in 2004.[16] Caviezel satisfies the brief of the "hot Christ," one who complies with a particular ideal of Caucasian or Eurasian beauty, with his chiseled features and slender, gym-toned body, much like the popular actors who play the role in Veloso's *sinakulo.* Actors I have interviewed who have enacted Christ in a *sinakulo* (Moreno 2010; Sorillo 2010; Madrigal 2005) all pointed to Caviezel's interpretation of Christ as a model for their approach to the role. Allen Madrigal, in speaking of *The Passion of the Christ,* observes, "I think it was a good movie and it sort of inspires me to play the role of Jesus Christ in some way at least closer to that." Migui Moreno, who played Christ in Veloso's 2009 and 2010 productions, recalls watching *Jesus of Nazareth* and *The Passion of the Christ* at the director's suggestion, seeking models for acting Christ in a "natural way, just like a normal person, not like Jesus Christ as god."

Filipinos may have been impressed by the "naturalness" of his acting, and many would have noted that he not only had the same initials as Christ (J. C.), but that when filming the movie he was the same age as Christ when he died (Ross and Woodland n.d.). Yet the point of commonality with Filipinos was that he approached the role in much the same way Filipino Christs do, with a deep and abiding faith, while seeking an experiential connection with the sufferings of Christ that he hoped would strengthen people's Christian faith. A conservative Catholic like Gibson, Caviezel, in an interview with televangelist Scott Ross, stated, "I believe I was called to play this role." While on the cross during the filming he was electrocuted and "miraculously" survived, and also undertook all manner of sufferings:

> It was so cold it was like knives coming through me. I had hypothermia. I don't know whether you've dealt with that, but on one day of hypothermia I was so cold I could barely get the lines out. My mouth was shaking uncontrollably. My arms and legs went numb. I was suffocating on that cross. (Ross and Woodland n.d.)

As with many of the Christs in the Philippines who take on the physical sufferings of Christ during Holy Week, Caviezel's faith was deepened by undertaking extreme acts that, in his case, involved risks to his life. Such acts are an external demonstration of one's faith, and they also encourage others to follow Jesus. Caviezel recalls that the following prayer "came from me" during the filming: "I don't want people to see me. I just want them to see Jesus. And through that conversions will happen." He reflects further: "That's what I wanted more than anything, that people would have a visceral effect to finally make a decision whether to follow

Him or not" (Ross and Woodland n.d.). Similarly, for actor Migui Moreno in Veloso's *sinakulo,* "our main goal is to touch those people's hearts. If we have one thousand in the audience . . . and if we touch at least one or two persons a night that's enough for me." Caviezel recalls the "other kind of a miracle" that happened while working on the film: "one of the guys working on the film was a Muslim. He was one of the guards who beat me, and he converted" (Ross and Woodland n.d.). That Caviezel the actor, the human being, suffered in the making of Gibson's movie is indeed part of its power, and that the pitiful nature of his suffering brought about a "conversion" of a Muslim is further proof to him of the value of his acts.

Though later denied by the Vatican, Gibson's coproducer Steve McEveety claimed that after seeing the film in a private screening, Pope John Paul II proclaimed "It is as it was" (cited in McCormack 2007, 24). In one interview, Gibson asserted that watching the film would be like "travelling back in time and watching the events unfold exactly as they occurred" (cited in McCormack 2007, 24). For many in the West who saw the movie, it was the extremity of the suffering that was so off-putting, especially on top of the much-critiqued strand of anti-Semitism that many felt ran through the film. As Susan Thistlethwaite observed, "In *The Passion of the Christ,* Gibson's message is: *No one* has ever suffered like this" (cited in McCormack 2007, 35). I would assert that it is through this common bond they share with Gibson and Caviezel—the need to connect experientially, thaumaturgically with the sufferings of Christ—that the *sinakulo* actors and directors I have interviewed view *The Passion of the Christ* as so authentic. Whether or not the Pope stated "It is as it was" is immaterial; the fact is that for many believers worldwide, including many who undertake the role of Christ as a *panata* in the Philippines, Gibson's film showed the sufferings of Christ in a way that was very much "as it was."

In the end, the external trappings of *The Passion of the Christ* are in the service of a much deeper, internal understanding of one's relationship to Christ. Filipinos enacting Christ in a Tagalog *sinakulo* respond to Gibson's movie because there are qualities in it that they recognize, not because they are blank slates for the imprint of foreign cultural influences. Throughout a decade of attending *sinakulos* at the three sites identified here and in the previous chapter, a concern repeatedly stated by those actively involved with the production of the *sinakulo* as actors, directors, or producers has always been with showing something "real" to the audience, making a "real" connection, or showing it as it "really was." Even in the Barangka Ibaba *sinakulo,* the "suffering Christ," Ferdie Santos, enacts the intensity of the suffering, making it "real," even while reciting verses no one can understand. The externals of acting and dramatic representation borrow from a range of sources, but what matters is what is done with those borrowings. In this case, all of it—the costumes, the scenic elements, the story, the psychology behind the "Best Friend Christ" and the "Suffering Christ"—are at the service of local communities as they gather together to connect experientially with the sufferings of Christ. And although some indeed do choose to make that connection through "the performance of pain and suffering," the vast majority find pleasure as well in the dramatic enactments associated with Holy Week. As we saw in the previous chapter, in the Barangka Ibaba *sinakulo,* audiences squeal with delight at the ridiculous antics of the soldiers who repeatedly come close to tossing Christ into the audience, and they hoot and holler at the posturing of their friends and relatives who sway from side to side to the *paso doble,* impressive in their Roman tunics, whereas in Boac the young, standing audience runs to the spot on the raised verge where Longinus is to be beheaded and they shout when the villain Judas hangs himself, remorseful over betraying Christ. The "Best Friend Christ" of Veloso's *sinakulo* sings a catchy tune while his disciples mime the catching of fish that symbolize the capturing of souls for Christ, whereas even on Good Friday, as Christ is being pursued by centurions in the streets of Boac, the mobile audience, charged with adrenaline, runs alongside their man, for reasons that, as I have suggested, seem driven by our bodies rather than our minds. We are compelled to be near Christ if we can keep up with the mob, not because we hope the actor playing Christ will actually be hurt by whips and blows, but because we somehow have the need to be part of something beyond ourselves.[17] With this final statement I have embedded myself in the action and may appear to be making large claims about the nature of participation. But when there, on the ground on which these events happen, it is hard, sometimes even impossible, not to be pulled into the action. There is a joy in this participation, even when commemorating something as terrifying and disturbing as the suffering of Christ, and it is because of the active participation of the entire community in these events that one feels connected to everyone else present and also to forces beyond our control.

CHAPTER 3

Panata, Politics, and the Morions of Marinduque

When setting out to undertake fieldwork on Holy Week performances in 2005, I was overwhelmed by the seemingly endless range of options as to where to start my research. Ultimately, I chose to rely on my instincts, ignoring the advice of a well-meaning colleague at the University of the Philippines to remain in Manila for Holy Week performances and instead setting off to the island of Marinduque for the Moriones Festival. I had been warned that its premiere attraction, the multinight *sinakulo,* examined in chapter 1, was tacky, unoriginal, and mimed by actors to an old recording of the dramatic text by radio actors, delivered through an aging sound system. Yet it was the image of the Roman-looking *morion* I had seen in photos that captured my imagination. Wearing full face masks and elaborate headpieces, these surreal-looking soldiers were shown parading through the streets in groups, looking as though they had stepped out of a Hollywood biblical epic but filtered through another series of unidentifiable cultural lenses. Many had visages carved into their masks that were almost absurdly hypermasculine, with large eyes, copious facial hair, and sneering, snarling miens that bordered on the comic in their excessiveness. Some wore massive headpieces of brightly colored flowers created with foil paper, whereas others bore crested helmets closer to the general shape and outline of the classic Roman centurion. I had a vague feeling that anything felt by a professional theatre artist to be this "bad" must be interesting for reasons having nothing to do with the dramatic value of the *sinakulo.* My hunch was not only that the larger, overarching Moriones Festival would offer up many rich layers of cultural complexity but also that the sheer oddness and high profile of the event would bring together the three domains that made the Philippines such an attractive place in which to do research, my personal "holy trinity" of interests and obsessions: politics, performance, and religion. Little did I realize then how spot-on my instincts were—the Moriones Festival turned out to be one of the most politically circumscribed religious events in the country.

The first part of the adventure was in getting there, an act that, as I later came to understand, was itself driven by political forces. Though the island of Marinduque is a mere one hundred miles southwest of Manila as the crow flies and part of the Tagalog region geographically and culturally, even guided by a travel companion with family ties to the island, the journey proved challenging by my usual *Lonely Planet* backpacker standards. For a start, there was the four-hour bus ride from central Manila that moved through the all-too-short divided motorway heading south and crept along a congested two-lane road winding through the provinces of Laguna and Quezon en route to Lucena, the provincial capital. From Lucena, there was the three-hour, standing-room-only ride on a dangerously overloaded ferry to the port of Cavite on the island. And from there another thirty or more minutes, either in a jeepney or a motorized vehicle known as a "tricycle,"[1] finally took me to the provincial capital of Boac, home of the festival. When I returned in 2007, once again undertaking the journey via bus, boat, and tricycle, I discovered that there was a regional airport connecting the island with Manila and further, that it was not operating. This seemed odd because it was the island's peak travel season, with large numbers of Marinduqueños returning home to be with friends and family during Holy Week. When I finally asked a local informant why flights were not running, he looked at me as though I had asked whether the Pope was Catholic and replied, "Because it's an election year." This response, which dumbfounded me at the time, marked the beginning of a decade-long education in the connection of politics and political patronage with anything that brings local citizens and especially working-class and poor Filipinos pleasure or comfort, or adds a measure of convenience to their lives.

In the years since then, I have come to see how air travel, roads, infrastructure, public buildings, and educational and social services are all frequently touted as gifts from local politicians, their names often permanently linked to the physical edifices of these "pork barrel" projects funded by the central government in return for political patronage or for "delivering the votes" in a particular province. I have also learned that running a "traditional campaign" for elected office means vote-buying, and although the price of a vote is relatively cheap (generally around 500 pesos, US$11), the fact that entire communities need to be paid off to ensure victory over any viable opponent means that the money often comes from diverting funds originally earmarked for local projects. Thus the Marinduque airport, like so many other projects in the Philippines that are "gifts" from local politicians, was closed for reasons probably known only to those seeking reelection at the level of the provincial government. For the ordinary citizen, its closure could be explained by the mere fact of an election year.

Community and the Individual

This chapter considers how a signature event such as the Moriones Festival, which is characterized by a vast range of performance practices and associated with a particular location, like the suspension of air travel, is interwoven with local and national politics as well as the broader history and legacy of the cultural politics of the Marcos era. I argue that although local and national political interventions have set the parameters for this regional festival, some individuals who variously participate in its many public performances do nevertheless recuperate agency through the web of connections linking them to others in their local communities and find expression in what Catherine Diamond (2012), building on Anderson (1991), has called "communities of imagination." As she observes of such communities in a wider Southeast Asian regional context, "Performers form special *communities of imagination* by virtue of the primacy they give to creating and performing imaginative ephemera—in contrast to the pragmatic imperatives dominating their cultures, and the world, in the twenty-first century" (Diamond 2012, 23). Though the communities I am writing about here are largely determined in the first instance by place, typically by sharing the same location (i.e., *barangay*, town, city), they define and express themselves as "communities of imagination" in much the same way that Diamond sets out.

Throughout the country during Holy Week, local performance traditions are markedly differentiated and it is important for groups and the individual participant to feel that what they do and believe is distinguishable in fundamental ways from practices elsewhere, even from groups in the same town. Groups creating these performances come together in ways that identify with and through a set of distinctive practices, whereas the more prominent and best-funded groups frequently rely on the patronage of powerful local politicians. It is at the personal level that politics influences these performance activities. In their situatedness in place, there is often a very strong personalistic dimension to the nature of the exchange in and through performance events. One does not just perform in a group; performing is an expression of what it means to belong to a particular group. Here I draw on Raul Pertierra's (1988) observations based on years of fieldwork on religion, politics, and identity in Ilocos Sur in which he concludes not only that Filipinos are a communitarian people like other Southeast Asians but also that the social order is based on deeply personal connections with others with whom they identify:

> The personalistic nature of Philippine society must be distinguished from the Western notion of individualism. Filipinos consider themselves as the center of a personal network of alliances based on ascribed elements such as family and locality. To this they add whatever personal ties become available as they progress through life. This world consists largely of consociates (including enemies) with whom ego shares personal experiences and moral orientations, outside of which are found strangers with vary-

> ing potential for assistance or hostility. In this world, and in the absence of trust in appropriate public institutions, strangers can only be assimilated by their conversion into consociates. (Pertierra 2002, 87–88)

This connection, as Pertierra suggests, need not be bounded by blood because it is also open to those with whom one shares an experience in a particular place over a lifetime. Only after three trips to Marinduque for Holy Week have I begun to understand just how appropriate Pertierra's formulation is for understanding the performance practice of the *morion* there, where allegiances and groups shift over time as do claims on lineages that relate to "authentic" practices. Thus it is to the practice of the *morion* in Marinduque that we now turn.

Emplacing and Embodying the *Morion*

The performance events and practices associated with the Moriones Festival in Marinduque extend from the apocryphal story of Longinus and involve individuals in the community in taking on the role of a Roman soldier, or *morion,* during Holy Week.[2] As we have seen, Longinus features prominently in the Boac *sinakulo,* particularly on the final night, Saturday, when his martyrdom becomes the dramatic focus of the play. The Moriones Festival offers an instructive case study both because of its complexity and because of the ways in which the personal and the communal are shaped and controlled as much by local political masters as they are by individual and community-based attempts to connect with "originary" practices. Indeed, as with the performative expressions found in many similar events elsewhere in the Philippines, the multiple and competing claims often made by individuals and groups with respect to "authentically" representing a tradition are impossible to prove in the absence of written records, thus enabling politicians and new groups to continually stake out the claim that they are "returning to tradition" as they support or drive alterations to the form, content, and meaning of performance. Many of these "traditions," which I once mistakenly believed were deeply consistent with some kind of originary practice, have been altered and reinvented during the years since I first encountered them in 2005. However, what has not changed are the ways in which the personal, the communal, and the political are interwoven. As with the airport that can suddenly suspend flights because it is an election year, the bands of men masquerading through the streets of Boac dressed as Roman centurions are also sometimes subject to political forces beyond their control.

To be a *morion* in Marinduque is to dress up as a Roman centurion, donning a mask and helmet that completely covers the head, and to masquerade through the streets of town during Holy Week. This practice, which is still largely the province of men, is believed to date back to the 1880s, when Father Dionisio Santiago, the first parish priest in the town of Mogog, sought to create a focal point for Lenten activities (Asuncion 2004, 29; Tiongson 1994c, 95; Mandia 2005; Obligacion 2007; Adachi 1994, 34). According to Alfred Marche, a French naturalist who spent a number of months in Marinduque in 1881, Mogpog, 4.5 kilometers north of today's provincial capital, Boac, was "an old village of bandits and of pirates very much feared by their neighbors . . . who were at that time active smugglers" (Marche 1970, 174). The "pirates" were presumably non-Christian "Moros" from the south of the country, the group that, as we saw in chapter 1, constitutes the villains in Filipino *komedya.* Because there is a widespread local belief that the much-feared Moro "pirates" threatened the island's inhabitants well into the nineteenth century (Asuncion 2004, 180; Adachi 1994, 39), it seems likely that Mogpog was one of the roughest and most unruly towns in Marinduque, and provided a significant challenge for parish priest Santiago, an Indio (native) Filipino from the province of Bulacan (Obligacion 2002, 50). An explanation for the origin of the term *morion,* put forth by senior Marinduqueños and sounding entirely plausible, is that it compresses the phrase, *Moro iyan,* or "The Moros are here," and they recall this being used as a threat to scare small children (Mandia 2002, 2005; Obligacion 2002, 49). In Mogpog, the weeklong penitential practice is known as Moryonan and those engaging in it are *moryons* and not *morions,* which to Obligacion suggests the very real possibility that the earliest *morions* in Mogpog were themselves Moro converts to Christianity (Obligacion 2002, 49).

Yet because the term *morion* has long been used elsewhere in the Philippines to signify men masquerading as Roman soldiers during Holy Week, alternative explanations have been put forward. Danilo Mandia, in his thesis on the *morion* (2002, 67), suggests that the term, which refers to the high-crested helmets worn by Spanish soldiers, was named after Domingo Moriones y Murillo, governor-general of the Philippines (1877–1880). Although this sounds like the most plausible of the explanations, the simple, historical fact is that a *morion* has long been the term used to describe the classic crested helmet worn by soldiers in the earliest days of Spanish colonization of the Americas in the sixteenth century. What is both fascinating and typical in these many explanations of the etymology of the term *morion* is that the "simple" answer never suffices; in the local expressions of forms found in many places throughout the Philippines there very often exists a local explanation for a key term or practice that is profoundly interwoven with and emplaced in a context determined by local identifications with history and place. These explanations, like relationships in the Philippines, are deeply personalized and rooted in the specific experiences that define a group of people in a particular place. Thus *morion* is not just a Spanish word for a type of helmet; instead it refers to a local practice, transformed by Tagalog wordplay, an important expressive feature of the language. Here in Marinduque, the term *morion* is formed by contracting Tagalog words, and is born out of local prewritten history, forged at a time when Moro raids are believed to have terrorized the population. Even when an explanation is offered more broadly (that it refers to the governor named Moriones, for example), it is still linked both to the Philippines and to a particular historical period, in this case the same period (1877–1880) in which the *morion* practice emerged in Mogpog. Essentially, local Marinduqueños are reinventing the term, making it their own, emplacing it in the local while making it personal. *Morion* becomes something other than a Spanish word for a thing; it is instead transformed into a deeply local practice, something reflected in complex ways by people's interpretation of the word itself.

To understand how and why Roman soldiers came to occupy the streets of the major towns of Marinduque during Holy Week one needs to consider the centrality of the story of Longinus. Given an extended treatment in the apocryphal tradition, Longinus is the unnamed Roman soldier who pierced Christ's side, mentioned in the Book of John: "But one of the soldiers with a spear pierced his side, and forthwith came there out blood and water" (John 19:35, King James Version). In the popular folk belief in the Philippines, also widely shared in the early years of the Church,[3] Longinus, who was blind in one eye, had his sight miraculously restored when the water and blood from Christ's wound sprayed into his eye after piercing Christ's side. In the *Pasyon Pilapil,* he is a soldier charged with guarding Christ's tomb along with other Roman soldiers, and after seeing the miracle of the Resurrection, he begins to proselytize, refusing to accept the bribes offered by the Romans and Pharisees for his silence, leading ultimately to his execution and subsequent martyrdom. Significantly, he is regarded as a kind of patron saint for soldiers, and the legendary "spear of Longinus" is believed by some to be encased in one of the pillars over the altar in the St. Peter's Basilica in Rome (Catholic Online 2014).

Father Santiago, most likely a relatively young man when he took up the position of parish priest of Mogpog in 1856,[4] may well have been responding to the fierce "Moro" energy in his new adopted home, seeking to find a productive way to channel it by setting up the *morion* practice. He is believed to have incorporated the *morions* into a staged reenactment of the Passion of Christ and, according to Eli Obligacion, the local expert on the history of the tradition, "The years thereafter saw the Christianized *moros* of the town preparing their version of the uniform of a Roman centurion at the approach of Holy Week . . . and doing their part in the chase and search for Longhino"[5] [Longinus] after he is condemned to death (Obligacion 2002, 49). Here Obligacion is pointing to what is known as the *pugutan* or beheading, the signature dramatic element of the *morion* practice, one that all sources agree was first practiced in Mogpog. The dramatized sequence of events is as follows: Longinus, seeking to evade arrest at the hands of Roman centurions (played by *morions*), runs through the streets of town in the late morning after Easter Mass and evades capture three times. The fourth time he is condemned and brought to a raised stage in the town square where he is beheaded by a *morion* executioner. Prior to the beheading, he delivers a speech testifying to the glory of Christ, and as the wooden axe falls on his head, the penitent playing Longinus slips his head back out of the elaborate mask and headpiece, which fall onto the platform, creating the impression of an actual beheading. In Mogpog in 2013, where this practice still takes place at noon on Sunday, pig blood was spectacularly sprayed into the standing audience as the axe knocked off Longinus' head. His "headless" body is then placed on a stretcher by other *morions* and removed for "burial."

In Mogpog and Boac the *pugutan* was a mass-participation event of long standing,[6] in which virtually anyone in town might be brought into the action because Longinus was traditionally free to enter any home in town while trying to evade capture. Teruya Adachi, an anthropologist who witnessed the *pugutan* in 1982, describes the chase or *habulan* in which the entire town of Mogpog provided the stage for this drama:

> Three times Longinus is captured, and three times he escapes. The chase takes him behind bushes, across open fields, along river banks, around rice paddies, up and down coconut trees, inside private kitchens, and under tables and beds. The thrill of the *habulan,* punctuated by the blare of trumpets and the beat of drums, surges through everyone and Mogpog erupts into a riot of colours and sounds. Finally Longinus, exhausted, is caught and his hands are bound by his captors. (Adachi 1994, 32)

Many of my informants described this practice from their childhoods in the 1950s and 1960s in Boac, citing similar details. One recalled how Longinus was chased not only through the streets of town, but up coconut trees and into people's homes, noting that "we were so scared of the *morions* [we] would hide under the bed," adding that "the *morions* at that time would come into the house and poke them with their spears." Another informant, also terrified of the *morions,* remembered a childhood taunt hurtled at *morions: Morion bungi may tae sa binti* (Toothless *morions* with shit on their legs), which is perhaps a reference to their inability to see their legs while wearing their highly restrictive masks (Madrigal 2005).[7] Thus the most dramatic portion of the *morion* practice was largely improvised, with the residents playing the parts of sometimes unwitting actors as they were pursued by crazed, vengeful *morions*.

On Holy Monday, the *morions* materialize on the streets of Boac, Gasan, Mogpog, and Santa Cruz—Marinduque's four largest cities—eliciting the attention of onlookers wherever they go and disappearing only in the afternoon on Easter Sunday after the *pugutan* traditionally concludes. In Boac, in addition to wandering the streets and actively participating in the scourging of the local actor/penitent playing Christ in the streets of the town on Good Friday, they also appear in the three-part *sinakulo* on Wednesday, Thursday, and Saturday nights. But the core work of a *morion* during Holy Week was and is to be present in the streets of town from Monday until Sunday, even during the heat of the day, which is often extreme during the hot, dry season that coincides with Easter. Moving in their respective groups (there are three major *morion* associations in Boac alone), *morions* sometimes assert themselves aggressively, playing tricks on children or snarling at passersby. Constrained by cumbersome masks and headpieces, they are unable to speak except in muffled tones. At other times, they can be found serenading local businesses with song, accompanied by a percussive bamboo instrument known as the *kalutang*, as the singers push back their visors to free their mouths while still keeping their faces covered with a balaclava. In their feigned fierceness, however, they are often the victims of tricks by children rather than the frightening, snarling centurions my informants remembered as terrorizing children by breaking into homes and running through the streets in the 1950s and 1960s. Trish Nicholson, who undertook an ethnographic study in Mogpog in the late 1990s, returning again in 2010, cites a common practice there where mischievous children tie a string across the path of the *morions* as they move through the streets of the town, knowing that because the tiny holes in their masks provide only limited, partial vision, they can easily be felled with a trip wire. As local *morions* are aware of this trick, evading it becomes part of a kind of cat-and-mouse game in the streets all week long. In Gasan, Boac, and Mogpog, *morions* also participate in competitions where awards are given out in a range of categories, while another important function is to accompany the many solemn processions of *karos* or floats bearing effigies of saints through the streets of the town.

Boac *morions* sport impressive capes in bright colors and wear breast plates, some with heavily sculpted, ripped abs that largely cover their tunics, while a skirt of a thicker, durable material such as leather or a synthetic facsimile, often adorned with studs or metal design work, covers the waist and hangs down over the thighs. Leggings and sandals complete the attire, and *morions* may also carry props such as chains, manacles, shields, and swords. The homemade, ingenious quality of these props was noteworthy when I first came to Boac in 2005, though more recently groups are moving toward greater uniformity with respect to both props and costuming. The defining feature of the *morions* is the elaborate mask covering the entire head, traditionally carved from *dapdap* or *santol,* soft local woods. Papier-mâché masks were also once fairly common among those who could not afford to have a mask made for them, and more recently, molded plastic masks have begun to appear in Boac. Masks are in two parts, with a visor covering the face that typically tilts back and a headpiece that in Boac and Gasan generally resembles the crested headgear of a Roman centurion. A practice closer to what is believed to be the original one continues in Mogpog, where a traditional headpiece or *turbante* consists of a bamboo or rattan framework adorned with elaborate, brightly colored foil paper flowers. The facial expressions carved, etched, or painted onto the mask generally fall into three categories: the extraordinarily fierce and often grotesque mien of the *morions* popular in the town of Gasan; the more refined and delicately sharp features of the traditional *bulaklakan* (flowered) *moryons* of Mogpog; and the stern, sometimes fierce expressions of the Boac *morions.* In practice, these categories all circulate between towns, and the stern Boac *morion* face is increasingly seen in Mogpog, sometimes paired with the flowered headgear. Boac has perhaps the greatest range of diversity in masks: one year the face of the disgraced but now rehabilitated former president, Joseph "Erap" Estrada, appeared as a *morion,* and I have seen more than one mask resembling a lightly pigmented Michael Jackson. Mogpog *moryons* evince the greatest range of materials used to construct both costumes and headpieces, and a citywide competition awards prizes based on the use of indigenous materials such as dried *nito* (an indigenous vine used for weaving), shells, feathers, and other natural materials or recycled materials.

In Boac, individuals typically took on the practice of being a *morion* as a *panata* over a seven-year period, after which they became eligible to play Longinus, with senior *morions* selecting the individual who would take on this honor. Although this is almost an exclusively male practice in Boac, women, particularly older women, freely participate as *morions* in Mogpog, wearing essentially the same costumes as the men, though with a female face mask. Nicholson describes the motivations behind the practice known there as Moryonan, observing that today, as in Boac, people may take on the *panata* for just one or two years or may well extend it over the rest of their lives. Her informants provided motivations for continuing to observe the practice over multiple years that mirror my own findings in Boac. One sixty-three-year-old woman who had been undertaking a *panata* for ten years explained why she did so: "I started out of gratitude for my good health because I had been sick and got better" (Nicholson 2011, loc. 644). A *morion* with

Figure 5. Boac-style *morion* entering Morion Park for Saturday night *senakulo*, Boac, Marinduque. Photo by author.

thirty-three years of experience offered a similar motivation: "From when I was in first year high school, I fell and injured my head badly on the concrete. I vowed to be a Moryon if it would get better, and I've done it ever since" (loc. 661). One of my own informants spoke of how taking on the physicality of a *morion* helped him heighten his masculinity and taught him how to be "a real guy and not effeminate," adding that a married friend undertook the vow "because he wanted a baby, and after four years he had one."

A week of constant outdoor activity while wearing cumbersome costumes and highly constrictive wooden or papier-mâché masks fitting completely over the head can result in extreme physical discomfort, which gives *morions* an experiential connection with the sufferings of Christ. One is expected to be uncomfortable and to push oneself beyond the limits of physical tolerance. One's identity as a *morion* was traditionally to be kept secret even from one's closest family members, a practice that in Boac has eroded in the past generation.[8] According to Mandia (2005), a *morion* used to "hide his mask at the back of the toilet, because the toilet in the barrio is separated from the main house." Mandia recalls that even in the recent past "everybody kept his face covered" and endeavored to keep silent about his *morion* identity until Easter Sunday. Today in Boac it is common to see the younger *morions* wandering through the streets in their "off-duty" moments carrying their masks under their arms. Nicholson notes that by contrast, though Mogpog is small enough for everyone to know who is behind the mask, anonymity is generally preserved in the public sphere.

In her account of Holy Week activities, Nicholson distinguishes between the Moriones Festival, which is in many respects a project developed during the 1970s under the watch of Carmencita Reyes, and the practices known as Moryonan that take place in Mogpog. She describes the Moryonan from the perspective of a participant-observer with intimate knowledge of the tradition and suggests that *morion*-centered practices elsewhere on the island have been commercialized and are at considerable remove from those in Mogpog.[9] Although there is a ring of truth in this assertion, my fieldwork suggests that Boac still has many individuals who take the weeklong commitment of being a *morion* seriously, and who engage in it for essentially the same reasons as those who take up the related practice in Mogpog. Furthermore, the Moryonan in Mogpog, as we will see later, is not entirely immune from the danger of being co-opted by local politicians, and it continues to change incrementally, even as what motivates people to take it up has not altered significantly. The history of the *morions* in Boac since the 1960s suggests that each time a collectivity emerges that appears to take the practice in a particular direction that others believe is contrary to the original spirit of what it means to be a *morion*, a new group soon emerges to reclaim what it believes is an authentic link to the original tradition. These collectivities, in turn, invent their own history, justifications, and credos that provide the group and its members with a collective identity as well as a moral and spiritual authority.

Panata, Politics, and Staging the *Morion*

Until the 1960s, individuals taking on the *panata* associated with being a *morion* in Boac were largely drawn from the poorer classes who lived just outside the town and participated as free agents, without being drawn into formal *morion* organizations. Poverty in the Philippines means that you come to know your neighbors because spaces that are large enough in which to gather comfortably are shared and few can afford to build structures capable of isolating their family from the noise and human activity of other families who live in close proximity. Access to water, cooking, bathing, and toilet facilities are often shared, and was the case particularly a generation or more ago and in the smaller centers or *sa probinsya* (in the provinces), the generic term for any place that is far removed geographically or culturally from the country's largest cities. As a small, relatively impoverished island province, Marinduque falls very much into this category. Thus for those living in poor *barangays* on the edge of Boac, the practice of being a *morion* was probably so woven into community life that no external organizations were necessary for much of its history. This changed in the 1960s, however, when formal *morion* organizations were established in both Boac and Mogpog. In 1961 the Samahang Moryones ng Mogpog (Moryon Association of Mogpog) was formed with recognition from the Church and local government (Nicholson 2011, loc. 1072). At around the same time in Boac the mayor's son, Agustin Madrigal, founded Samahan ng mga Moryon (Organization of the Morion), which in 1963 was renamed "The Order of the Moriones" at the suggestion of then-provincial governor Celso Preclaro (Mandia 2005). Influenced by popular movies and books of the time, particularly the Hollywood biblical epics, Madrigal, according to Mandia, "came up with an idea that a *morion* looked like a centurion," in contrast to the traditional *morion,* whose costume was handmade from the materials available to barrio dwellers living on the edge of town. The effect of this transformation over time, according to Mandia, was to increasingly marginalize the traditional barrio-dwelling *morions* as this new "elite *morion*" increasingly became the norm. Poorer would-be *morions* who lacked the resources to obtain elaborate centurion costumes and masks created by master carvers were made to feel they were diminishing the tradition by failing to attain this new and externally imposed standard of authenticity. It is widely believed that the style still largely present in Mogpog, with highly individuated costumes made of indigenous materials, capped by a flowered headpiece, reflects an originary practice that was common on the streets of Boac until the late 1950s.

Because Boac is the provincial capital, it is not surprising that there the practice first became increasingly linked to politics. Governor Preclaro (1963–1967), whom Obligacion remembers as having "looked the part," enacted the role of Pontius Pilate in the short playlet on Sunday in which he condemns Longinus to death by beheading, whereas the current provincial governor, Carmencita Reyes (2007),[10] also recalls, at that time, "the officials of Pontius Pilate were officials of the [Preclaro] government." That the local political elite would choose to publicly enact the roles of those who condemned Christ to death on Easter Sunday after Mass might seem to be either in poor taste or deeply ironic were it not for the long tradition of these kinds of enactments being led by local socialites and political powerbrokers. Resil Mojares observes that in Cebu during the Spanish colonial era the principal roles in Filipino *komedya* (known as *linambay* in that region) were reserved for the local elite (Mojares 1985, 91–92). Just as the Church used performance events to win over converts and consolidate their power, as the country moved into the Marcos years (1965–1986), local politicians increasingly placed many popular performance forms under their patronage and sometimes their direct control. Moreover, unlike the Mogpog *moryonan*, in Boac the tradition was not integrated into the official ritual activities of the Church (Nicholson 2011, loc. 1164), possibly making it easier for local politicians to manipulate.

The *morions* and the corresponding *pugutan* appeared on the national radar screen during the presidency of Diosdado Macapagal (1961–1965),[11] when Celso Carunungan, a well-known writer who was to later work on an expanded script for a multinight *sinakulo*, brought education secretary Alejandro Roces to Marinduque on a kind of cultural fact-finding tour during which the latter expressed the view that the "*moriones* is a dying tradition" in need of revitalization (Mandia 2005). But the primary force behind the politicization and commodification of the *morions* in Boac was not these individuals, but rather Carmencita Reyes, who in 2013 was elected again as provincial governor after having served as congressional representative, a position previously occupied by her son Edmundo. Her late husband, Edmundo Reyes Sr., held the powerful position of commissioner of immigration during the Marcos era, and since the 1970s the family has been the dominant force in governing the island province. Born into the socially high-flying Ongsiapo family, Carmencita Reyes is the country's oldest politician to have held major national and provincial public offices in recent times, and her famous socialite sister, Imelda "Meldy" Cojuangco, was one of Imelda Marcos' original "Blue Ladies." This group of socially prominent women constituted the first lady's inner circle, traveling with her on junkets, and appearing at significant social and cultural events. Gossip columnist Cindy Adams, a friend of Mrs. Marcos at the time, observes that "[t]heir job was to adore her" (Schulman 2013). Of this group Carmencita's sister was perhaps the most prominent, and some speculate that because she was raised in a more refined and rarefied environment than the first lady, she may have had a significant hand in shaping Imelda's public image as she emerged on the national and international stage as an Asian Jacqueline Kennedy. Like her sister Meldy, Carmencita Reyes, even in her eighties, remains an impressive lady with a sharp incisive mind, tremendous drive and energy, and great charisma. To be a guest in her home, as I have, is to come to understand how attractive and almost irresistible it would be to place your faith and trust in such an elegant lady, one capable of extending herself to all of her guests in a deeply personal way.

In 1972, as martial law was being declared, Imelda Marcos sought to bring the cultures of the periphery to the center in Manila through the creation of the Nayong Pilipino, a cultural village intended to represent the Philippines in miniature, with traditional dwellings from the major regions and small-scale replicas of natural wonders such as the volcanic Mount Mayon and the famed Cordillera Rice Terraces. Vicente Rafael observes that under Imelda's watch, "National culture was construed as so many gifts from above bestowed on those below" (Rafael 2000, 138). Reyes' first formal involvement with the Boac *morion* dates from this time, when, as she recalls, the First Lady asked her to "bring the *morion*es" to the park for a cultural performance that was aired on national television. Seeking a stronger foundation for the continuation of martial law, Ferdinand Marcos had the constitution redrawn in 1973, a process that eventually brought Reyes more fully into the political spotlight as the representative for Marinduque in the National Assembly (Batasang Pambansa) from 1984 until the fall of the regime a few years later.[12] According to Reyes, the idea of creating a longer passion play into which the story of Longinus would eventually be integrated came to her while watching the short dramatic presentation in which Longinus was condemned by Pilate: "[S]omewhere in the play Longhino says, '*Si Kristo ang isang dios,* Christ is the true God.'[13] And the children would repeat those [lines] and they would pray . . . and I was saying to myself, 'do these children know about Christ?' " In the 1970s Reyes invited the *sinakulistas* from Obando in Bulacan, north of Manila, to present their version of the *pasyon,* which extended from Monday to Friday in Boac (Reyes; Obligacion 2007), presumably as a model for a new kind of practice that would bring the *morions* and the *pugutan* into a more traditional *sinakulo* format. Reyes remembers the group's presentation in the Boac covered court in the middle of town as "so folklorish, really folklorish," and in the recitation of the Tagalog *pasyon* using standing microphones, "it was really more like comedy." Yet because continuous day and night readings of the *pasyon* are a common practice throughout the Philippines during Holy Week, it is probable that for the Bulacan *sinakulistas*, the power of the ritual extended from its completeness, not from finding an attentive audience willing to be present for the entire event.

Clearly, Reyes had another model in mind, one more grounded in theatre. For a start, she recalls, it needed to be shortened "inasmuch as people would . . . still work on Holy Monday and Holy Tuesday." Instead of starting on Monday, she "decided to shorten it, to make the Old Testament on Wednesday, on Thursday it would start with the baptism of Christ, the miracles of Christ . . . and then on Friday there was the *Via Cruces* [Stations of the Cross]." As we saw in the previous chapter, the Boac *morions* goad, beat, and cajole Christ as he passes through the streets of the town. Reyes notes that she retained this structure as it had "been traditionally depicted by the *morions*" and that "the only thing I did was to introduce that Christ would be buried (Station 14), when the next day, on Saturday, he would rise." Thus, by the end of the 1970s, the final Saturday night Boac *sinakulo* was to focus on the story of Longinus and end with his spectacular mock public execution, effectively disrupting the chronology of the week's events by placing the *pugutan* before the celebration of the risen Christ on Easter morning. In this way the culminating act marking the end of a weeklong *panata* by local *morions* was removed from its original context and placed into a theatrical presentation.

According to Reyes, what occasioned moving the *pugutan* from its usual Sunday morning time slot was an event of international significance: "In 1977 King Juan Carlos of Spain wrote the First Lady, Mrs. Imelda Marcos, that a group of Menorcan[14] pilgrims would want to go to the Philippines," to establish a case "for the beatification of Father Diego de Saura, a Jesuit priest who served in Marinduque in 1631." Reyes recalls that 120 pilgrims accompanied Father Saura's remains to Marinduque.[15] The process was followed by a 1979 Easter trip to Marinduque by the Spanish king who traveled with an extensive entourage. Before a Saturday night audience that included the king, Reyes staged a "twenty-minute presentation on the *pugutan*" using theatrical lighting borrowed from the Folk Arts Theatre at the Cultural Center of the Philippines (CCP). According to Reyes, "So when they saw the beauty of the presentation in the evening, they asked me to change the time and make it Saturday evening rather than Sunday morning." Thus, by 1979, the dramatic highlight of what was to become a three-night *sinakulo*—namely, the beheading of Longinus—was incorporated into a Saturday night program with stage lighting, under the watch of the governor herself and before an audience that included the Spanish king.

Given the obsession of provincial governments in the Philippines with promoting cultural tourism, it is ironic that incorporating the *pugutan* into the *sinakulo* appears to have been responsible for a decline in the popularity of the Moriones Festival with visitors from elsewhere in the Philippines and overseas. Obligacion (2007) recalls that during the mid-1970s a special cruise ship brought dignitaries from Manila to watch the Easter Sunday *pugutan*. Guests at that time included the 1974 winners of the Miss World and Miss Universe contests, Helen Elizabeth Morgan (UK) and Amparo Munõz (Spain), the former U.S. ambassador to the Philippines, William McCormick Blair Jr., as well as President Marcos' mother, Dona Josefa Edralin Marcos (Reyes 2007). Given the importance placed on beauty pageants in the Philippines and also the fact that the First Lady's point of entry into national political life was through the "Miss Manila" pageant in 1953,[16] this is as distinguished a lineup as one could find for any public event. One could speculate that subjecting such important dignitaries to the heat of the midday sun after Easter Mass may have made an evening *pugutan* program under lights more attractive. While it might be easy to dismiss such reasons, the spectacle of beauty queens, ambassadors, Imelda's Blue Ladies, and a host of dignitaries baking under the heat of the sweltering sun in the middle of the country's dry "summer" season is impossible to imagine,[17] especially during the ever-regal Marcos era.

The biggest shift to the traditional *sinakulo* script was that virtually all of the final night, Saturday, was given over to the story of Longinus. Whereas the Tagalog *Pasyon Pilapil* contains seventy-four stanzas of five lines each that touch on the actions of the Roman soldier,[18] Reyes recalls that she worked with writer Carunungan, adding new material "to make it more interesting" to bring a more "human touch" by adding the plot point that Pilate's wife, Claudia, was "infatuated with Longhino." Although Carunungan is credited as the writer of the text at the start of each evening's Boac *sinakulo,* and the exact nature of their collaboration is difficult to determine,[19] it is clear that Reyes provided the dramatic structure of each night's *sinakulo* by choosing the content to be dramatized. She also increasingly played a major role in determining the style of the presentation while providing it with a venue, production funds, and actors in the leading roles who were drawn primarily from the office of the provincial government.

The accounts of Longinus' actions contained in the *Pasyon Pilapil* invite representation, and also provide both the dramatic and spiritual foundation for the actions and attitudes of the *morions* not only on stage but on the streets of Boac throughout the whole of Holy Week. The instructive nature of the standard nineteenth-century Tagalog *pasyon* text, designed to teach lessons in ways that were accessible and consistent with the social, cultural, and spiritual values of the populace at a time when few had access to books of any kind, much less the Bible, is also reflected in the following selected segments of text that focus on Longinus. In the translated passage below, Longinus witnesses the resurrection of Jesus Christ while guarding his tomb with other soldiers, and unlike his compatriots, he converts immediately, not only refusing to cover up what he has witnessed but also starting to proselytize, setting himself up for conflict with Pilate and the Roman authorities:

> 2193. While the soldiers
> were sitting guard
> the hero Longinus
> was changed and converted
> when he saw this.
> 2194. His soul
> Was filled with fear and it trembled;
> he thought, remembered
> quickly he believed
> in Jesus the Lord Father.

2195. When they had come
to their senses,
quickly they agreed
to cover it all up
and not announce it.
2196. The hero Longinus
did not agree or follow.
Into the town, he entered quickly:
he came before and approached
the scribes and Pharisees.
2197. What he said
to the leaders:
"honorable ones,
that corpse of Jesus
now has come back to life.
2198. "We who stood guard
fell to our faces
out of great weakness
because of the exceeding brilliance
of that body of Jesus.
2199. "All this I declare,
believe in
for it is the truth.
A while ago at daybreak,
he came out of the tomb." (Nicholson 2011, loc. 1633–1666)

After testifying to a larger crowd about the Resurrection, Longinus is pursued by Roman soldiers, caught, and delivered for execution. In the passage that follows, Longinus expresses his willingness to stand in on an experiential level for the sufferings of Christ in a way that mirrors the pain and discomfort expected of anyone undertaking a *panata,* also embedding the Christ story into the body of the common man:

2214. He thought
in his own mind:
"God," he said, "the holy one
allowed himself to be insulted, slapped
when he is sinless.
2215. "While I
a deceiver and schemer

who always sins,
why should I not bear
these [*sic*] their punishment?" (Nicholson 2011, loc. 1713)

The final lesson or *aral* at the end of this sequence of verses makes clear that good Christians are expected to "imitate" the piety of Longinus by themselves undertaking a penitential act:

2241. Imitate the endurance
of the goodly martyr
for which his soul, indeed,
reaped joy and gladness
in heaven filled with glory. (Nicholson 2011, loc. 1792)

Returning to Reyes' initial proposition, namely, that the extended, multiple-night *sinakulo* grew out of her concern that children were not learning about the life of Christ in school or through the short skit that preceded Longinus' execution on Easter Sunday, what is one to make of an entire evening that focuses on a story not found in the Bible at all? Without reference to the Tagalog *Pasyon Pilapil,* the "popular Bible," the practice would make little sense. But in this *pasyon,* which features the biblical story of the passion as well as the basic highlights in the history of salvation, including the teachings of Christ and his miracles, a full 370 lines focus on Longinus, the individual who, like all of us listening to this tale, should be willing to take on the sufferings of Christ just as he has done. Longinus reflects on and acknowledges his sinfulness, and suggests that because Christ has taken on so much pain "when he is sinless," he himself should not hesitate to bear punishment at the hands of his fellow Roman soldiers. Longinus stands in for all sinners and his experience as well as the broader final reflection on it contained within the *pasyon* suggests that the biblical story of the Passion of Christ is not enough; those who believe need this extra degree of personalization embedded in the story, which demands that they actively engage with and are even willing to take on a degree of physical suffering. And in the local adaptation of the *pasyon* in Marinduque, the *morions* are required inasmuch as it is from the ranks of the sinners that the saint emerges. Those who serve as *morions* are themselves sinners just as the Roman soldiers were, yet because of the way in which they engage with the practice of being a *morion,* their actions become a *panata.*

Just as there is only one Christ in a dramatic representation of the *pasyon,* there can only be one Longinus, one soldier willing to face certain death to stand alongside Christ in his suffering and his sacrifice. For those *morions* who are not as spiritually evolved as Longinus (or those who have not yet earned the right to be Longinus because they have not yet undertaken the *panata* for seven years), they take on the role of his tormentors, and in doing so sacrifice time, energy, income, and opportunities to be with family and loved ones during Holy Week. As noted, this *panata* involves physical discomfort, particularly when the *morion* endures an entire week's worth of activities, sweating and at times breathing with difficulty under the weight of costume pieces and multiple layers of fabric, with his head covered by a heatstroke-inducing head covering and mask with only tiny holes for the eyes. Yet there is also some measure of fun connected with being a *morion;* there is an observable easy camaraderie and fellowship within each *morion* group, and the opportunity to be on public display and the license granted by the occasion and the costumes and masks allows for mischief-making and play of the sort that is bounded by strict rules. Thus it is to the communities of *morions* that we now turn.

Morions, Politics, the Collective, and the Individual

Throughout the Philippines, many politicians in key positions such as mayor, congressional representative, or provincial governor have traditionally had control over separate and often competing pots of money siphoned off from the public purse through a seemingly endless list of fraudulent practices, chief among them "pork-barreling," which typically means obtaining financial backing from the national government for large infrastructure projects in return for political support or "delivering the votes." In the absence of effective oversight and because "everyone else does it," this practice has meant that politicians at all levels have significant powers of patronage through the dispersal of these slush funds, though more recently there have been serious efforts to end pork-barreling as well as other questionable funding schemes. Patronage politics are further reinforced by the intergenerational transfer of power in political families; it is not unusual for families to run provinces over multiple generations, for example, as the Marcos clan now does in Ferdinand Marcos' home province of Ilocos del Norte, where octogenarian Imelda Marcos serves as congressional representative and her children Aimee and Bongbong serve as provincial governor and national senator, respectively. A similar form of dynastic succession has been in place at times with the Reyes family in Marinduque. This dynastic pattern in Filipino politics, an issue to which I will return later, reflects the personalistic expression of politics as well as the longstanding practice of vote-buying, which many of the country's wealthier families can easily afford to factor into the cost of running a "traditional campaign." There is little doubt that for many living in the poorer *barangays* around the country, voting for the family with the name, particularly if they offer 500 pesos for a vote, some free Tanduay rum for the men,[20] and support for the local fiestas, is an easy choice. Local politicians situate themselves into the *utang na loób* framework by "bringing you" things, setting themselves up as generous, even as crafty politicians, capable of attracting money and essential services that benefit the local populace. Because it is common in the Philippines to see everything from new freeway overpasses to basketball courts and even park benches bearing the names of local politicians who bestowed these "gifts" on ordinary citizens, their feigned generosity lives beyond them, making it even more likely that the majority will simply continue voting for the family name that is emblazoned on public works projects all over the region.

In such an environment, it is hardly surprising that one powerful, well-connected and charismatic individual has been able to alter the *morion* tradition so fundamentally by taking a relatively unorganized penitential practice from the streets and incorporating it into a dramatic presentation. It is widely believed among Marinduqueños that with respect to financial and in-kind support both the *sinakulo* and the Moriones Festival in Boac has been essentially a project of the provincial government, one largely overseen by Carmencita Reyes initially as the island's "leading lady," then later as governor and congressional representative. Indeed, the provincial governor's ambitions for the Boac event were never modest. She recalls how back in the 1970s, "I wanted to make Boac like a little Jerusalem, nobody using pants, everybody uses kaftans. I wanted to transform it into Jerusalem." When Imelda Marcos gave her the responsibility of taking care of the pilgrims accompanying the remains of Father de Saura, she remembers that those who saw her theatricalized version of the *pugutan* in 1979 "told me to go to Oberammergau." She had planned to attend the entire 120-day event in 1980, but, "a few days before I was supposed to go, my mother had a heart attack." According to Reyes, when those who went returned, "they told me, 'you know Carmencita, you can do better than Oberammergau . . . because your passion play is at the right time.'" When I interviewed her in 2007 she concluded that the Boac *sinakulo* "is much better than Oberammergau," adding, "The only thing is to . . . translate it into English," suggesting even more ambitious future plans.

Under Reyes' watch, it seems clear that the wild, sometimes anarchic energy that once characterized the *pugutan* has been tamed. By placing what had been a singular, stand-alone event within the context of the concluding Saturday night *sinakulo,* it is out of sequence with the tenor, tone, and content of Holy Week. On Black Saturday when Longinus is beheaded by the *morions,* Christ is not yet risen. The promise of the Resurrection has not yet been actualized, even though what is dramatized is the conversion, persecution, and martyrdom of the first Roman convert to Christianity. As Mandia (2005) flatly observes, "When we're celebrating, God's still dead," which conflates God with Christ in a way that is common among Catholics in the Tagalog region. The inference is that the celebratory tone of the final Saturday night *sinakulo,* with its grand dramatic concluding gesture and extensive use of *morions,* is not appropriate without the hope of eternal life that is the promise of the Resurrection. Though Mandia's concerns seem entirely reasonable to me, both he and Obligacion have earned the ire of Governor Reyes in the past for their outspokenness and criticism of the ways in which her interventions have altered the tradition.[21] Privately, Marinduqueños concede that there will be no significant changes to the *sinakulo* featuring the *morions* until Reyes has shuffled off this mortal coil. For as long as she lives and breathes, it seems unlikely that she will permit changes to the *sinakulo* to take place.

With respect to the *morions* in the street, as noted earlier, the theatricalization and indeed the Hollywoodization of the *morion* tradition in Boac began in the early 1960s when the then-mayor's son formed the group, the Order of the Moriones, taking what had been a largely barrio-based tradition and making it the province of the middle- and upper-class elite of the town, in turn presenting this slicker *morion* as a symbol of local pride in place. There is a long history of competing *morion* groups in Boac, with the favored groups at any given time often linked to whomever is exercising political power at the municipal or provincial level. In 2005, the dominant group was the Kapatiran, who in their physical presentation appeared very much like the images of Roman centurions that circulated in the mid-century Hollywood biblical epics. By 2007 the members of the Kapatiran group dominated the visual field of the multiple night *sinakulo* with their resplendent costumes and individuated masks. On Good Friday, they constituted a tight and highly disciplined group as they shoved, pushed, and beat Christ and the other two penitents in the streets of Boac, and in the Saturday night *sinakulo* it was one of their number who enacted Longinus. The overwhelming presence of this group also meant that any opportunities for social inversion that were once present when the tradition was dominated by men from the poorer barrios on the edge of town were now entirely absent. No longer could the poor run riot through the streets and invade the homes of the more affluent town dwellers, as my senior informants suggest they once commonly did until the late 1950s.

In 2003 a group calling itself Mistah was created by fifteen individuals who broke away from the Kapatiran (Vergara 2013), hoping to "promote the real lessons of the tradition" rather than the "politicized concept" of the Kapatiran with its "show-biz mentality" (Mandia 2005). Other informants echoed the view that Mistah sought out a more inclusive membership and wished to focus more squarely on *panata* as the core element in the *morion* experience during Holy Week. Affiliated loosely with the charismatic movement in the Filipino Catholic Church, the group, numbering more than two hundred by 2013, continues to engage in public-service activities throughout the year, including provision of gifts for the poor at Christmas. Mistah sought a return to the tradition where penitents "provide their own costumes, in their own different way, in any capacity they can . . . regardless of whether it's expensive or not" (Mandia 2005), in contrast to the relatively slick look of the Kapatiran *morions*. As Mistah member Ricky Vergara asserts, "Nobody can dictate what we do," noting that everything is "done for the benefit of the group." One informant observed that in 2007 the difference between the two groups is fundamentally about funding and government sponsorship, noting that Kapatiran "funds come from government's coffers . . . from the personal funding of the provincial governor." Indeed, that year many in Boac held the view that Kapatiran was favored by the provincial government and was therefore featured in the *sinakulo,* whereas the newer group, Mistah, though clearly a presence during Holy Week, was largely left to its own devices. In my trips there in 2007 and again in 2013, it was clear that Mistah had remained true to its commitment to stay outside of the political arena, and as its members celebrated their tenth anniversary in a public ceremony, they seemed to be a strong and cohesive group that reflected a broader constituency than Kapatiran.

By 2013, another new group had been formed and had found political favor. Claiming the moniker, "The Legion of the Marinduque *Morions,*" and known locally as "Legion," their very name staked a claim on the practices throughout the entire island. When incorporated in 2008, it had the support of Lord Allan Jay Q. Velasco (Obligacion 2013), then the provincial administrator of Marinduque and rising young star of local politics who served as congressional representative from 2010 to 2013. The group also garnered the support of Carmencita Reyes' son Edmundo, who took up his mother's congressional seat in 2007 so that she could again run for provincial governor.[22] Legion appear quite aggressively to stake a claim to a kind of authenticity, a return to some of the ceremonial traditions embedded in the Boac *morion* practices of the old Order of the Moriones. One of these "traditions" is that of "knighting and knighthood," and the bestowing of titles on visiting dignitaries such as the national secretary of tourism when he came to the island in 2011,[23] a practice that Madrigal's group had initiated in the 1960s (Obligacion 2013). Eli Obligacion, who has worked for Velasco, recalls how, at the competitive "Battle of the Morions" celebration in 2009, they presented a ritual drawn from the Hollywood film about King Arthur, presumably the 1953 cinemascope classic, *Knights of the Round Table*. The bonds of men and mateship are strongly but somehow curiously expressed in the motto emblazoned on their emblem:

"Brothers to brothers, rules, to life and death," a phrase that is difficult to interpret, as is the group's "preamble" that appears on its Web site:

> The specialization of historical studies, the importance of the tradition and culture of the *Morion,* broadly interpreted as the various religious beliefs of the nineteenth century and their impact on society, and the significance of tradition and culture of the *Morion* for century had prompted the formation of this organization and its incorporation on September 1, 2008 under the "Not for Profit Corporation Act." (Legion of the Marinduque *Morions* 2014)

In practice, it appears that the sources for the group's historical practices are largely derived from Hollywood movies. While "reviving" a ritual practiced in the 1960s drawn from a Hollywood movie from the early 1950s, one that was in turn created out of the legends of King Arthur in the late fifth and early sixth centuries may seem at odds with the group's commitment to "historical studies." Even more confusing is the use of the term "Spartans," which many informants used when referring to the group. Obligacion speculated that this moniker may have stuck with the group after their presentation of a Spartan "ritual" at the local "Battle of the Morions" competition, one inspired by yet another Hollywood movie.

Visually, the group projects a "Spartan" appearance through an aggressive presentation of a kind of hypermasculinity, heightened by the uniformity of costumes featuring heavily muscled and chiseled breastplates covering the chest, red capes, matching skirts made of hanging leather straps fitted with ornamental metal fastenings, high crested helmets, and masks that project a similar fierceness. The breastplate appears to have more in common with Spartan and Greek models than Roman ones, whereas the red capes and other costume features reflect the iconography of Roman centurions. Because all of their costumes match, they look more like an actual army than other *morion* groups. Inasmuch as the centurions were essentially the officer corps, each of whom commanded a group of around one hundred Roman legions (the ordinary foot soldiers), an "army" of centurions is a historical impossibility. However, none of these contradictions seems of particular concern either to the group or to the provincial government of Marinduque, which have in the past several years used the group to promote the *morion* tradition by sending them to events around the country. These have included religious festivals and the popular parade associated with the famed Panagbenga Festival in the city of Baguio, the gateway to the mountainous Cordillera region of north central Luzon. The costs associated with these junkets are considerable and funding appears to come from the provincial government. Not surprisingly, many of the key figures in this group are local government employees. What is perhaps unusual is that this group seems to have crossed the political divide, having been supported by both the Reyes family and their political opponent, Velasco. This group has all the trappings of a group supported by the political elite: clearly well-funded, slick, and uniform in presentation, and with many in possession of buff, gym-toned bodies that are rarely seen on the streets of a provincial town, they have staked out a claim with respect to the "tradition" that places them in the public eye both locally and nationally.

Holy Week 2013 fell a mere six weeks prior to the general election in which both mother and daughter were running for provincial governor and congressional representative, respectively. Carmencita, identified in campaign posters as "Nanay Reyes" and her daughter Victoria, "Ate Gina," were now presented as family members to Marinduqueños, as beloved "mother" and "sister," respectively. "Ate Gina," who lived in Los Angeles when I met her in 2007 and who then seemed to harbor no political ambitions, had in the intervening years returned to Marinduque, first to serve as provincial administrator under her governor mother, and was now running for the seat in the national House of Representatives occupied by the dynamic and youthful Lord Allan Jay Velasco. Perhaps realizing that there was no political capital to be gained by any further public connection with the *morions* of Boac or the *sinakulo* so deeply identified with her mother, in 2013 "Ate Gina" associated herself and her campaign with the *morions* of Mogpog, regarded throughout the island as the "most authentic" in both their practices and presentation. Mogpog *morions* have traditionally assembled on Easter morning after Mass to dance, and, more recently, to compete in a costume competition prior to the beheading of Longinus in the public square at midday. As in Boac and other provincial towns in the Philippines, the largest centrally located, open-air structure capable of sheltering people from the searing sun of the hot, dry season is the "covered court" used largely for basketball for most of the year. Thus it was on the stage of the Mogpog covered court that "Ate Gina," with her husband at her side, presided over the costume competition, handing out awards to winners in a wide range of categories, ranging from "oldest" to "youngest" participant, with further awards for best use of "recycled" or "traditional" materials. Because these *morions* dance to everything from the rumba beat to "Gangnam Style" while wearing costumes that are far more colorful, inventive, and homemade than the increasingly uniform costumes that hold sway in Boac, there is a light, joyful, celebratory quality to this event. As many of the masks bear an impassive, neutral gaze and women and children as well as men participate, watching them dance can put one into what feels almost like a hallucinogenic state as their brightly colored paper foil headdresses move and sway to the upbeat, up-tempo, eclectic musical selections.

Whether by accident or design, "Ate Gina's" presence was remembered long after the event, as she formally posed with each of the winning entrants when they came onstage to receive their awards. Parked outside the covered court in front of the Mogpog City Hall was the Reyes family Toyota Hi-Ace,[24] ready for a stylish exit and covered with campaign posters, some featuring a photo of her with president Noynoy Aquino, both sporting yellow shirts, the color associated with his mother Cory Aquino and the Liberal Party. While I found it distressing that Reyes appeared to be using this relatively homespun and locally emplaced tradition on Easter Sunday as a kind of campaign appearance while capitalizing on the popularity of Aquino, to most locals her presence was no doubt unexceptional. And nothing I saw would suggest that her presence altered the shape and form of the dance and subsequent costume competition. Yet there is little doubt that in the afterlife of the many images of winners appearing alongside "Ate Gina" circulated among family, friends, and social media, a subliminal impression was created that linked the Reyes family to this event in some way as patrons or sponsors.

The relationship between the Moriones Festival and politics brings to mind the well-worn phrase, "Politics *ay* weather weather *lang.*" Attributed to former president Joseph "Erap" Estrada, the cop-drama movie star elected to the top job who resigned in disgrace following a financial scandal in 2001 and who now serves as mayor of Metro Manila, it conveys both a sense of the ups and downs of political life and the seasonal nature of life itself: everything that goes around, comes around. Translated, it suggests that politics has the qualities that the weather possesses, that it is not merely "just like the weather," but that it is like what makes weather, weather—in other words, that it changes and is marked by seasons. The repetition of the word "weather" follows from a linguistic practice of intensification in Tagalog that comes with doubling the stem of a word, something that can turn a noun, for instance, into either an adjective or an adverb, as it does with the word *panahon,* which signifies both "time" and "season" as well as "weather" or "a period of time." Doubled, *pana-panahon* becomes "periodically" or "seasonal." Thus "weather-weather," observed one clever blogger in response to the question in an online forum, "is a derivative of '*pana-panahon,*' a Tagalog phrase that has a lot of connotation which did not actually refer to 'weather' per se. The original context was usually for social cycles, when the man in rags today could be a rich man by tomorrow, or when a preacher today might be wallowing in sin later" (Yahoo Answers n.d.). While interviewing informants in Marinduque in 2013 on the cusp of yet another election, many used the phrase "weather weather lang" to suggest not only the unchanging nature of local politics and how it is manifested but also how those who come into power ultimately engage in the very same tactics as those they ran against and displaced. No matter how much things appear to change on the political landscape, some things remain the same: those in power reward those who helped them get there, and those who are supported by those in power, be they *morions* traveling together as a group to a far-flung city for a festival or simply individual *morions* participating in a modest competition in the town of Mogpog, will never be immune from political forces.

Yet in spite of the interventions of local politicians and the competition between *morion* groups claiming to connect present practices with "rediscovered" traditions, individuals in Boac continue to experience their participation in the week's activities as *morions* as a form of *panata* and, however it may be expressed, that fundamental impulse remains consistent with the "tradition" established by Father Dionisio Santiago in Mogpog in the last half of the nineteenth century. The practice of Mogpog *moryonan*—despite the photo opportunities with "Ate Gina"—continue much as they have for decades, and the experience of the group Mistah in Boac suggests that even in the highly politicized environment of the provincial capital it is possible to hold to a particular set of practices that seem, in their inclusivity at least, to connect more clearly to the impulses behind the "original" tradition. Political authorities and power elites will continually and repeatedly stake a claim in any and all events such as these, particularly those where local culture and religious ritual come together in a festival context. Rather than using this as further evidence of a broken and corrupt political system, it is more useful to consider what it is about community-based performance in the Philippines that makes these interventions a political necessity. In the following chapters it will become increasingly clear how the community-based performance forms are so deeply embedded into what it means to have a place from which to stand that no Filipino politician can resist participating in them; further, they provide the foundation for what it means to be an empathic human being, and with that, also what it means to be Filipino.

CHAPTER 4

Dancing Natives, Dancing Nation

From *Bayan* to Bayanihan

On May 27, 1958, a new company composed of young dancers, many still in their teens, came halfway around the world from Manila to Brussels to perform at an international exposition alongside some of the world's most famed dancers and performers. Only this time they appeared not as a colonial project, the way Filipinos had been displayed at world's fairs in the past—notably the Paris Exposition of 1900 and the Saint Louis International Exhibition of 1904—but as the cultural ambassadors for a country that only twelve years earlier had gained its independence from the United States. Within the Philippines and among Filipinos in the diaspora, the "triumph" of the Bayanihan Philippine Dance Company at the 1958 Brussels International Exposition is the fixed point from which all considerations of the international reputation of Filipino dance inevitably start and to which they inevitably return.[1] The mythic moment when the company was catapulted into stardom is recalled by Bayanihan costumer and company resident chronicler Isabel Santos nearly fifty years later:

> It might have been the beginning of fairy tale. The participating countries were to showcase their cultural fare. Italy had Renata Tibaldi, Germany had Dietrich Fisher-daskau *[sic]*[2] and Japan had its Kabuki. The setting was the 1958 Brussels World's Fair. The Philippine cast had thirty-eight brown-skinned lads and lasses accompanied by a meagre 4,000 pounds of props and costumes, a substantial portion of them sun-dried bamboos. They were to perform on the same stage where Dame Margot Fonteyn and the Royal Ballet had enthralled dance critics the night before. Hardly anyone in that part of the world had heard of the Bayanihan Philippine Dance Company. On the chilly spring evening of May 27, the dancers nervously waited for the curtains to rise. Then, a magic wand seemed to wave for an hour and a half the Bayanihan held the audience in its spell. By the time the Tinikling peaked in its resounding, rapid staccato,[3] everyone was thoroughly captivated. The Grand Auditorium erupted in applause as the curtains fell. The Bayanihan had conquered Brussels.[4] (Santos 2004, 61–62)

The standing ovation audiences gave to the young, fledgling company, followed by the television broadcast of the "Tinikling" segment of their performance on the famed Ed Sullivan Show—seen by as many as forty million Americans (Ylanan and Ylanan 1974, 148)—achieved quasi-mythic status, but there can be no doubt that what happened in Brussels represented a historic opening for Filipino dance on the international stage. For those who participated and the dancers who came after them, these performances as well as the short season at New York City's Winter Garden Theatre the following year, validated by overwhelmingly positive critical responses, were and remain a huge source of Filipino cultural pride.

The cultural export of the Philippines as a nation could be said to start from this moment, and in many ways it could not have been better timed; the country was emerging as an independent nation after a lengthy period of American "tutelage," international air travel was becoming possible for greater numbers of travelers, and the United States and Western Europe were beginning an unprecedented period of economic expansion. From the regional perspective, the Philippines was poised to become one of the economic powerhouses of Asia, with a higher per capita income than all but a few other Asian nations in the 1950s.[5] Yet it was not the country's economic potential on display in Brussels or New York, but its exuberant, joyful, colorful culture, one composed of clearly differentiated strands. What later became known as Bayanihan's signature dance repertory was first presented internationally in Brussels, offering up an exotic cultural show, one that entranced many prominent Western critics. Responding to the Brussels show, Francophone critic M. R. Molenhoek of *Cette Semaine* opined:

> It was, this, in this century of anxiety, the most spontaneous expression of joie de vivre that we have ever witnessed. A song to the praise of life in paradise on those heavenly islands. With a peal of the gong, some dancing and a smile, the true happiness of man emerged from darkness.[6] (Bayanihan 2015)

Remarkably, the reviewer does not describe what was onstage, but rather his internal response to what was staged. Molenhoek, writing as the "ideal spectator" using the inclusive "we," suggests that the show was an antidote to the darkness of the nuclear age, one that was euphoria-inducing with its joie de vivre and glimpses of "paradise."

The two-week run at New York's famed Winter Garden Theatre the following year caused influential critics to be equally rapturous. No less than John Martin, the dean of American dance criticism and a leading figure in the development of modern dance in the United States proclaimed:

> So you think you have seen everything? Well, unless you have seen . . . Bayanihan . . . you couldn't be more mistaken. . . . It is completely different from anything that has been shown hereabouts, and it makes for an evening of enchantment. . . . It is primarily an engrossing evening of theatrical art, beautiful to look at, to listen to, and to "assist" at. . . . The evening is not only a brilliant one but is also pervaded by a rare and sweet grace all around. (Martin 1959b)

Martin, who championed the kind of modern dance that demanded an active response from the audience, found this quality of having to "assist at" the meaning-making process worthy of comment, constituting the value-added element in a peak experience. In his extended piece in the *New York Times* the following Sunday, he observed that this was "the first professionally organized example of Philippine art to be seen in this country," one for which "we are totally unprepared" due to the prior lack of cultural exposure. Of the myriad cultural influences integrated into the dance program, he observed that "the end result is totally individual, and it is no exaggeration to say that we have never seen a show like it. In this day of rapid communications, that is saying a great deal" (Martin 1959a). Martin praised the virtuosity, charm, and grace of the dancers as well as the originality of the overall creation. The dance program reflected influences from Spain, the tribes of the mountainous Cordillera region, Muslim/Malay culture of the south, and the rhythms and lifecycle of rural life in the Tagalog-speaking region, bringing them together as a singular Filipino culture, one reflecting extraordinary diversity; in a late 1950s context, it seems probable that Martin, like the vast majority of Americans, was unable to imagine such cultural complexity coming from a former colony, which just a few generations earlier was represented in the media as populated by "little brown brothers" in need of American tutelage.

A culture and people stereotyped for their lack of originality, or simply unknown to most in the West,[7] had come to their great cities and presented something extraordinary and singular of which many influential figures in the arts in the West were in awe. The ability to incorporate cultural influences from anywhere and everywhere and to Filipinize them is one of the distinctive features of the culture. It is, simply, part of what it means to be Filipino. As Manila-based performance artist-tour guide Carlos Celdran (2013) observes, using the name given to a popular iced dessert that combines a ridiculous number of diverse ingredients, Filipinos possess a "Halo-Halo culture," one where, long before Homi Bhabha (1994) waxed on about the perspicacity of the colonized subject's double gaze, ordinary citizens without higher degrees and access to international air travel were masters of intercultural communication and cross-cultural creation. Much like a good halo-halo, where ingredients that would not naturally be put together, such as coconut, mung beans, gelatin, and purple yam, produce a harmonious, satisfying, original—if somewhat garish-looking—dessert, Bayanihan judiciously culled, adapted, and manipulated a range of dance traditions and brought them together into a single, famous format, which has come for many to represent the entirety of the Philippines over two generations.

In order to make sense of what the Bayanihan repertory means in the community-centered dance contexts to be explored in the following two chapters, we must also consider the roots of the practices from which the company and its principal choreographers derived their methods. And this part of the story will take us back to the earliest sustained efforts at using culture in the service of nation before there was an independent nation, when a few individuals, chief among them young dance researcher Francisca Reyes-Aquino, began a process in the early 1920s that ultimately placed dance as one of the cornerstones of the nationalist project, one that would be extended onto the world stage in the late 1950s and into the decades that followed. First Lady Imelda Marcos took an active and often controversial role in developing the arts in the Philippines, and under her watch, local dance "traditions" became further fixed and identified with a particular region, while the infrastructure of the national Department of Tourism provided the framework and the mechanisms for these dance forms to repackage themselves as elements of a strong national culture that drew strength from its diverse traditions (Richter 1980, 1989). As politics came to shape and contain many of these local expressions, the foundational categories of folk and indigenous or tribal dance have become increasingly problematic. The following analysis does not identify or pay tribute to the contributions of a host of influential figures to the wider fields of folk dance in the Philippines,[8] because to recognize them here even in a truncated form would be beyond the scope of both this chapter and the entire book. Instead I will set out the foundational currents in folk dance as it emerged as a significant cultural force both at home and abroad, while considering the categories of "folk" and "indigenous" with respect to the foundational Bayanihan repertoire.

From Dancing Archipelago to Dancing Nation

The received wisdom among scholars working in the Philippines is that the Spanish relied on pre-Christian performance traditions as a means through which to successfully carry out mass conversions to Christianity (Villaruz 1989, 2006; Alejandro 1978; Tiongson 2003; Phelan 1959). Nicanor Tiongson articulates the commonly held belief that "The festivals of the Christian Philippines are, in reality, simply a continuity and expansion of the rituals and celebrations of indigenous times" (Tiongson 2003, 176). Similarly, influential dance scholar and critic Basilio Esteban "Steve" Villaruz asserts that the Spaniards, "knew our choreographic proclivity so even the priests used dance to convert us," observing that conversion took place not only "through the mind but also through the body" (Villaruz 2006, 31). Spanish colonizers, Alejandro and Santos-Gana (2002) argue, used dance as a means of control and as an enticement to conversion because it fed into the practices of folk Catholicism:

> High-ranking church and government officials were instrumental in propagating European social dances. In their attempt to combat the ancient heritage of pagan beliefs of the Filipinos and attract them to Catholicism, Spanish missionaries incorporated the less pagan of the native traditions into the rituals of the Church. (Alejandro and Santos-Gana 2002, 11)

In this way, concludes Alejandro, "dance became an important teaching aid in the Spanish educational process" (1978, 197).

This thesis appears to rely on a handful of early accounts by explorers and Roman Catholic priests who wrote of performances they witnessed or of song and dance in the context of worship services. One such account is from Antonio D. Morga's 1609 work, *Sucesos de las Islas Filipinas,* based on his experiences in the Philippines from 1595 to 1596 while serving as acting governor and captain general of the Philippines:

> At the same time that the religious undertook to teach the natives the precepts of religion, they labored to instruct them in matters of their own improvement, and established schools for the reading and writing of Spanish among the boys. They taught them to serve in the church, to sing the plain-song, and to the accompaniment of the organ; to play the flute, to dance and to sing; and to play the harp, guitar, and other instruments. In this, they show very great adaptability, especially about Manila; where there are many fine choirs of chanters and musicians composed of natives, who are skillful and have good voices. There are many dancers, and musicians on the other instrument which solemnize and adorn the feasts of the most holy sacrament, and many other feasts during the year. The native boys present dramas and comedies, both in Spanish and in their own language, very charmingly. (cited in Zafra 1967, 57)

Yet Morga attributes this mastery not to any native inclinations, adding, "This is due to the care and interest of the religious, who work tirelessly for the native's advancement" (ibid.).

Perhaps more persuasive is the 1663 account by Jesuit Francisco Colin describing a dance in the Visayas that communicated a narrative using choreographed movement:

> The dance is warlike and passionate, but it has steps and measured changes, and interposed are some elevations that really enrapture and surprise. They [the dancers] generally hold in the hands a towel, or a spear and shield, and with one and the other they make their gestures in time, which are full of meaning. At other times, with the hands empty they make movements which correspond to the movements of the feet, now slow, now rapid. Now they attack and retire; now they incite; now they pacify; now they come close; now they go away: all the grace and elegance, so much, in fact, that at times they have not been judged unworthy to accompany and solemnize our Christian feasts. (cited in Fernandez 1996, 43)

What is striking about this account is its detail, in spite of the chronicler's limitations with respect to writing formally about dance. The dancers moved to a changing beat, evoking in him the feelings of "surprise" and "rapture," moved with "grace" and "elegance," communicating intent through their actions, and conveyed meanings so profound that the viewer allows they were beyond his capacity to fully grasp. Further, and significantly for our purposes, he notes that the high level of skill displayed was such that dancers were called upon to "solemnize" Christian feasts, or what we would today call fiestas or festivals, an observation that seems to support the thesis that dance and performance skills were brought into the service of worshipping a Christian God.

Whereas a few accounts do not constitute conclusive evidence for practices across the entire archipelago, it is nevertheless significant that the belief that pre-Christian song and dance was used as the foundation for Christian worship is so widely held and often repeated by scholars and practitioners in the Philippines. This is possibly because they cannot imagine that mass conversions would have been possible without song and dance having assumed a prominent role in the process. Many Filipinos believe that dance is at the heart of Filipino culture for the ways in which it "cultivates precision and discipline, camaraderie and solidarity, articulation and eloquence" (Villaruz 2006, 15). Villaruz suggests that dance has a special capacity to bring the inner and outer soul into harmony:

> The soul is what is inside, our *loób*. It can range from empathy or *malasakit* to our sense of worship or *samba*. It is only understood when seen in or brought out by the body. So the soul is felt or practiced *sa labas* [on the

> outside/externally]. What's inside—the motive, the passion, or the idea—is projected outside via movement and as expressed through task or dance. (Villaruz 2006, 30)

Dance, more than any other performance form, is accessible to the greatest number, particularly though its folk expressions, providing an entire community with the opportunity to integrate an internal felt state *(sa loób)* with its external manifestation *(sa labas),* a key behavioral value and cultural norm. So how did dance shift from something that people did in the *barangays* and towns where they lived—from something they did that often had no name—to something that became studied, named, cataloged, linked to particular regions, tied to identity, circulated nationally and transnationally, then reintegrated into local fiestas through the mechanisms of the state? That answer to that question begins with the work of Francisca Reyes-Aquino.

In the 1920s, while a student assistant in the Physical Education Department at the country's flagship public institution, the University of the Philippines (Diliman), Reyes began traveling to remote areas of Central and Northern Luzon to document and record folk dance.[9] With the enthusiastic support of ardent nationalist Jorge Bocobo,[10] who served as president of the University of the Philippines from 1934 to 1939, and later as secretary of public instruction, Reyes' 1926 MA thesis titled "Philippine Folk Dances and Games" was followed by numerous books that had a significant, foundational influence on teachers of dance.[11] Course offerings on Filipino folk dance at the University of the Philippines began as early as 1926, whereas Reyes' collected opus, disseminated widely through her books, contains detailed information on more than two hundred Philippine folk dances. Mellie Leandicho Lopez echoes the view of dance teachers throughout the country when she characterizes Reyes' collective work as "the bible of Filipino folk dance teachers" (Lopez 2006, 232). Significantly, Reyes' research was developed and disseminated in the context of the national physical education curriculum when prominent Filipinos were pushing back against the political, economic, and cultural dominance of the Americans as they sought their much-promised and long-overdue independence. During the immediate postwar era and as the country gained its independence, Reyes served as supervisor of Physical Education at the national Department of Education, and from this time her work was circulated through the national curriculum for dance, offered as part of the mandatory physical education curriculum.[12] As Theodore S. Gonzalves observes, "While most scholars of Philippine dance are correct to point out that Aquino was founding scholar of folk dance, few link her contributions to the many curricular changes taking place in Philippine education during the U.S. colonial administration," training that as he asserts "constituted another aspect of a particular kind of disciplining of subjects" (Gonzalves 2010, 45). Thus Reyes' legacy was significant in two fundamental respects: first, it ensured that virtually everyone in the country learned a range of folk dances through formalized instruction on a scale possibly unparalleled anywhere else in the world; and second, it associated folk dance with pride in being Filipino at a moment when artists and intellectuals were especially preoccupied with uncovering a "Filipino soul,"[13] with the deepening understanding of what it meant to come together as a people, as *Bayan*.

Ethnographic research on performance by Filipinos had no precedent, much less a disciplinary home in the early part of the twentieth century, so Reyes largely created her own research methodology as she moved around the country collecting folk dances and later setting them out in her books. As Lopez observes,

> From a folklorist perspective, Mrs. Tolentino-Aquino's magnum opus, taken as a whole, is more a "how-to-do-it" manual with a strictly pedagogical approach. The author meticulously provides consistent and carefully described dance movements and terminologies, supplies the corresponding music for each dance; gives the provenance of each entry, but there is no scholarly contextual analysis of the materials. This is understandable for the work was written basically as a classroom tool to assist the physical education teacher to teach folk dances to students. (Lopez 2006, 233)

Indeed, as Reyes states in the foreword to *Fundamental Dance Steps and Music*, the book was written in response to "the dearth of teaching materials in physical education" and the demands from teachers "for materials in simple rhythms and fundamentals of folk dances which they could understand and interpret to their pupils, since they have found it difficult to follow the highly technical terms or expressions usually found in imported books on physical education" (Reyes 1957, i). Only in her comprehensive textbook, *Philippine National Dances* (Reyes-Tolentino 1946), does she offer a few brief paragraphs with contextual information about the dance form she presents, linking the dance to the region of the country from which it is taken and setting forth a few general concepts, mostly related to local terminology or the story behind the dance. But there is no indication as to the site where the dance was first observed, recorded, and notated, much less about how it has been altered so it could be standardized and set down in a textbook format that anyone who can read and count out beats can learn through repetition. Reyes conducted her research prior to the age of audio- or video recording, and during the Japanese occupation of the Philippines (1942–1945), according to a note from the publisher in her 1946 work, "all her other source materials, books, records, pictures, costumes, and musical instruments had been burned or wantonly destroyed by the Japanese" (Reyes-Tolentino 1946, iv). In spite of the lack of connection between the grounds from which the dance was taken and its final presentation in a textbook, Reyes is seen by virtually everyone in the field as the first of many "dance researchers" who scoured the country from one end to the other for folk dances before they disappeared. Yet what really happened is probably much closer to Gonzalves' assertion: "Aquino did more than research Philippine folkloric forms; she *invented* them" (2010, loc. 484).

The Philippines Women's University (PWU) became the next key player in the documentation, standardization, and dissemination of folk dance and it is from this institutional home that the Bayanihan company emerged. By the 1950s, building on the model provided by Aquino's already well-established practice, physical education teachers at PWU, supported by Helena Benitez (b. 1914), the daughter of the founders of the university and later the founder of Bayanihan, began to conduct their own folk dance "research." From their base at PWU in the 1950s, Lucrecia "Tita King" Kasilag, Aurora Diño, Jose Maceda, Manuel Cordova, and Lucrecia "Inday" Reyes-Urtula, ventured out into the field and gathered materials that eventually fed into Bayanihan's core repertory (Santos 2004, 7–10), although Reyes-Urtula was to be credited as the choreographer for much of the foundational repertoire. Lourdes Guillermo, who served as the company's public relations officer in its early years, recalls the birth of Bayanihan: "one day, people began to ask themselves why they should want to become Brown Americans. This questioning sparked the search for the Filipino identity. This search was another of Bayanihan's beginnings" (Guillermo 1987, 8). Veteran Bayanihan costumer Isabel Santos' account of the group's missions into remote locations relies heavily on the language of discovery and exploration, suggesting that the research "assumed a sense of urgency" because "there was a very distinct possibility that many ancient Filipino cultures could be lost forever" (Santos 2004, 10). Field sites are characterized as "happy hunting grounds" (11), and she notes with delight that the remote Cordillera region, "yielded the richest materials of all" as Bayanihan sought to "probe into the Filipino soul" (22).

National Artist in Literature Nick Joaquin uses similar language to describe this process of capturing the nation's cultural diversity through dance, only with an added twist by suggesting that lowland Tagalog Filipinos deserve the credit for their willingness to preserve minority cultures:

> Curiously enough, it's the Christian Filipino, now reviled for his cultural "impurity" and "inferiority" and "chauvinism," who has taken it on himself to preserve for the nation every bit of pagan and Muslim lore, ranging

> far and wide to search out and rescue and record even the most minor mimings of the minorities that he's supposed to scorn. Maybe he's doing it as a penance, but he's certainly alone in the doing. We still have to hear of some pagan dance troupe integrating into its tribal repertoire the Cariñosa of the lowlanders, or of some Muslim cultural group dedicating itself to the preservation of Philippine Christian dances. In this job of cultural integration, the pagan and the Muslim still have to produce a Kikay Aquino and a Bayanihan, not to mention a Leonor Orosa and her Filipinescas.[14] (Joaquin 1980, 9)

Like postcolonial elites everywhere, Joaquin offers a heroic tale of cultural restitution, one in which the dominant economic, cultural, political, and linguistic group, the Christian lowland Filipino, saves the undervalued cultures of "pagan" and Muslim from permanent erasure.[15] Failing to consider the benefits that flow to the center through this kind of appropriation of minority dance cultures, his suggestion that minority groups have not championed the dance forms of the lowlanders is offered as proof of the greater generosity of spirit of the group of which he is himself a part.

Filipino nativist cultural enthusiasts responsible for repackaging and disseminating these found cultural artifacts did so under conditions about which little is known apart from what was communicated through lore or hagiographic accounts of exotic field trips. In this regard, they were following in the footsteps of folklorists in Western societies, when, from the late eighteenth and early nineteenth centuries, as John Storey observes, "the 'discovery' of folk culture was an integral part of emerging European nationalism" (Storey 2003, 2). The notion that true, authentic culture was found not in the cities, but in relatively remote locations, was a foundational ideological position in the West just as it was among emerging cultural elites in Manila:

> Whether or not folk culture was understood as a product of the folk or merely something they had preserved, unaware of its true value, one thing that all the intellectuals involved agreed on, collectors and those who commented on the collection, was that production or preservation had only been possible because the folk had survived in primitive rural isolation. (Storey 2003, 6)

Indeed, as we have seen, Bayanihan researchers were especially wedded to this belief, that what was found in rural isolation was "authentic." Again, Santos provides the narrative: "Authenticity requires going out into the field to observe the dance at its place of origin, as Bayanihan has done" (Santos 2004, 35). As Storey notes, by going out "into the field" and returning with these riches, what is local becomes folk and popular culture:

> The concept of popular culture as folk culture was an invention made from ways of seeing the culture of men and women (and their families) who worked the land as agricultural laborers. It was their stories the collectors called "folk-tales," their dances they called "folk-dances," their song they called "folk-songs," their traditions they called "folk-lore," a version of their culture they called "folk-culture." (Storey 2003, 14)

The folklorist catalogs and "brings back" these cultural artifacts, which are quotidian, underappreciated, and unnamed where they live, and creates "a version" of their culture in another cultural space.

Preserving "authenticity" has from the beginning been important for those mining the choreographic riches of the far-flung archipelago as they sought to create and disseminate a distinctively Filipino identity through dance in the postcolonial era. This core value is reflected in the language used to describe the work of "Inday" Reyes-Urtula, who choreographed much of the foundational Bayanihan repertory in those early years, and whose staging of the famously exotic *singkil* dance remains even today one of the cornerstones of the company's repertory. Of her imprint on the repertory, company chronicler Santos asserts: "To Inday largely belongs the credit for transforming Bayanihan research materials into dances of theatrical excitement and artistry that remain true to the essence of the original" (Santos 2004, 198). Santos invokes the authority of *New York Herald* dance critic Walter Terry, who wrote of Urtula's choreography that "while preserving authenticity of step and regional color, Mrs. Urtula has devised designs of incredible originality, visual beauty and excitement" (ibid.). That a New York critic might be an arbiter of what is or is not authentic in the Philippines is not interrogated—rather his observations are taken at face value, reflecting the notion that authenticity somehow represents itself in a way that is universally recognizable. The concern with being true to an original source is one of the hallmarks of this emerging dance practice, even as the actual connection to the source of the dance is largely lost through the mists of time and the lack of surviving documentation. Thus, we now turn to the use to which source data has been put.

The Bayanihan Model

Given that everyone who creates folk dances in the Philippines is positioned within the culture as a "dance researcher" or "dance scholar,"[16] it is useful to consider what Bayanihan has said about what they were doing when they systematized this model of dance practices in the 1950s. Here I rely largely on Santos' observations, as they seem to reflect the official line of the company as reflected in their 2004 coffee-table book, *Bayanihan: Memories of Six Continents.* In the chapter "Creating Theatre," she outlines in considerable detail the process of translating raw materials into dance theatre. Far from seeking to retain some kind of absolute purity with respect to reproducing folk forms, Santos makes it clear that "one of Bayanihan's guiding principles is the adaptation of indigenous dance to the conventions and possibilities of theatre" (Santos 2004, 35). Indeed "theatre" is the key designation here, suggesting that the company was well aware from the outset that it was offering dance theatre and not the accurate representation of individual folk traditions, possibly recognizing that as soon as a folk tradition is taken out of its cultural context it ceases to function as a tradition of the folk. As we shall see later, in the national and transnational circulation of the Bayanihan repertory, the "theatre" in their choreography has often gone unacknowledged as dancers witness and themselves appropriate and recirculate these representations as folk dance rather than dance theatre with roots in a folk tradition. "Authenticity" to Santos and Bayanihan meant not refraining from making changes to a form, but rather staying true to the original impulses behind the dance, exercising care "not to lose the original flavour and feeling of the dance" (ibid.).

The process of translating dance obtained from folk sources into theatre thus involves three processes: "compression, highlighting, and enhancement." Compression is a requirement imposed by theatrical necessity, where performances need to be edited down to the length of a single stage show that "features a number of regional dance suites." This "involves eliminating repetition, restructuring the dance into sections of varying length, with due consideration for rhythmic and mood contrasts and, if called for, creating a clear narrative sequence" (Santos 2004, 36). Highlighting "ensures that each dance suite projects its distinctive character, even though it may be just a sequence from an epic," selecting and bringing it "to a climax of color and movement" using the techniques of theatre. Finally, enhancement requires "injecting a certain measure of theatrical exaggeration into traditional dances in order to suit present-day audiences" (37). This includes extending gestures and movements, adding bridging and group choreography, and using music and striking and colorful costumes to heighten the overall effect of the work on the audience. Indeed even today, these techniques of compression, highlighting, and enhancement, as we shall see in chapter 6, underpin the aggressive, fast-paced choreography in the large-scale, competitive street-dance routines seen at the country's largest civic and religious festivals.

The Bayanihan company's foundational practices encouraged a particular kind of packaging of dance, in which multiple dances from a range of related traditions—typically those originating within the same geocultural region—are compressed into discrete and clearly differentiated suites, originally five, but now four in number.[17] These suites, collectively representing *bayan* or nation/people writ large, range from those featuring the dances of the (formerly) non-Christian tribes of the mountainous Cordilleran region to the lowland and Hispanicized dances most clearly identifiable as fitting squarely within the category of "folk" dance. Of the dances from the Cordillera that traditionally started the program, Santos observes: "the traditional rituals depicted have no foreign influence whatsoever, whether Western or Asian, and are therefore truly indigenous to the Philippines" (Santos 2004, 42). Thus Bayanihan starts with what is most "untouched" by the outside world and ends the program with a dance celebration of lowlander village life.

The "Cordillera" or "Mountain Suite" begins with men in traditional G-strings dancing vigorously and assuming aggressive stances, whereas the women sway gracefully with pots on their heads, leading to a courtship dance in which the aggressive spirit of the men is tamed, followed by a dance of thanksgiving in which all are united together. This progression, from battle, to being touched by feminine charms, through courtship and ending with celebration, is typical of these suites. Each one compresses what might traditionally have been quite lengthy dance sequences or makes up new choreography altogether to fit within a single narrative frame with a clear beginning, middle, and end. When I was invited some years ago to participate in a relatively simple two-step folk dance at the Adivay, a festival of thanksgiving in this region, the dance itself could have been extended for an hour if the other dancers and musicians were willing to continue, something that when translated into theatre, clearly requires editing. And although the women of Kalinga Province do have a dance known as the *banga* where each woman carries up to five pots on her head, which would once have been part of everyday life in this mountainous region, it was traditionally presented to entertain visitors at feasts (Capuyan 1994, 63) and was not necessarily offered to attract male attention that would lead to "courtship." Thus Bayanihan in this example and in their other suites recontextualizes, edits, and creates a new theatricalized entity based on real and sometimes invented dances from a particular region, in this case perhaps unwittingly adding an overlay composed of a Christianized narrative of "courtship."

Following the "Cordillera Suite" is what is often referred to as the "Spanish" or "Maria Clara Suite," named after a graceful, passive heroine in Jose Rizal's *Noli me Tangere*. This is essentially an homage to the grace and beauty of the refined and urbane Hispanicized culture, offering, as Santos observes, "a dramatic contrast between the primitive, elemental strength of the tribal dances and the graciousness and old-world charm of the Spanish suite" (Santos 2004, 46). Featuring guitar music, elegant women, and gallant young men, "the dances of this suite exude an air of gracious sweetness and refined urbanity" (47). Villaruz comments on the progression of these two suites from the tribal to the civilized, imagining them positioned before an "ideal" Christianized, Western viewer: "Imagine all of them turning from brassy primitives to polished Christians" (Villaruz 2006, 358). This "progression" mirrors the cultural positioning of the so-called pagan Igorot and Christianized Visayan villages at the 1904 Saint Louis World's Fair, where Americans had the opportunity to view firsthand the results of hundreds of years of colonial enterprise, where the native was essentially turned from a seminaked savage into a refined, churchgoing colonized subject (Kramer 2006; Delmendo 2004).

Up next in the traditional repertoire is a suite bringing together Muslim dances from Mindanao and Sulu in the south. Again, another contrast is set up, this time from the Christianized, Hispanicized world, to what Santos calls "an exotic world of sultry colors and sinuous movements," one "[i]n vivid contrast to the languorous strains of the guitars in the Spanish suite" and where instead "the percussive *kulintangans, gandigans* and other beaten instruments hold sway, echoing Arabic and Indo-Malayan origins" (Santos 2004, 48).[18] The suite begins with an adaptation of the famed *singkil* dance of the Maranao people in which a sumptuously clad princess, while gracefully manipulating two hand fans, moves lightly and sure-footedly through three crossed sets of double bamboo poles that are clapped together rhythmically. The dance is most often said to represent the princess's flight through a forest of crashing trees during an earthquake. The rhythm is provided by the company members manipulating the poles, with one at each end beating them together in unison, then tapping the floor on the off beats as the princess moves into the center, stepping out on the next beat, each time narrowly avoiding having her ankles crushed. She maintains tremendous poise throughout and after a languid display before her sword-bearing suitor, the couple dances together in the center of the stage, while other dancers move into the two remaining areas. Villaruz describes the sequence as a "flirtation based on male bravado and female coy assurance—a kris-flashing prince and a (red) fan-expert-princess dressed in gold, . . . together with a troupe of dancers walking through bamboo traps like gods on turbulent but festive waters" (Villaruz 2006, 358).

The spectacular *pangalay ha patong* from Sulu follows as part of the same suite, featuring a sumptuously clad young woman executing elegant and intricate hand and foot movements on raised bamboo poles resting on the shoulders of two men. As is characteristic of *pangalay,* the form from which this dance is derived, the smooth, elongated gestures of the women are accentuated by their lengthy fingernail extensions known as *janggay.* This final, elegant display of the female form serves the four-part narrative of the "Muslim Suite" well: initially fleeing through the forest, the princess stops and dances for the prince, then dances with him, and in the end is brought out most spectacularly on raised bamboo poles. Villaruz describes the sequence from elegant flight to display, capturing its dramatic qualities, as well as its cross-cultural and highly engineered complexity: "Add to these a gliding, running solo paced and laced a la Loie Fuller, the awesome *pag-alay* on two hoisted bamboo poles with vinta-effect, and you have another play on crescendo, from the languid to the frenzied" (ibid.).[19] If the Igorot are the fiercely proud, independent warrior people, the Muslims are here offered up as the ultimate refined exotic.

The fourth suite, which has been sidelined from the current repertoire, brought together a range of ritual, animistic, and mimetic dances from tribal groups in the south, notably the Bagobo, Subanon, and T'boli minority ethnic groups in Mindanao. The most eclectic of all the suites, the "Tribal Suite," has been known by various names over the years, including "Regional Variations," "Tribal Images," and more recently "Tribal Tapestry" (Fisher 2006). It melds dances used to heal the sick, celebrate a wedding, initiate the planting cycle, and respond to the natural world into a single dance piece that incorporates a series of clear and contained narratives. Individual dances from this suite live on as dances popular at regional dance competitions that serve as markers of local identity. As we shall see later, the reach of Bayanihan is such that dancers within the region from which a dance originates often look to the repertory of the national company and its range of instructional videos for modeling "authentic" local practices.

The fifth suite in the original lineup, and one that for much of its history concluded the program, offers an exuberant and joyous celebration of rural life. Santos sets out its theatrical and dramatic function: "It expresses the people's pleasure in work and in working together, their natural love for dance and music, and their delight in the simple things—a good harvest, the rhythmic sound of clacking bamboo, and birds gamboling in green fields" (Santos 2004, 54). Ending with the signature dance piece, the *tinikling,* in which rural folk skip through rapidly moving bamboo poles rapped against the stage to an insistent, ever-increasing rhythmic beat, the audience's emotions rise to a crescendo as the rapid movements of the dances race to a thrilling conclusion. For international audiences as well as urban Filipinos and those in the diaspora, it offers, as Christi-Anne Castro observes, "a mythologized portrait of a simple agrarian-based way of life" (Castro 2011, 96). Of the music and dance, she observes that it "evokes a kind of wonderland somewhere near or far from the city, in a place one might wish to return to if circumstances permitted" (ibid.). It is a place of nostalgia for those who have roots in the countryside as many Filipinos do and for the cosmopolites, it provides a glimpse into "that paradise on those heavenly islands" that the European critic Molenhoek saw onstage when the company made its dramatic international debut in Brussels in 1958.

As a whole, the program of five suites is, in spite of its reductionism and lack of cultural specificity, a meticulously crafted piece of theatre. It is sequenced to achieve the maximum emotional effect on the audience, a formula so winning that it has changed little for over half a century. On the other hand, in spite and even perhaps because of Bayanihan's success and global impact, it can also be seen as having contributed to the commodification of folk and indigenous dance, and the transnational dissemination of a view of the Philippines as a hyper-fiesta-sized country, singing and dancing itself into a frenzy, especially as the dances themselves are detached from the traditions from which they were derived. Villaruz gives voice to this anxiety:

> We stage our dances as if they were set on a Broadway stage, and the whole system of life that the dance represents is changed in the representation. In the end, we do not *inform* but *reform* a cultural expression. The representation then enters the possibility of illegitimacy and becomes a commodification of a way of life. (Villaruz 2006, 211; emphasis added)

Yet, even as he calls for Bayanihan to evolve into "a more decolonized style of presentation," he concludes that "The Bayanihan remains the beloved. With the most meaningful name for any dance group and unwavering excellence in stagecraft . . . the Bayanihan Philippine Dance Company remains as spectacular and endearing as ever. It always promises and delivers a broad spectrum of sheer dance delight" (Villaruz 2006, 359).

It seems that there is no way to completely escape the appeal and charm of Bayanihan. In Castro's impressive and systematic investigation into the relationship between nation and music in the Philippines, even her pointed criticism of the ways in which the repertoire serves to "enforce hierarchical structures" (Castro 2011, 101) is tempered by her larger, concluding observations about the value of the company's work over time. Referring to the vision of the Bayanihan founder, Helena Benitez, she observes,

> Yet, Benitez's vision of the role of the folkloric in authoring and strengthening nationalism, or at least the idea of nation, still holds great significance. There are innumerable folkloric groups based on the Bayanihan model in Filipino communities all over the world. The very real solidarity and sense of cultural pride they engender through social gatherings and events within and external to their own ethnic community are nothing

> short of a practice of national belonging, however far-flung and variegated that nation might be. (Castro 2011, 101)

It is perhaps in what Bayanihan does that its greatest value lies. Across the world where it has been seen by audiences, and as it circulates through Filipinos in the diaspora, it brings communities together, providing fixed points of reference in which individuals can collectively experience joy and happiness in being part of a celebration of what it means to be Filipino. Bayanihan, with its foundational suites that extended from the work of Reyes-Aquino, has created, perhaps unwittingly, a practice and way of thinking about the function of dance in the Philippines that extends back three generations.

Yet the cultural positioning of the Bayanihan company remains problematic, especially because it mirrors the ways in which diasporic Filipino performing artists and scholars I have encountered speak privately of how they are continuously subject to pressure to use their art and scholarship to express pride in nation. By choosing to live outside their homeland, the unspoken subtext is that they are expected to repay a debt to the nation by virtue of having left behind a poor country and gained entrance into the very small club of Filipino academics and scholar/practitioners who lead cosmopolitan, transnational lives. The notion that art should promote people and nation is a foundational principle in the development of folk dance in the Philippines extending back to Reyes-Aquino, enthusiastically supported by nationalist Jorge Bocobo. This tension between art and obligation to nation or people is embedded in the word *bayanihan* itself. The stem word, *bayan,* has an expandable meaning, based on the feeling of association that one has with others constituting nation, country, motherland, city, municipality, neighborhood or *barangay,* and the people or citizens of such places. The standard definition of the term *bayanihan* is "working together for the common good" and indeed that is the phrase most commonly invoked by the company (Benitez 1987, 6; Bayanihan 1961; Cal Performances 2010). Thus *bayanihan* suggests the spirit of cooperation and mutual support within a group constituted by virtually any collectivity of people that identifies as a community.

In an essay by Guillermo Gómez Rivera prominently featured on the Bayanihan company's Web site, *bayanihan* is defined as "patriotism or love of country," an understanding that removes it from the ethos of collective action and identity and suggests allegiance to a singular external force—that is, the nation. An even bolder claim is made in the following sentence: "[W]e dare say, that each one of those involved in *Bayanihan* are literally national heroes and artist *[sic]* who reiterate through dance, music, percussion, dress and action what is Filipino." Using similar language, former president Gloria Macapagal-Arroyo famously lionized

Overseas Filipino Workers (OFWs), whose remittances prop up the national economy, as the country's *bagong bayani* (new patriot-heroes) (Philippines, Government of 2006). The Web site of the Bagong Bayani Foundation, a nonprofit organization that gives awards to the most "outstanding and exemplary" OFWs, articulates the services of this group to the nation:

> The awards seek to recognize and pay tribute to our OFWs for their significant efforts in fostering goodwill among peoples of the world, enhancing and promoting the image of the Filipino as a competent, responsible and dignified worker, and for greatly contributing to the socio-economic development of their communities and our country as a whole. (Bagong Bayani Foundation n.d.)

Most OFW *bayani* make huge personal sacrifices—leaving behind the safety net of friends, family, and even one's own children—to work long hours for low wages in wealthier countries. The noun *bayani,* although it contains the root word *bayan,* is frequently translated into English as "hero," although in its actual usage it conveys the sense of being a "hero for the nation," thus coming closer to the meaning of the word "patriot." It is noteworthy that the only real act of heroism is to make sacrifices of time and labor for the sake of the *bayan* because it conjures up not individual acts of heroism that are associated with the English word "hero" (e.g., the fireman who rescues a child from a burning building), but rather the notion that to be a hero one makes a sacrifice for the sake of a larger group with which one identifies. It is thus perhaps not surprising that cultural workers are workers like any others; their labor, like that of the OFWs, is meant to contribute to the task of nation-building. And there is an extent to which Bayanihan were the originators of this project of being the *bayani* for the nation through the labor of their dance.

One of the important legacies of Bayanihan within the *bayan* as constituted by nation has been the recirculation of dances from the company's foundational dance suites back to the country's regions, where they are staged at local festivals and regional competitions featuring dance. The power and appeal of the Bayanihan repertory, combined with the collective oeuvre of Reyes, which over the last half of the twentieth century constituted the "Bible" of Filipino folk dance, can be seen as collectively constituting a hegemonic practice of imagined authenticity. Because the Bayanihan repertory has been identified for so long with the "real" local tradition, it replaces what may have been there in the past, which may still exist in isolated pockets or in the bodily archives of a region's oldest residents. Dancer Joseph Patricio (2010) gives the example of dancers from the Maranao region in the south sourcing material from Bayanihan's "Muslim Suite" in staging their own cultural dance. One could argue that these dancers have been doubly colonized: first when the raw material of their dance was extracted and shaped by Bayanihan, who, as Castro (2011) observes, freely borrowed music and presumably dance steps from Reyes, and then a second time when their own native dancing bodies move in culturally encoded ways mediated through this exchange and altered and reconfigured as dance-theatre by an external source. Cultural critic Epifanio San Juan Jr.'s observation about the colonization of the Filipino body in America might well be applied to folk dancers dancing their traditions through the lens of the cultural outsider: "What is at stake is not just our souls, but more crucially our bodies and those of our children" (San Juan 1996, 86). It could well be that in the "search for the essence of the Filipino soul," so central to the Bayanihan foundational mission as Santos (2004, 1) observes, has come at the cost of embodied knowledge, even as dance "research" continues to be at the heart of what makes the company vital and forward looking.[20] Thus it is to the issue of the relationship between folk, indigenous, and *bayan* as constituted by both small and large collectivities and by nation that we now turn. I will argue that what dance means for those who participate in it is driven by the interlocking relationships between these categories, which were essentially willed into existence through the dance archive created by Reyes-Aquino and Bayanihan and furthered by the countless other dance teachers, choreographers, and companies who have reinforced their foundational practices.

Beyond Folklore: Who's the Folk?

Fifty years after their New York debut, in 2010 Bayanihan came up with a new theme for their international tour, proclaiming that they were going "beyond folklore" (Gómez Rivera n.d.). What was evidently meant by this catchphrase was that the season would offer a deeper engagement with Filipino history, including a revival of folk dances that were historically present but largely overlooked in the contemporary repertoire, particularly those of Filipino-Hispanic origin, and by the time of their 2012 tour, a dance tribute to artist Fernando Amorsolo (1892–1972). Writing for the *Washington Post,* Pamela Squires (2012) observes, " 'Beyond Folklore' is the company's own phrase, and it is a terrifically good one because it banished the burdensome question, 'How authentic is or isn't it?' " But the core question of what is folk and who is constituted in and by this category cannot be sidestepped because it is central to understanding how dance functions in the Philippines both within smaller communities and as a symbol of the nation. As we have seen, the core historical repertoire of Bayanihan relied heavily on dance traditions drawn from minority ethnic groups for three of the five original suites: The "Cordillera Suite," which used a range of dances from the Igorot, itself a designation for a number of different tribes; the "Tribal Suite" (also known as "Regional Variations" or "Tribal Tapestry"); and the southern "Muslim Suite." Traditionally, dances in the first two suites have been designated as "indigenous" or "tribal," whereas those that constitute the "Muslim Suite" appear to be in their own category, circulating domestically and especially in the Filipino diaspora as "Royal Muslim dances." Because of their royal provenance—which as we shall see at least in the case of *pangalay* is a fiction—and even though they exist outside the Christianized mainstream of the country, they have been appropriated as symbols of *bayan*-as-nation. Thus in this section I will contrast the cultural position of Muslim dances from the south with those from the Cordilleran region to show how the expandable concept of *bayan* enables the nation to appropriate the former as "folk" and keep the indigenous outsider in his place outside the circle of *bayan* by virtue of his indigeneity. In the case of so-called Muslim royal dances, we will see how they have been enthusiastically embraced as symbols of a proud, pre-Christian past.

At this point it is appropriate to first ask the question: What makes dance folk and what makes it indigenous? While all Filipinos can potentially make a claim to be indigenous just as anyone from a particular place may choose to so identify, in its common usage in the Philippines "indigenous" is a label applied almost exclusively to the less-assimilated, non-Christian or rather more recently Christianized ethnic minorities of the country. Writing about the Isneg people in Apayo Province, Scott has characterized this process as one in which through "the magic of colonial alchemy, those who changed most became today's Filipinos while those who changed least were actually denied this designation" (Scott 1982, 40–41). Similarly, in dance, assimilation into the political, cultural, and economic framework of the national culture would appear to separate traditions that are "ethnic" or "indigenous" from those that are folk or "royal." In his essay on "The Ethnic Tradition" in dance in the *CCP Encyclopedia of Philippine Art,* Villaruz observes that "ethnic dances are found among the ethnolinguistic groups scattered all over the Philippine islands, who have not been substantially westernized, either by Spain or the United States" (Villaruz 1994a, 28),[21] echoing Scott's trope of the "magic of colonial alchemy" that renders minorities as "ethnic." Yet Villaruz's 2006 compendium of dance criticism contains an essay that uses the term *katutubong sayaw* (indigenous dance) when writing about dance that extends from older animist, pre-Christian or pre-Muslim traditions, which he renders into English as "ethnic dance" (Villaruz 2006, 33–41). In Tagalog, *katutubong* means being endemic, literally of a place, suggesting that connection to the land is driven by place, not by the more mobile, even migratory quality of ethnicity. Representing this construct of *katutubo* as place-bound is one of the most famous and iconic images from the Marcos era, the painting known as *Si Malakas at Si Maganda* (The Strong and the Beautiful), which depicts strongman and "war hero" Ferdinand and the beautiful Imelda emerging naked from bamboo stalks as the first man and woman. This Filipino pre-Christian creation myth, appropriated with unselfconscious vulgarity by the First Couple, reflects the notion of all Filipinos being *ab origine,* from the place, rather than created through an external force such as a sky God who emplaces humans in the natural world. Yet, ironically, even as she appropriated pre-Christian iconography, on a daily basis Imelda Marcos herself cast herself not in the mode of an indigenous native, but as a Hispanicized, cosmopolitan Filipina, famous for wearing elaborate versions of the *terno,* itself a Filipinized version of a Spanish dress in which the skirt and the blouse are joined seamlessly at the waist. Like Argentina's Eva Peron, Imelda was most fabulously a symbol of *bayan,* and she appropriated all, bringing it to her and to the center in Manila. In a similar fashion, that which is outside *bayan*-as-nation has a history of being culturally appropriated, even though part of it remains outside the periphery of the circle that constitutes the larger, collective *bayan.*

When applied to dance, *katutubo* can be said to be emplacing humans back into the natural world; thus *katutubong sayaw* is somehow closer to an origin, less mediated by other places and cultures. Oddly however, and as is the case with many of these categories, these terms work differently depending on one's position inside or outside the English/Tagalog cultural/linguistic divide. A Google Translate search of the English "folk dance" into Filipino renders the term as *katutubong sayaw,* whereas when reversed, the Filipino *katutubong sayaw* is translated into English as "indigenous dance" rather than folk.[22] Thus the ability to differentiate between folk and indigenous, present when looking in through the Filipino lens, is lost in the other direction when for English-speakers the terms are conflated—at least for those relying on Google Translate! But fundamentally, *katutubo* remains about place, where one is from. To be *katutubong sa Pilipinas* is to be "native to the Philippines," of the land, rather than simply *mula sa Pilipinas,* or "from the Philippines."

A significant body of dance within the Philippines is referred to as "neoethnic," which has come to mean using indigenous (nonfolk) sources and transforming them into work more squarely situated in the traditions of modern dance or ballet. As Agnes Locsin (2008), one of the choreographers most famously associated with this practice, observes, "It is the responsibility of the choreographer to delineate what is ethnic and what is neo-ethnic." Fundamentally, dance becomes neoethnic when it is deemed to be so by those creating the work. Bayanihan does not position its work within this category by virtue of its claim to having been obtained from an original source and by making changes to the source dances through the conventions of their own internal dance-theatre practices rather than the conventions of modern dance or ballet. My reason for not using the moniker "ethnic" dance is simple; to characterize dance of the nonassimilated minorities of the country in this way as to differentiate their traditions from those of the "folk" suggests that the majority population are themselves not ethnic or are somehow "ethnic-neutral" by virtue of being able to claim majority status. This position would be difficult to defend under any circumstances, but especially in a diverse, far-flung archipelago with so many regional languages and distinctive local cultures. If one group in the Philippines is termed "ethnic," surely all groups are potentially "ethnic" as well, as Scott's wry commentary suggests.

As we have seen, the traditional Bayanihan program typically began with the "Cordillera Suite," featuring ceremonial dances from the ethnic minorities of that region. Its position at the top of the program, according to Santos, was due to its lack of "foreign influences," thus marking it as "truly indigenous" (Santos 2004, 42). Though the notion that these dances are "not Asian" seems absurd, insofar as they are derived from a people who have lived and developed a complex culture over the course of millennia on an island that is geographically within Asia, what marks them as "indigenous" in her formulation is that they are also untouched, which thus places them in a separate category—that of the Other. In relative terms, the "purity" of the ritual and mimetic dances featured in the "Tribal Suite," extending from the formerly animist Bagobo, Subanon, and T'boli minority ethnic groups in Mindanao, is more difficult to assert, as these are relatively speaking more porous cultures, whereas conversions to Islam and Christianity long ago disconnected these dances from their original ritual and to some extent from their social functions as well. Thus, while they fall within the category of *katutubong sayaw,* for the sake of clarity and also because they are no longer part of the repertory as a single suite, these will be excluded from the analysis that follows. The midpoint in the original Bayanihan program was the "Muslim Suite," with its thrilling *singkil* romp through the clacking poles and *pangalay*-style dance on raised bamboo poles, both dances that circulate widely within the Philippines and transnationally in conjuring up a vision of an "authentic," exotic, shared pre-Christian past. Within a *bayan*-as-nation framework, the signature movement style of *pangalay* as well as the practice of raising men and women on poles to dance is much-used in large-scale competitive street dance routines, the subject of chapter 6. The cultural positioning of Igorot dance also has a similar history of appropriation and colonization as we shall see, though it offers a vision of a less refined culture, in which dance reflects the relationship of an animist people to the exigencies of life in a region where a rugged topography kept tribes separated from one another or in conflict over scarce resources. Thus the reworkings of the cultural artifacts of these two cultures—the Muslim of the south and the Igorot of the north—provide a study in the ways in which the exotic Other can serve to enhance the cultural capital of *bayan,* whether constituted locally, nationally, or transnationally.

The indigenous people of the Cordillera have long been emblematic of a proud and fiercely independent culture that has resisted colonization. Paul Kramer asserts that the American colonizers viewed them as "noble savages," the "moral, masculine, and military superiors of Christian Filipinos" in need of the U.S. empire "to preserve their nobility" (Kramer 2006, 368). The traditional dance forms of this diverse indigenous population living in north-central Luzon, known collectively as the Igorot,[23] have for nearly a century been presented both domestically and internationally as the headliners who showcase the country's rich cultural heritage. As the mineral-rich region became increasingly dominated by external forces throughout the twentieth century, its dance traditions have been exported as embodying an important strand of Filipino strength and resilience; whereas the people of the region resisted political, economic, and military domination by the Tagalog-speaking majority of southern Luzon, their dance forms became incorporated into the wider cultural fabric of what it means to be Filipino.

The Cordillera region encompasses the country's largest mountain range, which starts some two hundred kilometers north of Manila and forms an imposing spine that runs through the northern half of the island of Luzon. Though the Spanish repeatedly sought to gain access to the goldfields in the region during the nineteenth century, a succession of failed military campaigns demonstrated that their forces were no match for the legendary fighting prowess of the mountain tribes. As Scott observes, "Spanish records themselves leave no doubt that these mountain peoples fought for their liberty with every means at their disposal for 320 years, and that this resistance was deliberate, self-conscious, and continuous" (Scott 1994b, 2). Unlike other areas of the Philippines that were colonized and converted to Christianity from as early as the sixteenth century, this region remained relatively off-limits to outsiders until well into the American period, which began in earnest with the creation of the Mountain Province in 1908. The civil, municipal, and legal structures imposed by the Americans in the decades prior to World War II rapidly transformed this mountainous and previously inaccessible region and as Gerald Finin (2005) argues, laid the foundation for the eventual emergence of a pan-Igorot consciousness in an area where a harsh geography had historically meant that individual mountain cultures lived in a state of isolation often characterized by mutual enmity. With the completion of Kennon Road, named after the U.S. army colonel credited with its construction, the region was opened up to mining and timber interests. In the postindependence era, Benguet Province, the more densely populated province and the gateway into the region, has been increasingly populated by Tagalog-speaking lowlanders, resulting in what has often been an uneasy relationship between those who were indigenous to the region and the relatively more prosperous newcomers who viewed the tribal cultures of the Cordillera as less civilized than their own.

Today, the diverse cultural groups known collectively as the Igorot continue to be marginalized and colonized within the nation. As Sally Ann Ness notes, "The attribution of cultural inferiority to so-called Igorot communities has been used to justify both the history of colonial domination in the Cordilleran region and the contemporary programs of internal colonization carried out by the Philippine national government" (Ness 1997, 71). The cultural traditions of the region have a long history of being exoticized, the most prominent early instance of which was the wholesale import of Cordillerans to the United States to populate the Igorot Village of the Philippine Reservation at the massive 1904 Louisiana Purchase Exposition, also known as the Saint Louis World's Fair.[24] Drawing nearly twenty million visitors (Vergara 1995, 111), the event in many respects defined the early relationship between Americans and their new and largely unknown colony in the Pacific. Occupying a focal point within the geographic centerpiece of the fair was a Cordilleran "Igorot Village," which provided a sharp contrast to the villages created to house other, more "civilized" Filipino ethnic and cultural groups. Mirroring Santos' language with respect to the position of the dance of the Cordillera in the Bayanihan repertory, David R. Francis, the president of the exposition, noted that "The Negritos and Igorots" were consciously chosen to represent the "least civilized" groups (Vergara 1995, 120). Visitors to the exposition witnessed the daily life of what were billed as "The Bontoc Head-Hunters" and, according to the fair's *Official Guide,* were treated to entertainment in which "the Bontocs go through a realistic pantomime in the use of shield and spear, advancing, retreating, posting and thrusting" (cited in Vergara 1995, 125).

Dance from the Cordillera continues to reflect this iconography in the Bayanihan programming, which typically starts with a sequence foregrounding the warrior-like qualities of the men of the region,[25] followed by the *Banga Salidsid,* a dance that combines a couple's courtship dance *(salidsid)* from the Kalinga region with the practice of women carrying pots *(banga)* on their heads. In this fusion of the practice of transporting water with a courtship dance the man circles around the female, presenting both himself and a ceremonial blanket, while the focus shifts to a line of women who move gracefully, arms extended, with up to eight pots stacked on their heads. Reconfigured in this manner, the dance becomes about displaying the agility and grace of the women, while the man circulates in and through them. Thus the dance becomes a "courtship dance with pots" *(banga salidsid),* which, at least in part because of its prominent position in the Bayanihan repertory, has become a signature "traditional dance" of the region, one that can be seen at regional dance competitions in the Cordillera.[26] Indeed, the image of women with clay pots stacked on their heads has become an iconic symbol for virtually all indigenous Cordilleran women.[27] Today the Igorot remain the most exoticized of groups within the Philippines, and images of Cordillerans in traditional attire are ubiquitous in the tourist literature both in print and online. Significant cultural capital both at home and abroad has been gained by setting out the dance from the Cordillera region as the reflection of an independent and vigorous Filipino national identity.

On the ground from which they sprang, dance forms in the Cordillera were connected with ritual activities and indeed many still are, another marker of *katutubo* rather than folk. Traditional rituals fell broadly into four categories: (1) those that were based on giving thanks; (2) those associated with the cycles of the planting and harvest season; (3) those tied to betrothals, marriage, birth, and death; and (4) other rituals designed to appease a vast array of sky-dwelling and earthbound spirits, including the spirits of the deceased. Dance has long featured prominently as a component of the *canao,* a Kankanaey word that has come to mean a thanksgiving feast or gathering but that traditionally refers to "several and quite different feasts celebrated for the purpose of appeasing spirits of departed ancestors, curing illness, ensuring prosperity, and promoting social status in the community" (Bagamaspad and Hamada-Pawid 1985, 94). Well aware of the symbolic power of the *canao,* in 1974 Imelda Marcos brought Miss Universe Pageant contestants from Manila to Baguio for a *canao,* a field trip that was meant to showcase the traditional culture of the region at a time when its dance forms had already been synthesized into folkloric dances by Bayanihan. Subsequent attempts to turn this indigenous ritual practice into a drawing card for tourists during the early 1980s were met with protests from "Igorot professionals and student activists" (Malanes 2000). Even today, the larger *canao,* now sponsored by the provincial governments, is largely an indigenous affair with few tourists or outsiders present.[28]

The region's famous circular dance, known generically as the *tayaw,* has long been the signature dance used to express Cordilleran identity, and it remains an essential component of any *canao.* Commonly danced by the Ibaloi, Kankanaey, and Ikalahan people at weddings, death anniversaries, and healing rituals (Capuyan 1994, 25), the dance is a core element in virtually all public ceremonies that feature indigenous Cordillerans (Baguio City 1960, 56). Often danced by a man and a woman, the man wears a long, handwoven blanket over both shoulders and the woman is wrapped in ceremonial cloth as they move in a counterclockwise fashion around a circle, hopping to the beat of musicians who dance with them carrying handheld gongs. The dancers move with their arms open and palms extended, bringing down the blessings from above, stopping the forward motion periodically to dance in place while opening up their dance positions by moving from side to side. The *tayaw*'s characteristic chant, "Ooooo Wai, Ooooo Wai, Oy! Oy!" marks the end of a sequence and is believed to be derived from a dance known as the *Kadaring*, or Spirits' Dance in which the dancers "impersonate the spirits of dead ancestors" (Baguio City 1960, 64). At a contemporary *canao* where dancers may have consumed considerable quantities of rice wine, dancing can reach almost manic proportions. Because they are dancing in a circle with the musicians, the effect of this dance on the bodies of the participants is almost hypnotic.

Indeed, when participating in this dance in a large group some years back with the Filipino band Pinikpikan, I felt as though I were stepping into another dimension of reality where I was connected to everyone through our shared movements, the unending trajectory of the circle, and the heartbeat provided by the gongs. My body still retains the sensation I had then that I was capable of continuing this dance forever, even if I faced death from overheating, dehydration, and exhaustion. To have died while dancing would have seemed a blessing, or so it seemed at the time. There was a moment when my mind kicked in and, realizing that I was past the limits of my physical endurance, I withdrew from the dance circle. But it seemed to me then as it does now that only the reptilian brain imperative for self-preservation saved me from passing out at the very least. My body remembers longing to remain a part of that collective body of dancers, which points to the foundational impulse behind the *tayaw*, that of drawing a community together through celebration. These dances bring people together as a collective organism, not as a reflection of some larger notion of *bayan* through cultural display. Dances reconfigured as theatre, as the Bayanihan *banga salidsid* is, offer spectacle, but are far removed from their efficacious functions that are not just about offering thanksgiving, but about actualizing the bonds between individuals in the community and emplacing them into the bodies of participant-dancers.

Another signature dance at the *canao* is the *bendian*, a mass participation dance from the Kabayan region of Benguet Province. Meaning "untiring" or "indefatigable" in Ibaloi, its name signifies the belief that those engaged in this victory dance will never tire (Baguio City 1960, 66).[29] Associated with victory in battle (Bagamaspad and Hamada-Pawid 1985, 90; Capuyan 1994, 25), a dance line is formed behind gong players and a leader, with men, then women dancers following the leader's arm movements while stamping with the left foot and moving forward on the right. When large numbers participate in this dance, it provides a fitting counterpart to the *tayaw;* whereas the former encloses the energy of the group in a circle, giving it strength and power as it is created and shared as a single organism, the *bendian* is the point of entry, the coming together as the dance line becomes longer and longer, assuming a spiral pattern that draws everyone from the outside in. These are remarkable and powerful dances, but their power derives from the shared experience of the group that is also possible because the dance steps are not complex to master, although an accomplished dancer is free to add his or her own signature moves into the mix.

Occupying a similar position of exoticism and precolonial authenticity is the dance style of *pangalay,* a product of the Tausug, Samal, and Badjao peoples of Sulu, an archipelago of some five hundred islands in the southern Philippines, an area that, like the Cordillera, has historically been the most resistant to colonization and inclusion into the nation. Like Thai classical dance or Javanese and Balinese court dances, *pangalay* involves the hyperextension of the arms and wrists, coupled with complex and fluid finger and hand movements.[30] Female *pangalay* performers sometimes attach ornamental extensions to their fingers, giving them a heightened focus similar to that found in Thai classical dance. As with Indian classical dance and other forms of Southeast Asian traditional dance, the female body's center of gravity is low and centered over the pelvis, with the bottom half of the body capable of moving fluidly, vigorously, and quite independently from the top. While the torso remains relatively rigid, complex movements of the arms, hands, and fingers invite the audience's gaze, and throughout, the dancer's body retains the S-curve line most famously associated with Balinese dance. *Pangalay* is performed to the accompaniment of the *kulintang,* a traditional set of instruments similar to the Javanese *gamelan* that features bronze gongs of various tones mounted horizontally on a rack. A complete ensemble consisting of eight sets of bronze gongs as well as larger hanging and handheld gongs and a drum is typically scaled down in the context of a dance performance.

Santos writes of Bayanihan research conducted in Sulu in the 1970s (Santos 2004, 19–21), out of which emerged another signature dance choreographed by Urtula, the *Vinta,* which she recalls "proved to be a showstopper when it was premiered in 1976" (21). The *vinta* is based on the *pamansak,* a dance found in the Sulu Archipelago that features a woman dancing atop two bamboo poles resting on the shoulders of two men while a male suitor dancing below her seeks to impress the woman with his martial arts moves. With her distinctive metal fingernail extensions drawing the focus to her gracefully moving arms, the dancer's feet and lower body constantly shift her position on the raised poles, as she appears to rotate in the air like a ballerina atop a music box. In Reyes-Urtala's Bayanihan version this is turned into the presentation of a royal bride and groom as both are brought onto the stage on raised bamboo poles.[31] Today, the practice of raising dancers of both genders aloft on bamboo poles is a feature of many of the competitive street-dance presentations that come from the region. Just as women with pots on their heads wearing the traditional red wrap skirts form an iconic representation of the Cordillera, raising dancers on bamboo poles in Muslim-influenced ceremonial attire has come to represent not so much Muslim as pre-Christian culture for the entire south of the country.

The *singkil,* the other dance featured in the "Muslim Suite," is one of Bayanihan's signature dances, and in many ways it epitomizes how a dance can be recreated and repositioned to mean something different to one group of people than to another group. Bayanihan's version of the tale positions it as a "royal dance," but it is far likelier to have been a folk dance much like the *tinikling,* to which it bears striking similarities. The nature of the core action of the dance—moving with absolute precision between clacking bamboo poles to a rapid beat—is precisely the kind of activity one would expect in a popular folk form where a community gathered together to celebrate, show off, and compete with one another. The overlay of dignified, regal movements of the princess, followed by her parasol-wielding attendant as she glides through a minefield created by three pairs of clacking poles, might be almost comical to watch were it not set up with such delicacy and grace by the performers. That dance was ever the province of Filipino Muslim royalty is most likely a complete fiction that serves interests of the nation, local oligarchs, and the Bayanihan company[32] rather than actual Muslims in the south. Ligaya Fernando-Amilbangsa, the preeminent scholar of *pangalay* who has devoted most of her life's work to deepening the understanding of this form of dance from Sulu and disseminating it nationally, argues quite convincingly that the form of *pangalay* and its many dances were not an art cultivated by royalty:

> A formal system of dance instruction and the so-called "royal dances" failed to evolve in Sulu and Tawi-tawi, despite the fact that the region was the seat of the Sulu Sultanate, the first organized state in the country. At no time in its history did dance training and presentation depend on members of royalty or on royal patronage. Most probably, court life and tradition used to inhibit members of royalty from providing dance training and entertainment. In fact, until the death of Sultan Jamalul Kiram II in 1936, female members of the royal household were not allowed to dance in public. While it can be surmised that they danced among themselves, if only for private amusement, the dances thus performed were not assumed to be *royal* dances; neither is the term *royal* affixed to the dances performed in recent times by any member of royalty or in their presence. (Fernando-Amilbangsa 1983, 52)

Fernando-Amilbangsa also observes that the attraction of Islam in the pre-Christian era was precisely that it was the religion of the common man, and that it did away with the castes found in Hinduism and the hierarchies associated with animism and a priestly class. Given that the Sulu Sultanate was the preeminent among many in the region, the notion that the Maranao people developed the *singkil* in the context of a court culture seems even less likely. Fernando-Amilbangsa concludes: "Seen against this background, the application of the term *'Royal'* to certain traditional dances is an anachronism in Sulu and Tawi-tawi, and perhaps in other parts of the Philippines as well" (Fernando-Amilbangsa 1983, 52).

As we saw earlier, Filipino Muslims are still often called "Moros" (Moors in English), a legacy of Spanish colonization, which began in the sixteenth century, three centuries after Muslim traders first arrived and made a significant imprint on the culture of what is today the south of the Philippines. As was the case in the Cordillera, the Spanish never successfully conquered the Muslim-dominated areas of the south, and even the present degree of control over the region has only been achieved over the past century. U.S. colonial administrators encouraged the resettlement of Christians from the densely populated islands of the north to the less populated island of Mindanao, where Muslims had traditionally lived as hill people rather than landowners (Steinberg 1994, 92). Thus, what had once been a traditionally Muslim region has been radically transformed since independence from the United States into a predominantly Christian one. During the Marcos era, the intensity of the conflict between the government and Muslims in the south increased significantly. Many had by this time fled to the much smaller island of Jolo, where in 1974 President Marcos, by then functioning as a virtual dictator, bombed the predominantly Muslim city of Jolo (Gaerlan 1999, 271). Over the past three decades, an estimated 100,000 individuals have died in the nearly continual fighting between Muslims and government forces in the south,[33] making it the most bloody and protracted conflict in contemporary Filipino life. In an article on Filipino American dance, Barbara Gaerlan maps out the ways in which dances in the "Muslim Suite" quickly emerged as "signature pieces" of the country's national dance troupe shortly after its founding in 1957 (269). During the Marcos era, the exalted position of Muslim dance took on a special irony:

> It was at this time that the non-Christian dance suites of the Bayanihan assumed even more prominence than they had previously achieved. During this time the Bayanihan, with its "signature piece," the *Singkil*, became a special project of First Lady Imelda Marcos, who provided new costumes, encouraged frequent trips abroad, and arranged Bayanihan performances at the presidential palace as often as once a week. (Gaerlan 1999, 271)

The irony that Muslim dance was the most extensively used cultural symbol of nationhood at a time when relations between Muslims and the government were especially troubled was apparently overlooked by the First Lady and her people, as it continues to be today.

The sheer length of colonial rule over the Philippines makes it especially difficult to find performance forms that reach back to a time before Catholicism and contact with Spanish or American culture. Thus the largely unexamined and unquestioned use of *pangalay* as a national dance style to represent all of the Muslim south, and the appropriation of *singkil* as a "signature" national dance is perhaps inevitable. Wrapped in the mantle of an authentic pre-Christian past, their strongest expression may be in the transnational circulation of Filipino culture, particularly among Filipino-Americans seeking to connect with their "roots." In California and Hawai'i, where "Fil-Am" culture is especially strong, the *pangalay* style is replicated in the cultural dance nights created largely by and for a young, Filipino-American audience. Bayanihan's signature style has had a profound effect on Fil-Am college students yearning for contact with a home culture from which they are often estranged (Gonzalves 2005, 2010; Gaerlan 1999). Students who grew up in the suburbs of California's larger cities eagerly latch on to the exoticism and orientalist tropes implicit in Bayanihan's depiction of a remote, mythic past, which, in the case of the "Muslim Suite," is replete with rajas and harems observing the dance from the stage. These students reconstitute the Bayanihan performance style—one basically frozen in time as the company has moved on—in the context of Pilipino Cultural Nights (PCNs),[34] a popular event on college campuses such as the University of California, Los Angeles. The featured musical instrument in most PCNs is the *kulintang ensemble*—an instrument not present in the cultures from which most North American Filipinos descend—which is used to underscore the languorous, exotic moves of the female dancer using a *pangalay*-derived movement vocabulary and the vigorous martial-arts-inflected moves of the Muslim men,[35] forming an experiential pathway into their own imagined cultural roots. Theodore Gonzalves details the cultural history of the PCN based on years of observation and detailed ethnographic research, observing how in the context of American identity politics, "the traditional PCN possesses elements which demonstrate that Filipinos do have a culture, that they are visible, despite the persistent, institutional erasure from U.S. American 'official' history" (Gonzalves 2005, 37). Another circle of *bayan* then is constituted transnationally and extraterritorially as first- and second-generation Fil-Am youth look back to the land of their parents and grandparents.

Within the Philippines, the combined legacy of Reyes' work and its institutionalization as a compulsory subject in the national physical education curriculum and the massive reach of Bayanihan has been twofold. First, because dancing in groups is something that everyone does from a very young age, in many communities it has become the primary means through which local identities are reinforced and projected externally. Second, the standardization of dance forms and its increasing theatricalization in the post-Bayanihan era has meant that dance has become increasingly focused on generating spectacle. The following two chapters expand on these two important strands in dance, concluding with a consideration of how dance has come to bring communities together as *bayan,* while setting out a *bayan*-centred model in which to situate the places, forms, and communities of dances and dancers examined in all three chapters.

CHAPTER 5

Time and Transcendence at Ati-atihan

One of the first things I came to learn from talking with informants after I started attending local festivals in the Philippines was how many were compelled to return to the same event every year, some traveling great distances across the archipelago or from overseas to participate. As we have seen, religious and civic festivals are typically the largest public events of the year in the hometowns and cities in which Filipinos live, and for this reason, they possess a strong, singular pull. And where overseas Filipinos cannot go home or have set down roots in a new adopted country, they find ways to re-create these festivals in their new home. In their local expression and re-creation, Filipino festivals in the diaspora are often linked to place and not merely practiced as generic cultural or religious events shared and celebrated in the same way by most other Filipinos. As an archipelagic nation with cultures that grew up quite separately prior to independence, these local practices are still highly differentiated within the Philippines, with one group in a particular *barangay* or region having an understanding of the practice and a mode of expression different from another, even when they are sometimes geographically contiguous communities. Unlike Divali or Chinese New Year, these festivals are in many cases particular to a region or a group of believers who come together to venerate the local patron saint, or in parts of the Philippines, the Santo Niño, the Holy Child. Thus the major festival in a particular region or town may not be shared by groups of individuals anywhere else in the country, which marks these events as quite different from cultural or religious festivals in other Asian countries. For instance, Sinulog, the festival that venerates the Santo Niño, is celebrated with Mardi Gras-style exuberance in Cebu City on the island of Cebu, while another, quite different festival known as Ati-atihan, also honoring the Santo Niño, is held a week earlier in the city of Kalibo on the island of Panay. Yet neither of the events, which are re-created in the diaspora among populations from those respective areas, is celebrated in a significant manner in Manila or outside the Visayan region. Many Filipinos return home each year for these local festivals, and not for Holy Week or the Christmas season.

It is as if, for many, what happens at these events enters the body and the bloodstream, and these experiences thus require annual renewal. These festivals are often of great duration, with preparations starting many months before the range of events associated with a single festival formally commence, occupying time and reflecting great commitment and preparation, which adds to the anticipation feeding the festival. In this respect, they constitute labor that is worth undertaking, which gives them additional importance in a country where so many are bored with their jobs, underemployed, or struggle on a daily basis to feed, clothe, and provide shelter for themselves and their families. It is no accident that the most faithful and numerous adherents and participants are frequently either local residents of the poorer barrios in a region, town, or city, or those with the financial resources to return home each year from elsewhere in the country (typically Manila) or from overseas.

The central position that dance occupies in many of the festivals suggests another pathway into our understanding of these events and how they are experienced by individuals. Dance, more than any other embodied practice, has the greatest potential to offer the greatest number of participants at a festival entry into what Mihaly Csikszentmihalyi (1992) termed "flow" states that place us into a zone of altered consciousness. While Csikszentmihalyi was concerned with happiness, the descriptions given by participants in his study of what they experience while in this "flow" state are not situated in the conventional ways that happiness is understood. Instead, his framework points toward a state that transcends ordinary, daily experiences and, as such, leaves a deep imprint on the body. Such experiences can literally place us into a different mode of being, into another way of experiencing time. This is what makes them pleasurable, even if they are not within the framework of what we might otherwise identify as a "happy state," and it is through their operational characteristics that we are able to transcend our quotidian lives, making us want to repeat these experiences as they sear into our brains and bodies. As Susan Isorena-Arcega (2013) observes of this pull, while dancing, "It's like riding the roller coaster for 70 seconds and you want to do it again," an experience so strong that even "those who live overseas they just have to come home."

Thus in this chapter I seek to go inside the experience of dance at the Ati-atihan Festival in Kalibo, located in the province of Aklan on the island of Panay. I have participated in this festival honoring the Santo Niño four times, three of them as part of a family that has essentially adopted me and therefore expects me to return annually as does virtually everyone in their extended clan. In the days leading up to the third Sunday of January, in their company I watch the processions and troupes of street dancers from the balcony of their ancestral family home and participate in social activities, most of them centered around eating and talking. The culminating event and the reason for the gathering is to dance with the family through the streets of Kalibo from the late afternoon and into the evening on Sunday in front of the *karo* (cart/float) carrying a nineteenth century carved effigy of the Santo Niño that belongs to the family,[1] at a festival many believe is more than eight hundred years old. Not a practicing Catholic, I was raised as a Lutheran and spent a number of summers in my young life presiding over a makeshift church for family members and neighbors at our family's cabin, preaching and providing musical accompaniment to hymns on the trombone. My relationship with Christianity has from childhood been performative and thus the practice of "taking it to the streets" is not constitutionally foreign to me. My adoption into this family I suspect has much to do with my birth position as the eldest child and grandchild in a large, extended family, thus providing me with a point of entry into Filipino families that seems to have been recognized by Filipinos before I identified it within myself.

When I dance in this place with this family that comes together once a year, and with the thousands of others who flood into the streets, I lose myself in others as I feel more fully myself in that surrender, and time bends, opening into infinity so that temporal markers of timekeeping that would otherwise imprint on my body are absent. I feel transcendent and fully alive in this moment that seems in its temporal dimension to be both an instant and an eternity, and I carry it with me into the rest of my life as an essential component of how I feel emplaced in this world. These are the most tricky and difficult components of flow to identify and quantify, that state where concern for the self disappears, but emerges more strongly after the experience, and where time slows down, expands, even stops, and where we are so overtaken by a sense of "deep enjoyment" that we are willing to expend huge amounts of time and energy "simply to be able to feel it" (Csikszentmihalyi 1992, 49). Dancing facilitates this flow state, while this kinesthetic practice provides the additional layer making the ritual, which at its core is a devotional act to the Santo Niño, an experience in which even a non-Catholic can enter into a transcendent state. Although aspects of this experience might well be replicated in other mass-dance events that are not focused on the Santo Niño, the particular way dance functions on the streets of Kalibo in the days preceding the third Sunday in January provides the peak experience that compels one's body to return year after year.

This chapter seeks to map out a phenomenologically grounded anthropology of perception that extends from what the body experiences. Thomas Csordas (1990), responding to Edward Casey and Maurice Merleau-Ponty, asserts that "the goal of a phenomenological anthropology of perception is to capture that moment of transcendence in which perception begins, and, in the midst of arbitrariness and indeterminacy, constitutes and is constituted by culture" (Csordas 1990, 9). If the body is central to this experience of creating culture, while also being bound by it, then what happens when the body dances is key to our understanding of an event such as Ati-atihan where the rhythms of the overarching festival become emplaced in the body, compelling one to move. Merleau-Ponty posits the possibility of this kind of deeply embodied knowledge: "Our bodily experience of movement is not a particular case of knowledge; it provides us with a way of access to the world and the object, with a 'praktognosia,' which has to be recognized as original and perhaps as primary" (Merleau-Ponty 1962, 162). This "practical knowledge" that accesses the world through the body is especially important when considering the relationship of the body to space and time. As I have suggested, in a flow state the body enters into space and time in a way that does not separate the body from those modes of operation. As Merleau-Ponty observes:

> In so far as I have a body through which I act in the world, space and time are not, for me, a collection of adjacent points nor are they a limitless number of relations synthesized by my consciousness, and into which it draws my body. I am not in space and time, nor do I conceive space and time; I belong to them, my body combines with them and includes them. The scope of this inclusion is the measure of that of my existence; but in any case it can never be all-embracing. (Merleau-Ponty 1962, 162)

Although not all-embracing, the body is constituted in space and time, not created through consciousness that situates the body in space and time through thought. The body is not merely another way of knowing; the body, and particularly the body in motion, the body engaged in proprioception, the body that thinks with the body, is positioned in time and space.

Place, as Casey observes, is mutually constituted by space and time: "But the phenomenological fact of the matter is that space and time come together in place. Indeed, they arise from the experience of place itself" (Casey 1996, 36). The space of Ati-atihan is not disinterested and generic. It is constituted as place by the body and the mind existing within it: "Similarly, to be emplaced is to know the hollowness of any strict distinction between what is inside one's mind or body and what is outside, or between what is perceived and what is remembered or imagined, or between what is natural and what is cultural" (ibid.). My sense of emplacement at Ati-atihan is inseparable from the experience of dance and from what I feel of my body as constituted in and through time and space. This inquiry thus also seeks to evoke place with reference to my embodied experience at this event, while considering the ways in which moments of transcendence constitute and are constituted by culture in ways that generate intragroup empathy, and in so doing, contribute to happiness.

In *Choreographing Empathy: Kinesthesia in Performance,* Susan Leigh Foster sets out the ways in which understandings of choreography, empathy, and kinesthesia have shifted radically over time, even within the relatively narrow range bounded by Euro-American culture. She argues that "any notion of choreography contains, embodies within it, a kinesthesis, a designated way of experiencing physicality and movement that, in turn, summons other bodies into a specific way of feeling towards it" (Foster 2011, 2). Her book provides examples of a range of dances that collectively "show how empathic connections occur in multiple and diverse ways." These dances, she suggests, "enact the process" through which the production of empathy with others takes place while "empathy forms the basis upon which knowledge of self and other is generated" (218). It is this concluding point Foster makes that I feel is worth pulling out and building toward; this chapter will demonstrate how a particular practice is the "process" through which the self in relation to the other is experienced. Thus the chapter relies on data gained from four years of fieldwork at this site as local informants situate their embodied practices in the places that constitute Ati-atihan. The indigenous Filipino cultural tropes and models invoked in previous chapters also have application here and are often invoked by participants, creating what I believe will be a productive conversation between ways of knowing through what Csordas terms the "phenomenological anthropology of perception" and ways of knowing that are deeply local and deeply emplaced at Ati-atihan.

Following a brief overview and contextualization of Ati-atihan, the account that follows charts my experiential pathways in and through the five principal days of this event from Wednesday through the third Sunday in January. In that I have experienced the festival in 2009, 2010, 2012, and 2014, I will identify the primary forces and responses of the body on each day, noting specific experiences linked to moments in particular years whenever relevant by way of expansion and illustration. As a phenomenon touches on or activates the body to move, to respond, and ultimately to dance, the descriptive account will open up to consider both the internal microcharacteristics of the experiential dimension and the external cultural and religious beliefs that support and interact with what the body is experiencing. At times I will stop at a moment of the experience as it unfolded and attempt to dig into the inner experience before moving out to consider frames that contain and activate it.

The Way In

In his local incarnation at the Ati-atihan Festival in Kalibo, the Santo Niño is mischievous and playful, yet infinite in his capacity for bestowing divine grace upon believers, serving as the de facto patron saint for residents of Kalibo and indeed the region. The first complication in what might otherwise be a singular narrative is that the veneration of the Santo Niño at Ati-atihan is conflated with two foundational mytho-historical events: the displacement of the darker-skinned indigenous Ati population by ethnic Malay stock from nearby Borneo in the thirteenth century, and mass conversions to Roman Catholicism three centuries later. Thus this festival has two points of origin: the meeting of indigenous and settler cultures more than eight hundred years ago, supposedly marked by a kind of thanksgiving, and the baptism of one thousand inhabitants of the area in and around present-day Kalibo (de la Cruz 2001; Roces 1980; Tirazona 2009a; Cruz 2009), the provincial capital of Aklan province, by Father Andres de Aguirre in 1569. These two once separate events were merged, probably by a local priest, at some point in the eighteenth century (Tiongson 1994a, 1:67). On a national level the festival has been promoted since the 1970s as a kind of Filipino Mardi Gras, even though the event has no connection with the transgressions and excesses of Fat Tuesday in the Lenten calendar. Over the past few decades the focus of tourism development has shifted to the two nearby festivals, Cebu City's Sinulog and Iloilo's Dinagyang, both of which have become famous for presentations of theatricalized street dancing that will be briefly considered in the next chapter. Indeed, when I tell most Filipinos that I repeatedly return to Ati-atihan, those without a personal connection to the festival find it hard to understand why I have not yet been to Sinulog or Dinagyang, insofar as they are held up nationally as the two major festivals of which Filipinos should be most proud. Manila taxi drivers frequently tell me that I should go to one of these festivals on my next trip because the assumption is that I am a foreign tourist and thus would prefer these spectator-focused festivals to the relatively tatty Ati-atihan, which is now seen by many from outside the region as a kind of poor cousin of these glitzier events.

But even before arriving to commence fieldwork in 2009, it was clear that Ati-atihan would not be like other festivals. To begin with, there appeared to be no place to stay. There were only a few hotels in Kalibo and when I contacted them months in advance by phone, proprietors wanted me to wire money to their bank accounts, a practice that seemed odd to me at the time, but which I later came to understand was designed to maximize income during a one-week tourist season while taking advantage of the very few who came to this town without having friends and family with whom to stay. In the days leading up to the main events on Saturday and Sunday, up to a quarter of a million people flood into the city streets (Alcedo 2007, 110), more than four times the resident population of this provincial town. Arriving on Wednesday and settling into a motel far from the town center, I expected to have a day to gather my thoughts and formulate interview questions when my hosts told me that the street dancing had already started. Not only had it started, they added, but it had been going on all week. Indeed, as I later found out, some of the youngsters start dancing in the streets with marching bands a month earlier.

Fearing I would miss something essential to my understanding of the event, I took a tricycle into town and followed the sound of a marching band to the town center, Pastrana Park, a prototypical Spanish colonial era civic square bounded on one side by the Kalibo Cathedral, and on the other by the classic, two-story traditional homes found in many provincial centers. In such homes the ground floor is given over to businesses, and the living quarters occupy the upper level, many of which feature sliding latticework panels that open onto a balcony overlooking the street, as they do in Kalibo. Everything needed to sustain life was here on the square: a hardware store, a bank, an English-language school, the central police station, and what is for many middle-class and poor Filipinos a significant social space and container of memories for birthdays and other milestone events that take place outside the home, the ubiquitous Jollibee, a fast-food restaurant and virtual cultural institution that serves combination plates such as the ever-popular fried chicken and spaghetti dishes. The square itself features a raised, covered stage at one end, and spaces for food vendors at the other. What I could never have imagined, as the sound of the band drew me toward this square in January 2009, is just how intimate I would become with this square over the next five years, how I would come to know every broken tile, every opening in the crumbling cement walls containing parts of the square, every spot of pavement surrounding it, and the two public toilets, one of which I soon learned was best avoided during peak periods on Saturday and Sunday when urination took place from any position in which one could stand.

On the day and time of that first encounter, however, it was sound that beckoned me toward the square, a wave of sound generated by multiple marching bands, all heavy on the percussion, particularly the bass drums. In the absence of brass instruments such as trumpets and trombones, the melody line is typically picked up by handheld metallophones known as "lyres," a sound which, over the course of the rest of the week, is completely drowned out by the dominant beat of the snare and bass drums, which repeat seemingly endlessly the same sixteen- to eighteen-beat cycle. The soundscape is created largely by young boys, many of them not much bigger than the enormous drums they beat mercilessly with sticks.

The sound of the bands and the repetitive beat known locally as the *sad-sad*, provides an adrenaline rush, one that at times has propelled me past the point of exhaustion. Dancing in front of these bands on Wednesday are contingents of street dancers, many clad in matching T-shirts identifying themselves as members of groups ranging from local shooting clubs to vocational schools. While some have lines of what one informant will later characterize as "Red Indian war paint" drawn on their faces, most are unadorned, without the headpieces and elaborate costumes worn by the dancers who will fill the streets in the days to come. Each day was to prove a warm-up for the following day, a slightly scaled-back, less noisy, less populated, less colorful version of what is to come.

The *sad-sad* beat is believed to replicate the "primitive" dancing of indigenous Ati. One informant characterized the *sad-sad* as "the way the Atis dance, like the [American] Indians," adding that this is "how they danced before" the Malay settlers arrived. Indeed, many ceremonial dances among the indigenous Cree and Ojibwe people in the part of the United States from which I hail offer a similarly repetitive beat that is found in many other ritual traditions as well. Though the two-step dance is a devotional practice, it also fits within the framework of Filipino folk dance set out by Mellie Lopez:

1. *"It is traditional"* in the sense that while it lays claim to "some traditional lineage" it is "subject to change" as a living organism;
2. *"It is expressive behaviour"* in that it reflects "an affective behaviour developed within the cultural milieu of the folk group";
3. *"Simple, basic rhythm dominates the folk dance and establishes the pattern of movement."* Because these forms were meant to be danced by all members of the community many of the basic steps and formations must be "simple and easy to perform";
4. *"An unknown choreographer or communal efforts create a folk dance"* and the category does not include "art and classical dance";
5. *"It performs a function in the life of the folk"* notably the "social expression of customs and traditions, as communal amusement, and as a solemn ritual." (Lopez 2006: 234–235)

The dancing of these groups consists variously of a step back or to the side, a stationary step and two steps forward. Younger kids can improvise fancier and more energetic footwork, but there are no formal steps, just moving to the beat, which impels movement. The *sad-sad* is the beating heart of Ati-atihan activating the street dancers and taking over the bodies of all present so that by Saturday and Sunday everyone is compelled to participate. Local informants observe with pride that mass participation is what distinguishes Ati-atihan from Sinulog and Dinagyang (Janbog 2009; Orbista 2009). The repetitive beat both draws one in and keeps one going, offering as one senior informant observed, "a never-ending sound" (Aguirre 2010). Referencing a popular television advertising campaign, she claimed, "It's like an energy that keeps on flowing and flowing. . . . It is like the Duracell battery. . . . It keeps going and going and going" (ibid). Another senior figure noted that the beat of the *sad-sad* is deeply embedded into the bodies of local children and is part of how they play: "[O]ur children . . . during their play are actually copying the Ati-atihan Festival. . . . They look for tin cans and then beat them and dance in their play." He added that, "If you're a true-blooded Kalibonian at any time of the year and you can hear the Ati-atihan beat being played your feet will force you to do the dance" (Tirazona 2009b). That the beat is so much a part of life, and something that can be so easily mastered while done in communion with others, mirrors the first of Csikszentmihalyi's conditions for flow: participants have the capacity to carry out what is being asked of them, in this case without having to stop and think.

The heartbeat of the festival connects it to its ancient mytho-historical past. Ati-atihan is believed by its organizers and many locals to date back to 1212, when ten *datus* (nobles) and their families fleeing the tyranny of Sultan Makatunaw (ruler of Sulawesi and Borneo) arrived on the island of Panay on which Kalibo is situated.[2] While it seems probable that such a population displacement did occur at some point, where it turns into legend is with the much-repeated local narrative of the "Barter of Panay." According to the story, the prime pieces of real estate along the coast were ceded to the new settlers from today's Borneo in exchange for an elaborate piece of gold headgear *(salakot)* and a necklace, on the condition that they would be provided with a share of the harvest from the seas, a promise that was never honored. In the account circulated by Ati-atihan organizers, what followed was "a glorious celebration to seal the negotiation" that provided the foundation for the tradition:

> The unending flow of the native wine (*tuba*) and the sumptuous meal motivated the start of merry-making. The Malays in their effort to show appreciation, sincerity and further befriend their hosts smeared themselves with soot from their cooking utensils to look like the *Aetas* [Ati].[3] The uninhabited *[sic]* spontaneous dancing of the two races lasted till the wee hours of the morning to the beat and music of the native songs, bagtoes and drums of the *Aetas* and the Malays.[4] (Tirazona 2009a)

Lacking a contemporary account of this encounter, there is nothing to suggest that this detailed and somewhat fanciful story of the first Filipino thanksgiving is anything other than wishful thinking. Nevertheless, this foundational story is embedded in the event, reflected in the iconography and dancing of the competitive street-dance routines on Friday and Saturday, and honored by many even if it is believed by some to be a fantasy.[5] Thus there are two foundational and exceptional embodied practices at this event: the persistent beat of the *sad-sad* that compels us to dance and the practice of blackening the body, adopted by the groups competing in the popular "Traditional" and "Tribal" categories of street dancing.

The *sad-sad* also provides the link to the central feature of the event, the veneration of the Santo Niño. Kalibonians believe that by offering the dance as *panaad*—which would seem to be close to the Tagalog *panata* or vow—we are honoring and physically connecting with the Santo Niño who will not only preserve us, but offer us the energy that enables us to keep going beyond all physical limits, like the bunny in the Duracell battery television advertisement. That here one can express *panaad* through dance rather than through the enactment of pain and suffering also points to regional variations in how one understands, experiences, and expresses one's relationship with Christ. Benigno Beltran's exhaustive survey involving nearly ten thousand participants suggested that while a plurality of Catholics (37 percent) thought the image most Catholic Filipinos identified with was that of the suffering *Hesus Nazareno* (Jesus the Nazarene),[6] nearly as many (34 percent) suggested it was the Santo Niño (Beltran 1987, 38). Were a similar, exhaustive survey conducted in Cebu and throughout the Visayan region where Kalibo is situated, that figure would represent the vast majority of practicing Catholics. The Santo Niño, as the lovable, impish boy-child, who in his Kalibo incarnation is even capable of being a bit of a trickster, requires and responds to a different expression of adoration. As Julius Bautista observes,

> Rather than being seen as a sign of vulnerability, the childlike aspects of the Santo Niño constitute its very amenability to being related to one's immediate experience, either through modification or localization. After all, or so goes the popular logic, a cute and lovable child can get anything from the Father, even more so than a bleeding and crucified Son. (Bautista 2010, 44)

The centrality of the Santo Niño here has deep historical roots, in that Christianity was bestowed on the region with and through the iconic power of not the crucified Christ, but the Santo Niño. The story of the Santo Niño extends back to the arrival of Magellan in 1521, who is believed to have brought the first effigy of the Santo Niño to the Philippines, gifting it to the leader of Cebu, Rajah Humabon, and his wife as a symbol of the alliance and to mark their conversion to Roman

Catholicism. Many believe that this relic of the Holy Child Jesus was recovered intact from the ruins of a burned-out building, nearly two generations later in 1565, by Spanish explorer Miguel de Legaspi, thus proving its miraculous powers. The Santo Niño is a symbol of the birth of the Philippines as a Christian country long before it became a nation. Indeed, Cebu and by extension much of the Visayas are seen as markedly different from other regions, in part because of the claim to having been the first area to be Christianized. In 2010, while watching the question-and-answer segment of the national Reyna ng Aliwan (Queen of Aliwan) contest in Manila, I heard Rizzini Alexis Gomez, who represented Cebu and later won the crown,[7] characterize her native region as "the civilizing heart of the Philippines," a phrase I have heard many times. Such a claim might seem arrogant if one did not consider that the Manileños to whom she was speaking do indeed seem to regard Cebuanos as more refined and sophisticated than the diverse inhabitants of their large, sprawling, congested city.[8]

The Santo Niño entered the local belief system at the time of mass conversions in 1569, when Father Andres de Aguirre is said to have baptized one thousand inhabitants in and around present-day Kalibo (de la Cruz 2001; Roces 1980; Tirazona 2009a; Cruz 2009). At this time, it is believed that the town's former name of Madyanos was replaced with Kalibo, which contracts part of the phrase "isa ka libo," or the "one thousand" (de la Cruz 2001). Thus the town's "rebirth" and renaming is linked to conversion. According to one version of the story, upon conversion, the locals and the Spaniards danced together to the beat of drums exclaiming, "Viva kay Señor Santo Niño," or "Long live the Santo Niño" (Cruz 2009), thus creating a connection between dance and veneration of the Holy Child Jesus. This link is embedded into street dancing today when, after a lengthy period of dancing tirelessly, the marching band suddenly stops as all dancers shout in unison, "Viva kay Señor Santo Niño." This exclamation is often preceded by the dialect phrase, *Hala bira puera pasma,* which local informants suggest means "Let's keep on going (dancing) and never get sick." Although the Spanish root word *espasmo* refers specifically to spasms, *pasma* is used throughout the Philippines to cover a wide range of ailments and thus constitutes what might be called a "folk illness" (Tan 2007). In 2009 this link between the dance and *panaad* was invoked by Monsignor Jose Dollete, the head of the Catholic Church in Kalibo, before a crowd numbering well over a thousand at the Sunday morning Mass on the final day of Ati-atihan. He suggested that when prayers or petitions to the Santo Niño are answered, we are compelled to offer "the *sad-sad* as *panaad.*" Because "we love the child who answered our prayers," "love moves us to *sad-sad* and *panaad*" (Dollete 2009). The monsignor's comments bring this devotional practice into our bodies by suggesting that to dance is to express our devotion to the Santo Niño and that dance, even when excessive in its demands on the body, itself constitutes *panaad.* To dance is to ask for our prayers to be answered, and to dance excessively is to take on a measure of pain through physical exertion that demonstrates our love for the Santo Niño. In this way, the indigenous *sad-sad,* the rhythmic beat of the event, is what moves us to dance, and while we dance for the Santo Niño, the dancing is possible because of the Santo Niño's intervention that allows us to continue dancing past the point of exhaustion.

Dancing to the Beat of the *Sad-Sad*

The beat of the *sad-sad,* literally pounded into the body by the drumbeats of roving bands of enthusiastic boys, continues on Thursday, as the number of dance groups and bands in the streets begins to increase almost exponentially. On this day, which is still very much the prelude to the main event—though it might seem more like a Fourth of July parade in a U.S. city—local businesses and employees of the provincial and local government march as groups wearing T-shirts and sporting banners proclaiming their work affiliations. The parade route expands to accommodate these numbers, circling around the town's central square and being fed by and continuing down the two parallel streets that bound Pastrana Park on the north and south sides. These streets—one named after Kalibo-born Gabriel M. Reyes (1892–1952), the first Filipino archbishop of Manila, and the other dedicated to the nineteen local martyrs executed in 1897 for joining the Katipunan in their fight against the Spanish—serve as the principal arteries moving tens of thousands in and around the square over the next four days. Even the pathways trod in this event reflect and combine local pride, the power of the Church, and *bayan* as nation. By Saturday and Sunday, the route expands even farther, connecting to a larger loop that comes back into the square from the north. There are no real barriers between participants and spectators as people wander freely in and through groups of dancers as they move in the streets. From the start, it is an event set up to maximize participation inasmuch as virtually everyone who lives and works in and around Kalibo has some potential affiliation with a group that will dance together in the streets, whether it is through work, school, or a club.

When I first came to Ati-atihan in 2009 I felt it essential to experience every event on the schedule during the five principal days of the festival, not understanding that each day provides a different kind of experience for different groups, and that it is only on Saturday and Sunday that everyone comes together in the streets and the beating heart of the event is most in evidence. One event that attracts a significant audience on Wednesdays is the *Higante* (Giant) competition, which features papier-mâché effigies three to four meters in height being wheeled, pulled, and driven through the streets of town. In 2009 I was greeted in the town center by a *higante* of Barack Obama as a scantily clad Ati warrior, just days before his inauguration as the first African-American president of the United States. That he was "blackened-up," presumably to appear more like an indigenous Ati, was especially striking and it presaged what I was to experience on Saturday, when the competitive dance groups took over the streets, many of them blackening their entire bodies. Days later, when I saw actual Ati appear on the streets in small numbers and in a few dance groups, they seemed like shy people, who were uncomfortable being watched by others from outside their clan, quite far removed from the bold statement of ersatz native pride exemplified by the Obama *higante* effigy. In the years that followed, the Ati, so essential to the iconography and mytho-historical basis of the event, were noticeable not by their presence, but by their absence. I later discovered that their presence in 2009 was due to the intervention of Patrick Alcedo, an anthropologist at a Canadian university who hails from Kalibo, who used funding from a grant to bring in indigenous Ati for participation in the street dancing. Today the Ati on the island of Panay are essentially a dispossessed people, the poorest of the poor, occupying a position similar to that of the Aeta in Luzon.

In addition to the *higante* parade and competition, another scheduled festival event was a dance-drama performance on Thursday night enacting the story of the "Barter of Panay," the foundational myth at the heart of the claim that Ati-atihan is eight hundred years old, paired with the coronation of the Reyna ng Ati-Atihan (Queen of Ati-Atihan/Miss Ati-Atihan). Inasmuch as the festival is named after the indigenous Ati, suggesting in its doubleness (Ati-Ati) that it involves "becoming Ati" or that it is "really-really Ati," I assumed that the presentation would constitute a key element of the week's events and would be well attended. Instead, along with a small audience composed largely of the local political and economic elite, in 2009 I witnessed a mimed enactment of a meeting between a group of richly bedecked settlers in generic, quasi-Muslim theatrical garb that resulted in the darker-skinned folks trading away their land for a gold crown and some fancy beads, followed by a bit of partying around a campfire. As with similar civic events elsewhere in the Philippines, the ruling triumvirate (mayor, representative, provincial governor) were given seats of honor and the opportunity to speak at length prior to the start of the festivities on two popular themes: the value of traditional culture in a modern/globalized world and the government's plans to help stimulate economic growth. While watching the contestants of Miss Ati-atihan, all in possession of the classic Mestizo looks and light skin of most beauty queen winners in the Philippines, it struck me that I was witnessing a celebration of the triumph of whiteness over the dark-skinned Ati population, one that literally ended with a coronation. Both events were staged in a controlled space that required payment of an entry fee, which explained why everyone watching was lighter-skinned and better dressed than those on the streets. This experience was deeply unsettling, a reminder that there often exist two parallel universes in the Philippines at civic events with foundational political, cultural, or religious significance—one in which the power elite perform by and for themselves, while the mass event unfolds outside the gates and walls, in the streets, which is observed by the elite only from a safe, detached position such as a raised stage, where dignitaries sit for the Aliwan dance competition, or from the balconies of their gracious homes.

Dance troupes in elaborate, handmade costumes fill the streets of town on Friday, accompanied by bands of drummers as they gear up for the Saturday morning street-dance event, in which groups compete in the categories of Balik-Ati, Tribal, and Modern. Literally meaning "return to Ati," Balik-Ati groups are to use only materials found in nature for all costume elements, whereas tribal groups, although required to carry the traditional shield and spear, may use commercial materials. Effigies of individuated, black-faced Santo Niños are grasped with both hands and essentially danced with by some of the more senior members participating in the Balik-Ati category, while they are raised aloft by leaders of the dance teams in the Tribal categories. In all categories, the Santo Niño typically wears miniature versions of the costumes worn by the dancers. There is no group choreography, about which the official rules on the festival Web site are quite explicit: "All participating tribal groups must adhere to the age-old tradition that made Kalibo Ati-Atihan famous—Dance Steps and Drumbeat must be Kalibo's original and not copied from the other festivities. Choreographed dancing is not allowed" (Kalibo Ati-atihan 2013). Another requirement is that "Exposed faces and parts of the body of participants must be covered with black soot *(buling)* using painting material." In addition, lest dancers or anyone present forget the religious dimension of the festival, the rules also require that when presenting before the judges, "Each group must, from time to time, chant or shout-in joy, triumph, and unison 'VIVA KAY SEÑOR STO. NIÑO!' to boost the spirituality of the festival. Failure to chant or shout in all corners of the street will be a point deduction on *[sic]* participating group of the Ati-Atihan contest." That there are penalties for failing to "boost the spirituality of the festival" is noteworthy; even while undertaking competitive dance routine, when the largely youthful groups of dancers might well be thinking more about winning or looking good in front of their friends and family members than about praising the Santo Niño, they are required to call forth his presence. As we shall see in the next chapter, it is not unusual for choreographed, competitive street-dance routines associated with festivals elsewhere in the country to incorporate such rules because adherence to these formal features is often the only thing that distinguishes the dancing of one group from another.

The streets are packed on Saturday morning for the dance competition as groups wend their way through the complete parade circuit, ultimately presenting themselves in front of judges in Pastrana Park. The best views are along the street, and this is the only time when the physical boundaries between spectators and dancers are enforced, though sometimes with limited success. Forty percent of the judging mark is devoted to costuming, with points awarded for design, craftsmanship, and use of materials, and an additional 20 percent is awarded for endurance, which includes "enthusiasm and liveliness." Discipline and rhythm equally compose the remaining 40 percent; with no marks given for choreography as apart from the movement of dance lines that break apart as in marching band formations, it is the *sad-sad* and not choreography that activates the costumes. A typical costume for the Balik-Ati and Tribal groups consists of a large headpiece, which for the former group includes extensions made of reeds or natural plant fibers, and for the latter is made of thin but sturdy plastic tubing. Additional costuming pieces may include a breastplate that fits over the shoulders and extends along the front and back of the dancer adorned with hand-painted designs, shiny or brightly colored objects, or pieces of plastic, and with extensions that expand its size and shape. Skirts or lower garments often follow the same basic principle and design aesthetic, and matching leggings typically complete the ensemble. The foundational architecture of the costume with its multiple layers and attachments greatly extends and exaggerates the dancer's movements. Because the bodies and faces of dancers are jet black and their costumes more completely envelop the human form, it is sometimes difficult to determine whether the dancers are coming or going. Viewing some of the larger groups of fifty or more participants is almost trance-inducing as they break into dance lines and weave around and through groups of other dancers, generating the impression of a massive, swaying, living single organism moving in ways the eyes cannot fully take in and the brain cannot anticipate.

By Saturday afternoon, the competitive groups are joined in the streets by a colorful and eclectic mix of individual costumed participants, devotees of the Santo Niño with personalized effigies, and smaller groups of dancers, many sporting wildly elaborate and fanciful themed costumes. The Papag Blues group has for many years had a significant presence on the streets, providing New Orleans-style jazz accompaniment for Tay Augus, who danced through the streets in elaborate Folies Bergère-style costuming until his death at age eighty-two (Alcedo 2007). Danilo Gonzales, a senior participant who has been coming to Ati-atihan since the 1980s, continues this tradition of elaborate cross-dressing, creating an

Figure 6. Dancers are sometimes barely visible beneath their elaborate costumes. Pangawasan Group (Tribal Category), Ati-atihan 2010, Kalibo, Aklan. Photo by author.

original costume every year that bears more than a passing resemblance to those worn by the famously leggy Rockettes at New York's Radio City Music Hall. Yet Gonzales (2010) pulls it off with great chutzpah and style, noting that his costume must be new each year because, as he puts it, "that's my pledge to Jesus the Christ." On Saturday many are carrying Santo Niños dressed in costumes that match their own, holding them aloft as they process and dance through the streets. A handsome man in black body paint handles a live snake, while a local *bakla* in a massive, fanciful butterfly costume sashays through the streets, stopping every few meters for a photo opportunity with participants who rush into the streets to pose with her. The effects of heat, dehydration, lack of sleep, and for a not inconsequential number, excess alcohol consumption mean that making it through Saturday can feel like a feat of endurance. By Saturday afternoon, the loose boundaries between those on the streets and those watching becomes increasingly porous, as more and more people are compelled to come down to the street from balconies, raised positions, and the sidewalk to physically connect with dance groups and those engaged in a wide range of idiosyncratic expressions of devotion to the Santo Niño.

Enter the Santo Niño

On Sunday the Santo Niño takes center stage everywhere, and the wild, at times untamed spirit that has been likened to Mardi Gras is fused with the veneration of the Santo Niño. But it is more than worship; on this day the Santo Niño not only compels one to dance, but pushes one beyond the limits of physical exhaustion, all done for his sake and with his help. For the faithful and the sober, the day starts at 6:30 a.m. as thousands gather in the Pastrana Park as the sacred carved effigy of the Santo Niño emerges on a *karo* from the cathedral and into the square for an outdoor morning mass. Following the sermon and communion, and as the Santo Niño returns to the cathedral, a hush descends over the square. This moment and what follows immediately afterward is for me and for other participants why we get out of bed on Sunday morning, exhausted and spent, and make our way into this square. In this sacred moment, which seems to linger as it opens up a connection with the cosmos, to something greater than the "I" or the collective "we," the dance groups and bands formerly scattered all around the square, clumped together with their headpieces, costumes, props, and instruments, all rise together from the earth, transforming themselves from ordinary human beings into a grand collective organism of swaying, pulsating life, color, and movement, activated by the crescendo of the drums of dozens of bands. I have spent much time and energy seeking to understand this moment and having my response to this and similar moments interrogated by others. I believe that the power of such moments is not in the display and the reveal, or what I call the "Leni Riefenstahl moment" when, as in her infamous Nazi propaganda film, *Triumph of the Will,* the spectacle unfolds into a massive, gorgeous totalitarian display that short-circuits the mind and overwhelms the emotions; rather this is the time it takes for life to be created anew, the coming-into-beingness of these dispersed groups, and as they come to life they retain their singularity as groups, even as they form a collective whole of which you too are a part. This is a moment that is empty and full at the same time; empty in that it starts with silence and a gentle rustling of costumes being slipped onto bodies, but full in that it is the collective potential of all present, connecting with the same life force, activated by the beat of the drums, calling us forth back into life. It is the moment when every year for me time opens up and stops, when my body falls into another state of being, and where in its suspendedness, I exist outside myself and, possibly as Levinas famously termed it, also "being for the Other" (1969, 304). This state, far from negating the "I," is the very thing that calls the "I" into being; further, it is while in this state that we enter into that point of transcendence where we experience that which "can not be encompassed," where the other, as that which has "signification prior to my initiative, resembles God" (293).

The Greeks had a dual concept of time capable of holding on to this moment and recognizing it, marking it as separate from *chronos,* or chronological time that can be measured. They conceptualized the time when something happens, when one is processing an experience and while inside this moment, as *kairos,* literally the space between time (Agamben 2002, 6). Giorgio Agamben sets out the relationship between the two from the ancient text, the *Corpus Hippocraticum:* "the *chronos* is where we have *kairos* and the *kairos* is where we have a little *chronos*" (ibid.). Thus there is no possibility of time opening up without it existing in chronological time, while chronological time requires the possibility of the space between time in order to have meaning and even existence. Christian theologians going back to Saint Augustine built on this double understanding of time, positioning *chronos* as illusion and real time as being the time of soul, measured by entering into messianic time. Philosopher Jürgen Mittelstrass observes that for Saint Augustine, the "founder of the anthropological concept of time," it "was not a property of the world but a property of the soul. Time, understood as *lasting presence,* is not 'measured' by motions in the world or in nature, but is 'measured' by the *soul*" (Mittelstrass 2001, 25). Agamben argues that this time, which he calls "messianic time," is "*the time it takes for time to come to an end, to accomplish itself.* Or, more exactly the time we need in order to accomplish, to bring to an end our representation of time" (Agamben 2002, 5). Thus the time that we seize within the larger framework of messianic time is the time that matters:

> While our representation of chronological time, or the time *in* which we are, separates, divides us from ourselves, and makes us the powerless spectators of ourselves, observing without time the time that runs away from us, messianic time, or operational time, in which we grasp and accomplish, is the time that we *are,* and for that reason, the only real time, the only time that we *have.* (Agamben 2002, 5)

If chronological time is "the time that runs away from us," the time over which we have no control, then those moments in which "we grasp and accomplish," those moments of "operational time" are the only real time we have. What I have endeavored to demonstrate here is not that what happens in this moment at Ati-atihan for me or for anyone else is bounded by Greek philosophy or a Catholic theology of messianic time, but rather to suggest that this experience, one that has been described in its external features and considered phenomenologically and as a condition of flow, is remarkably consistent with these theological understandings of time. Does this make moments such as this at Ati-atihan a "holy" experience?

I am suggesting that whether one is a devotee of the Santo Niño or not, this operational mode of time, where it opens up and there exists a sense of being in and outside, is consistent with what is for many at the heart of the religious experience.

The Santo Niño enters into this experience of time and place and stands beside and with one's self on Sunday afternoon and evening, as thousands move through the streets dancing and around *karos* bearing carved images of the Holy Child. My observations here build on Julius Bautista's framework, which responds to "the question of who Filipinos *say* the Santo Niño is" (Bautista 2010, 207). Sunday is the culmination of a process that for many began months earlier, as bands started to rehearse and hundreds of elaborate costumes in the competitive groups came to be designed and constructed. And as some informants have observed, the process never really ends inasmuch as the *sad-sad* is always present in the body, waiting for the beat to activate it. After days or even a week of drumming, dancing, sleep deprivation, and, for some, excess alcohol consumption, at the conclusion of mass on Sunday one might well retire back to bed to prepare for the new week. However, this is not what happens, because although the Santo Niño has been much present through the week's activities, he has not yet been made fully manifest. Almost unbelievably, as life staggers to its feet again at the conclusion of Mass early Sunday morning, the party would appear to begin anew as riotous dancing and drumming again spills out onto the streets from Pastrana Park. But by early afternoon the party ends as the square and the area surrounding it become packed with dozens of *karos* bearing effigies of the iconic, white-faced Santo Niño, most belonging to extended families. Typically festooned with fresh flowers, these structures, pushed and pulled through the streets by friends and family members, resemble the tops of elaborate wedding cakes, with steps and platforms guiding the eye upward to the crowning glory of the *karo*, the individualized, sacred effigy of the Santo Niño that has been taken from its position on altars in family homes where it lives 364 days a year.

That these Santo Niños are so profoundly individuated is a reflection of the relationship that Catholics in this part of the Philippines have with this particular manifestation of Christ. The Santo Niño functions as a kind of personal patron saint, though this is of course a theological impossibility (see Bautista 2010, 123–124). Although Our Lady of Guadalupe and Saint John the Baptist are the respective official patron saints of Cebu City and Kalibo, neither would seem to offer the same possibilities for a personal relationship between believers and the deity provided by the Santo Niño. Not only did Christianity come to the Philippines in the form of the Santo Niño, but it is believed that he was chosen by Rajah Humabon's wife at the time of her conversion:

> Contemporary accounts of the Queen of Cebu's Baptism in 1521 narrate that she was presented with three figures: the Virgin Mary, a crucifix, and the Santo Niño. Her choice of the latter is said to establish that the "Filipino love of Children" was the means by which the figure itself gained acceptance among Cebuanos—that the adoption of a foreign doctrine was made possible, even easy, because it was foregrounded by the pervasiveness of kinship. (Bautista 2010, 134)

Thus the Santo Niño, a repository of pre-Christian values and the symbol of the "civilizing" heart of Cebu, is everywhere in the Visayas region, of which Kalibo is part. He lives on the private altars in family homes, but is equally on display in public places and businesses. As Bautista observes, "veneration is enacted in thinking of the Santo Niño as a kind of alter ego, a comrade in earthly hardship instead of a divine ruler or provider" (41).

The belief that the Santo Niño is in it with you, that he is copresent for your life and there to take on your burdens and suffering as you share your heart with him, is reflected in the iconography of individualized niños who, in the context of Ati-atihan, are often dressed in the same clothing as the individual who bears the statue of the Santo Niño in public on the final Saturday and Sunday of the festival. At this time the public space is full of cheery niños, carried by devotees as their own powerful, personal effigy, and as the mascots of dance contingents, where as previously noted, he typically precedes the group, dressed in a miniature version of their often elaborate costumes. When dancing with the Santo Niño, he is held aloft, swaying with the dancers. He is there an extension of the self: "The Santo Niño as alter ego does more than symbolize a divinity that is readily accessible to its devotees. It also symbolizes the humanization of the divine, variously interpreted in line with the concept of *pakikisama* (fellowship, or camaraderie)" (43).[9] In a similar vein, Resil Mojares observes that the "idiosyncratic, localized, and personified" nature of religious icons in the Philippines, "take on 'a life of their own' apart from what may be the original or intended meaning, fostering tensions between the idol, as the iconic image of some immaterial original, and the insistent materiality of the fetish" (Mojares 2002, 151). The display of the Santo Niño in this way does not lessen his power by making him more human, but rather invites his presence and his direct labor and intercession:

> The Santo Niño's inclusion within a concept of social camaraderie *(makisama)* is here not seen as an erosion of its divine status and powerfulness *(maykapal)*. While it is present in people's common struggle, its devotees are still very much aware of its capacity to free them from the

> hardship and toil of making a living. The Santo Niño's alter ego-ness, then, is not a desire to co-opt its labor power as such. Displaying it as one's alter ego, rather, is understood as a way of petitioning its intervention, inviting it to "take pity upon them" by sharing the experience of their hardship and struggle. (Bautista 2010, 43)

Here the Santo Niño takes on a function beyond that of the "Best Friend Christ" or *Kaibigan* Christ present in the Manila Mobile Theatre's *sinakulo.* He is not merely someone you would follow or put your faith, hope, and trust in, he is vitally, fundamentally, even physically connected to those who parade and dance with him. Aches, pains, and even more serious ailments can be cured by the women administering a massage (*pahilot* in local dialect) using small plaster casts of the Santo Niño in an area set aside for such a purpose next to the Kalibo Cathedral. The Santo Niño is in every way there for you while also serving as an extension of you.

It is believed that one cannot tire while dancing in praise of the Santo Niño. And for many years I have put this to the test along with thousands of others who dance along with the *karos* of the Santo Niños winding through the streets of Kalibo, following the same expanded parade route occupied by dancers on Friday and Saturday. This is a significant durational event that starts around 4:00 p.m. and continues until the last *karo* loops around the town and returns to a spot directly in front of the church, generally around 9:00 p.m. Thus many dance with the *karo* for up to five hours without a break. Many *karos* are accompanied by bands hired by the family or sponsor of the *karo,* and thus the same percussive *sad-sad* that provided the beat for the street dancers on the previous days provides the heartbeat for the final procession through the streets on Sunday. As the sun sets, *karos* are illuminated by homemade lighting systems, many powered by gasoline engines, the sound of which is completely overwhelmed by that of the bands.

On Sunday I dance with my adopted family and, as with so many of my experiences in the Philippines, the initial connection with them came through the process I identified in the introduction as "natural selection," in which I was selected by them on the basis of a kind of mutual self-recognition. In my first year with them, I danced through the streets for five hours wearing rubber flip-flops, surely the worst possible shoes for lengthy periods of street dancing. Yet the next morning, just as I had been told, I had no aches or pains and oddly enough, not so much as even redness where my toes had been so tenuously connected to a rubber sole—something that was difficult not to attribute to the protection of the Santo Niño. More than this minor miracle, what compelled me to return the following year was the experience of timelessness, being with the group and apart from it, a sensation I felt ever more strongly the following year when I threw myself into the spirit of the dance with greater abandonment, dancing with family members and strangers who fell in and out in front of our *karo*. The memory that year is of one smooth, seamless flow, in which I fully surrendered to Csikszentmihalyi's final two states, where the boundaries between self and others seemed to be erased and where time was both compressed and boundless.

On my first visit to Ati-atihan in 2009, I met with Benny Tirazona, one of the festival organizers, a native Kalibonian with a long personal connection to the event. When I asked why he returned every year like so many others, he related the following story:

> In the Marcos years I was then a political detainee . . . because I was then a leftist. When I was detained at the local military outpost is the time that I prayed . . . [to] . . . a Christian God. I said to him that "if you exist then let me be released before the Ati-atihan." And I was released . . . [on the] . . . Friday [before Ati-atihan]. I was the only one in Aklan released. The funny thing is . . . in my arrest paper I was included in the list of priests and pastors which I am not [*he laughs*]. On the list of Panay and Negros leftist fathers and pastors, I was included as number seven. There were six of them. So I was released on Friday and said my vow has begun. Because I think maybe God really exists and I made a vow that every year—I was then working in Manila—that every year I would go home to participate in the Santo Niño and the *sad-sad*. Because of office problems in Manila I was not able to go home in 1977. I met with an accident after that, my foot was broken, I had to be hospitalized for six months in the orthopedic hospital and then stayed out of work for more than one year. So here I am in the Ati-atihan office because of that vow. (Tirazona 2009b)

Tirazona's compelling story, set against the backdrop of the political repression of the Marcos years, reflects the core belief held by virtually everyone whose participation is grounded in *panata;* whereas the Santo Niño protects, preserves, and can respond to one's prayers, failing to honor him in the context of Ati-atihan is to lose the benefits of his power.

My experience suggests that *panata* is deepened and rewarded by the act of street dancing and that moment of silent communion shared with thousands of others, a sensation that is extraordinary and that imprints deeply on the body, emplacing one in the time and space of Ati-atihan—emplaced in Kalibo—long after the event. My body tells me that once Ati-atihan is in the body, it remains there for life. And the power of this embodied state is not just in its coming-to-life in place, in the body, and in and through time, but also that it can be reconstructed in and through the body later. These experiences that we put back together through the complex process of memory imprint both in place and body. As Edward Casey observes of body and place memory:

> Here the pivotal phenomenon is place memory, that is, the fact that concrete places retain the past in a way that can be reanimated by our remembering them: a powerful but often neglected form of memory. Body memories are not just memories *of* the body but instances of remembering places, events, and people *with* and *in* the lived body. In commemoration, body and place memory conspires with co-participating other in ritualized scenes of co-remembering. (Casey 2000, 11–12)

The memory of the Ati-atihan experience on the final Sunday imprints on my body but is also carried by my body, living on through it, compelling me to return. Thus, even on a cold, wet autumn day in Leiden, the Netherlands, as I write these words my body is on the other side of the world in Pastrana Square with thousands of souls on a hot summer morning as we stagger back to life, floating somewhere between body and place, between memory and infinity.

CHAPTER 6

Street Dance and a Bayan-*Centered Framework*

Street dancing, a theatricalized form of dance executed on the streets or in a public square in line formation with up to one hundred dancers, is the largest single mass-participation performance phenomenon in the Philippines.[1] Virtually all civic, regional, and religious festivals incorporate street dancing in teams or groups organized within a particular *barangay* or municipality, displaying features of their cultural heritage through a signature "local" dance tradition. This chapter considers street dancing at large festivals, using as a case study the Aliwan Fiesta,[2] a mega-event that brings winning dance groups from regional festivals to Manila to compete for prizes in what has emerged as the mother of all street dancing competitions nationally. The festivals that feed into this singular event are beyond counting,[3] insofar as virtually all medium-size municipalities in the country offer festivals or fiestas that feature street dancing. This chapter will contextualize the practice of street dancing, particularly as it emerged from a longer tradition of dance at religious festivals, before proceeding to an account of what the Aliwan Fiesta experience looks and feels like for the spectator, while also describing the features of a winning dance routine.

Because competitive dance teams rely on the largesse and financial support of local businesses or politicians, street dancing is also a mode of cultural production circumscribed by local and national politics. For local business leaders and provincial government officials, street dance from their regional festivals reflects a local identity and expresses it externally for purposes of drawing tourists to these events, and also as a source of pride-in-place for those who participate. This final layer has led to the increasing spectacularization of dance, whereby the relationship of this spectacle to actual local practices, both in the present and the past, has been subject to a disconnect. The way in which dance has been disseminated, taught, and inscribed on local bodies has made the form especially subject to appropriation by local elites and the center, where dance is in the service of *bayan* writ large, where it designates the larger frame of what it means to be Filipino, refracted through the lens of national cultural elites and perpetuated through the national cultural infrastructure. The chapter concludes with a consideration of the ways in which key dance forms, variously emplaced locally, nationally, internationally, and transnationally by Filipinos in the diaspora can be situated in a *bayan*-centered framework where the boundaries of *bayan*, differently constituted, expand, contract, and overlap.

Festival Dance

Dance as part of festivals in the Philippines has a long history, one reflected in what John Phelan (1959) termed the "fiesta system,"[4] a mode of political and social control that the Spanish successfully used in Central America (Smith 1977).[5] While in the Philippines as elsewhere the rhythms of agrarian life no doubt created long periods in which individuals could come together to trade, feast, and celebrate long before the arrival of the Spanish, Phelan's point is not that the Spanish brought performance to the Philippines, but rather that the construction of a local church, typically bounding a large, public space, created both an institutional reason for people to gather together through religious rituals and a space in which to enact larger public celebrations. The Spanish friars, Phelan asserts, were quick to incorporate song and dance into Christian festivals, and indeed, he argues that performance was a key inducement not only to participate in these events, but was part of the successful strategy in bringing a dispersed rural population under the control of Catholic religious orders as villagers were brought into the aural range of the church bells:

> The fiesta system and the founding of sodalities, on the other hand, reached out to embrace the whole scattered population of the parish. Although the majority of Filipinos preferred to live near their rice fields, they could be lured periodically into the *cabecera* village. The enticement was the fiesta. There were three fiestas of consequence to the Filipinos, namely, Holy Week, Corpus Christi, and the feast in honor of the patron saint of the locality. The parishioners flocked to the *cabecera* villages for these occasions. Not only did the fiestas provide a splendid opportunity to indoctrinate Filipinos by the performance of religious rituals, but they also afforded the participants a welcome holiday from the drudgery of toil. (Phelan 1959, 73)

Religious festivals today typically offer a range of performance activities, including processions, dance, music, theatrical presentations, elaborate floats and effigies of saints, and even beauty pageants. In Doreen Fernandez's inquiry into Philippine theatre history, the title of her work incorporates the Tagalog word *palabas*, a word that, like *bayan*, has an expandable meaning:

> *Palabas* indeed it all is—performance, show, entertainment, fun. *Palabas*—outward—it also is: people-based and community-oriented, whether it be school play or fiesta spectacle or protest theater. . . . All of it comes from a people to whom performing is part of living. (Fernandez 1996, viii)

Palabas in a literal sense conveys not only "to show" but also "to bring out" (Balance 2008, 97), suggesting that *palabas* is about extending outward that which is internal, mirroring the process of seeking to externalize *(sa labas)* that which is felt internally *(sa loób)*.

Fernandez mined Spanish-language sources for accounts of the earliest theatrical activities in colonial Philippines, finding considerable evidence in the historical record that events then already had much in common with contemporary festivals in terms of structure, content, and even political organization. One noteworthy early fiesta, held on June 20–21, 1611, was associated with the beatification of Saint Ignatius Loyola and featured "artillery salutes, fireworks, the pealing of bells, poetic jousts, processions," as well as a group of students from the parish of San Miguel presenting a "brief colloquy in the Tagalog language." There, events were interspersed with three dances described as follows:

> [O]ne with the dancers dressed in Spanish costume; the second dance done in the native manner, with lance and shield; and a third which showed the maimed, the halt, and the blind staggering and falling over on another, then falling on their knees and asking the *beato* to cure them, and when cured leaped to their feet to "perform a Tagalog sword dance with great skill and agility." (Fernandez 1996, 52)

The literary contest associated with the feast was judged by a panel that included the lieutenant general of the Moluccas (then under Dutch control), the vicar general of the Manila Archdiocese, the chief of staff of the armed forces, and a papal official (ibid.). Like contemporary religious festivals, this event was organized around the veneration of a particular saint. It included a range of ancillary activities such as fireworks and processions that involved or were seen by the general public, and it featured a competitive event that was overseen and judged by the highest governing authorities of the day, which in the seventeenth century were religious and military leaders. That the dance presentation involved not one but three representative types of dance is significant: the first was presumably a re-creation of a Spanish folk dance; the second showed the "native" as a hunter or warrior executing moves that were immediately recognizable to the viewer; and the third showed the power of the Christian faith by depicting a cure at the hands of a Christian *beato* or "blessed one." The native is not merely restored to health, but he leaps up to execute a sword dance with "great skill and agility." This kind of mimetic representation of story through dance is one of the key elements of street dancing routines presented competitively at festivals today, as we shall see later. The way in which these three dances mirror three of the five foundational suites in the Bayanihan program ("Maria Clara Suite," "Cordillera Suite," "Tribal Suite") is also striking.

That these early Catholic festivals incorporated not just dance, but a range of other performance events is also documented. Another festival in Manila just a few years later in 1619 carried out Pope Urban III's official decree "authorising public celebration of the Feast of the Immaculate Conception," resulting in a fifteen-day celebration featuring fireworks, bullfights, masquerades, song, dramatic presentations as well as a procession described in a contemporary Spanish account as "remarkable enough to have appeared in Madrid" (Fernandez 1996, 53). Inasmuch as Manila was little more than a village at the time and Madrid was the wealthy capital city of one of the world's foremost maritime powers with a population in excess of 60,000 (Ringrose 1973, 761), this is high praise indeed, and the language used is typical of many Spanish accounts, which points to surprise at the quality of these feasts compared to their own frame of reference, but also speaks to the enthusiasm with which Filipinos embraced these events. Given that by this point in history these chroniclers had comparative points of reference in the Americas, their observations have additional merit.

While today religious festivals provide the model for fiestas all over the Philippines, many of the larger regional festivals today are not religious in orientation. With the push toward the development of cultural tourism that took off during the Marcos era, regions without unique Church-based fiestas have created festivals that focus on signature traditions or features of the region that are offered up for consumption or as distinctive markers of a local identity or pride-in-place,[6] whereas those from areas with a strong Muslim heritage place culture rather than religion on display. Tiongson identified four generic categories of festivals based on their historic-cultural origins: (a) the animistic; (b) the Muslim; (c) the Christian; and (d) the secular (Tiongson 2003, 165). While these categories still largely hold, I offer the following expanded list of categories, based on my own observations and Susan Isorena-Arcega's (2012) breakdown of Aliwan Fiesta participants, although it bears noting that some festivals cross categories:

1. Festivals celebrating indigenous culture or that are connected with displaying or enacting pre-Christian myths or historical legends, including those that celebrate harvests of the land or sea;

2. Religious festivals, most of which are devoted to a local patron saint or a deity such as the Santo Niño (the Holy Child) who in parts of the Philippines functions virtually as a patron saint;
3. Festivals from the south of the country that celebrate aspects of Muslim culture and history, or those that celebrate interfaith and intercultural cooperation and mutual respect;
4. Festivals of a more recent origin that promote municipalities or regions, including: (a) those associated with a city's "Foundation Day," typically dating from the American colonial period; (b) those associated with the development of tourism that champion the products associated with a particular region (e.g., flowers, fish, crabs, woven mats, mangoes); and (c) those that extend from local government priorities such as developing adventure tourism or promoting environmental sustainability.

Most informed observers believe that the contemporary practice of street dancing emerged with many of its key characteristics first at the Ati-atihan Festival (Jardin 2010; Isorena-Arcega 2012). Marketed in the 1960s as "The Mardi Gras of the Philippines," Ati-atihan came to be seen as a driver of tourism, and in other cities and provinces the political and business elite came to see festivals as having the potential to deliver economic benefits. Other festivals soon took on some of the external trappings of Ati-atihan, including increasingly exotic Carnival- and Mardi Gras-style costuming that was fused with local practices, much as Bayanihan had done with their principle of "enhancement," along with the use of mobile marching bands to accompany dancers as they moved through the streets and danced in formation.

Because dance has been a compulsory physical education subject in the national curriculum since the 1950s, the majority of the population alive today would have had both instruction and experience in dancing in groups, while dance has long been a popular extracurricular activity as well. Winning dance teams are a source of great pride to a school and to the region from which they hail. Informants working in the performing arts who grew up in the 1960s and 1970s recall the importance of dance from their earliest days of elementary school. Nestor Jardin, former president of the Cultural Centre of the Philippines, remembers dancing as a six-year-old in a "field demonstration," held in the open area typically found in front of most schools throughout the country (Jardin 2010). Alex Cortez, a prominent theatre director and choreographer based in Manila, has similar memories of what is generally called "Field Day," which involved dancing on a designated day, often in the latter part of the school year during the hot, dry season, before the school's principal, assembled teachers, and top bureaucrats from the regional offices of the Department of Education (Cortez 2010). It is important, however, not to romanticize street dancing or to suggest that participation in this form of dance, especially at school where it is a compulsory part of the curriculum, is universally loved and embraced by all. As Cortez observes, the experience has a martial quality to it, as students start rehearsing in the last part of the school year "from day one." He notes that "every morning they will have this little exercise. And the next day they will have additional things to do and so on and so forth," while throughout "they know that this is what they're going to do for the contest." When the routine is eventually presented in the open yard in front of the school it is preceded by the dignitaries speaking of "your contribution to the growth of Philippine tourism and culture," words that he remembers as seeming "meaningless." He speculates that for the leaders watching the performance, "it's really the satisfaction of the higher authorities watching young kids perform in harmony and with energy and gusto." For him, the form in which most young people first experience this kind of dance is "really a self-aggrandizement or a self-adoration," reflecting a "very selfish motive among the leaders." Other informants over thirty years of age remember this kind of enforced participation in a group activity as something they failed to master and did not enjoy.

Around the time Ferdinand Marcos declared martial law in 1972, street dancing throughout the country became more organized, emerging as an increasingly prominent cultural phenomenon that was frequently used to serve the ends of the state. First Lady Imelda Marcos took a strong personal interest in the arts, and though her legacy is sometimes seen as that of creating and leaving behind an expensive and arguably unnecessary physical, Manila-centered infrastructure for the arts designed for international high culture, she was also influential in bringing amateur groups of regional folk dancers into the national spotlight. National Dance Artist[7] Leonor Orosa-Goquingco suggests that the First Lady was the key player in the process of using dance to express pride in nation:

> Dance is the most ephemeral of the arts, and as of this moment, only a Fairy Godmother—perhaps in the person of the First Lady of the Arts in the Philippines, Madame Imelda Romualdez Marcos—could keep it, in all its many ramifications, projections, and reflection, vibrant and alive in the Philippine scene. (Goquingco 1980, 234)

Identifying and supporting regional diversity through dance was a strategy adopted in building a tourism industry; groups came up to Manila to perform at the Folk Arts Theatre or the Nayong Pilipino, a cultural village showcasing six of the country's regional cultures, with some groups also appearing on national television. Mrs. Marcos was famous for having students "lining up the streets to welcome dignitaries" (Cortez 2010) and, indeed, the way she mobilized vast numbers of children and adults for these displays of quasi-totalitarian state adulation provides fodder for an entire field of public performance that is yet to be fully analyzed.[8] Responses from my interviews with older informants at multiple sites throughout the country are virtually all in agreement that during the 1970s street dancing began to assume much greater prominence both in the country's regions and also nationally.

The legacy of the national tourism infrastructure created during the Marcos years has meant that many of these festivals, and in particular the core activity of street dancing, share key features. Competition dancers are typically young, generally students at a local middle school or high school, or a collectivity based on their *barangay*. The shape and form of their costumes often include elaborate headpieces that extend the human body into space, while the architectural spines that provide the foundation for these costume extensions are typically flexible, and thus move and sway with the dancer's body, magnifying the effect of relatively small bodily movements. Top choreographers who have coached prize-winning groups move around the country and offer their services to the groups who can afford their fees, and the competition judges of the larger festivals also circulate nationally, creating a dense network of artists and judges, many of whom themselves are former dancers. Over the past few decades, these factors have contributed to the formation of uniform models for creating and judging this form of dance presentation that come together nationally at the Aliwan Fiesta.

The final element that set the stage for a national practice of street dancing and a corresponding national festival has been the increasing spectacularization of street dance since the early 1980s at two key regional festivals, Cebu City's Sinulog and Iloilo's Dinagyang. Both festivals, like the older Ati-atihan, are devoted to the veneration of the Santo Niño, and also pay indirect homage to the indigenous Ati by having dancers blacken their bodies. Unlike the latter, however, where everyone present, regardless of whether or not they are attached to groups, dances seemingly endlessly through the streets of the town for days, the festival centerpiece at Sinulog and Dinagyang is a theatricalized dance presentation that functions primarily as a spectator event. These presentations of elaborate dance routines, typically five to six minutes in length,[9] feature as many as one hundred dancers in colorful, neoethnic costumes, hundreds of constantly shifting handheld props, and enormous mobile scenic elements that are more abundant and massive than one would find in a typical Broadway musical. In many respects, the movable scenery, pushed through the streets by the dancers and moved in and out of position with drill-team precision, is as much a star of the show as the costumes and the dancers themselves.[10] This relatively recent practice of theatricalized street dance is the basis for the national dance competition at Aliwan, where participating groups ship set pieces to Manila by truck and boat from all over the Philippines, providing ingenious, massive, movable stages that work in tandem with the choreography in ways that are inventive, low-tech, and unique globally. The ability of sets and costumes to rapidly transform is a key feature in the routines, adding greatly to the delight the audience experiences while watching dancers in their competitive segments, as we shall see below.

Dance at Aliwan 2013

Sponsored by the Manila Broadcasting Corporation, the Cultural Center of the Philippines, and the cities of Manila and Pasay, as well as a raft of corporate sponsors, since 2003 the Aliwan Fiesta has provided a showcase for winning street-dance troupes from regional and local fiestas around the country to compete for prizes at the national level. Spread out over three nights from Thursday through Saturday, the festival includes song and dance acts by well-known singers and pop stars, comedy acts, competitive games with built-in audience participation, a procession of floats and street dancers through the streets of Manila, the sale of locally produced crafts from participating regions, and a Reyna (Queen) Aliwan or "Miss Aliwan" Beauty Pageant held on Thursday and Friday nights. The street-dance competition typically starts late in the afternoon on Saturday, staged frontally before an audience viewing it from a fixed position, and beauty contest winners are announced along with the results of the dance competition on Saturday night in front of the Aliw Theatre in the Star City Complex at the Cultural Center of the Philippines, capped off by a spectacular fireworks display. This excess of activities, and the fact that participating in all of them over three days would challenge the endurance of even the fittest individual, is a characteristic shared with festivals around the country. Though festivals may be famous for a singular event (e.g., the street-dance routines at Sinulog or Dinagyang), they are never fully defined by any one thing. Participants are fully expected to throw themselves into as many festival activities as possible, and exhaustion is often part of the shared experience. In festival events that are religious in nature, excess and exhaustion are part of the devotional act of the participation, as we saw with Ati-atihan in the previous chapter. The following description, based on fieldwork conducted in 2013,[11] focuses largely on the Aliwan street dancing competition though ancillary events are also touched upon.

The featured event, the Saturday dance competition, began at 4:00 p.m. and was staged in front of the massive Quirino Grandstand in Rizal Park, which seats up to ten thousand people. Because of the two-dimensional nature of the dance presentation and the massive set pieces used, there is only a small optimal viewing area where spectators can witness the staging to its fullest advantage. Given that the best seats and standing positions in this central section are occupied by the emcees of the event as well as judges, dignitaries, sponsors, and photographers with passes, for most people in the grandstands viewing the presentation at an angle rather than full-on, the visual experience is less than ideal. Just as in French neoclassical theatre, where the king occupied the ideal viewing position, seated centrally at about the same remove from the stage as the stage was deep, here the panel of eight judges occupies a corresponding position. A larger, secondary audience exists for the event on television, where a two-hour version of the highlights of the competition is later broadcast to television audiences around the country through local stations. More recently, additional audiences see the routines of local and winning contingents through the endlessly proliferating videos posted on YouTube and embedded in the many personal blogs that feature dance.

Each dance number is preceded by an impressive logistical and choreographic feat as up to one hundred dancers wheel in a staggering array of scenic elements and in a matter of minutes transform an empty street into an elaborate theatrical space in which colorful costumes, props, and scenic elements come together to form an impressive visual tableau. Groups include not just dancers and technical crew but also mobile bands with up to sixty musicians, generally young men and boys playing loud percussive instruments dominated by the beat of bass or kettledrums. Dance groups are judged on the basis of four criteria: (1) theme/concept, which includes relevance and its connection to local culture (35 percent); (2) choreography, which focuses on successful transitions and movement patterns in large formation (20 percent); (3) performance, which includes precision in execution and energy level (30 percent); and (4) effective use of costume and props (15 percent).[12] Ballet dancer and Aliwan judge Lisa Macuja-Elizalde describes her evaluative process:

> I look at the execution, their alignment, formation and precise techniques. I look at the choreography against the theme they submit—concept versus execution. I check the way they structure the dance, how unique their moves are . . . how they synch the music with movement. There is also the personality factor—the appeal of the dancers. It's so different when you see them smiling and "*ganado*" [very enthusiastic] with what they're doing . . . they have to be enjoying themselves. (Macuja-Elizalde 2012)

In spite of the searing heat coming up from the street and the hours of waiting in the midday sun while wearing massive headpieces and heatstroke-inducing costumes, when they are presenting, the dancers are uniformly smiling, energetic, and appear to be having a good time.

The 2013 Aliwan winner, the Tribu Panayanon group from Iloilo City National High School in the Visayas, had earlier in the year won the top prize at the Dinagyang Festival, one of the most competitive and best-funded of such events in the country. Because in all key respects their performance reflects the successful application of a formula that has come to govern this dance form, it is instructive to describe it here in detail. The storyline they used for the dance is based on a local legend in which a dragon-like creature known as *Bakunawa* rises from the ocean and is swallowed by the moon, which causes lunar eclipses to occur. Choreographed by Rommel Flogen, as the seven-minute work opens, a massive hand-painted visual tableau created by a series of flat screens covers the width of the central performance area. Depicted are scenes from pre-Spanish contact village life, including nipa huts, fields of rice, a male figure seated around a fire, women and children playing and gathering food, and a woman seated on a raised platform praying to what are presumably animist spirits. A drum volley on bass and snare drums makes the already attentive audience even more alert, and as a melodic flute line weaves through the heavily percussive base, two *bakla* performers in flowing white sequined gowns and large sparkling headdresses are carried in on the shoulders of men in colorful pseudo-tribal attire, their skin blackened by body paint, presumably meant to represent indigenous Ati.[13] The two elevated, extravagantly attired performers repeat a series of large circular gestural patterns with their arms, which, when accentuated by the size and flow of their gauzy sleeves, suggests a large white circle, presumably meant to represent the moon. A female villager in a brightly colored rural folk costume appears between the two "moons," displaying a statue of the Santo Niño, the spiritual heart of the Dinagyang Festival. The effigy wears a costume identical to the dancer's, and she thrusts the statue out toward the audience as she moves, much as a dance-team leader would when marching through the streets with a troupe at a festival.

As the dancers peel off to the sides and disappear behind the flats in the upstage position, a contingent of male dancers, nearly half of the total company of one hundred, emerge bare-chested and with their bodies blackened, clad in generic tribal attire. Wearing elaborate feathered headpieces that move and sway, G-strings covered by beadwork in orange and yellow, and leggings that draw attention to their leg movements, they execute a series of warlike gestures from the "upstage" area, burst forward in lines toward the audience, then carry out a rapid-fire series of arcs, crosses, and kicks with arms moving out and up or from side to side. More line dance than folk dance, the men are joined less than a minute into the sequence by blackfaced women in large purple skirts with orange, blue, and white petticoats. They move in and around the men, taking positions between each man in lines as they shift their bodies backward in a body roll and raise their arms above their heads, swaying from side to side. The men, now dancing with the women in a quick movement that would be unseen to most of the audience, pull from the waistband of the women's skirts, and, in just one of many moments of rapid transformation, they wrap the skirt in the opposite direction around their female partners, causing the color palate—dominated by the size of the women's skirts—to shift to green and yellow, hues that in turn link them to the painted village backdrop behind them. Suddenly, the legendary *Bakunawa* appears, a massive ten-meter-long sea monster with a huge head, snaking through the central playing area, driven by the human power of approximately twenty young men who control the massive internal infrastructure of the monster, a series of metal frames on wheels.[14]

The upstage backdrop suddenly parts and the tribal men stream out, now wearing bright, verdant green headdresses and two-dimensional forearm coverings in yellow and orange, the three dominant colors of the set behind them, suggesting their emergence from this pictorial representation of a tribal, pre-Christian world. The backside of their forearm covering bears a stylized blue and gray wave pattern, and as they leap forward and jump from side to side, moving jerkily like birds, these extensions take on the appearance of wings, allowing them to radically alter the audience's visual field by simply shifting their forearms in as a group from front to back, shifting rapidly between luminescent yellow-orange and blue-gray waves. Suddenly, appearing to fly in behind them is a row of seven *bakla* in flowing white costumes that race across the width of the playing area on wheeled platforms. A group of men with huge ceremonial spears of yellow and orange move in rapidly from the stage left position and as the first group of men run offstage, the *Bakunawa* weaves its way through the throng, joined by moving, raised platforms transporting the white-clad moon-*bakla,* one of whom is dramatically devoured by the monster as she appears to fly into its open mouth. A group of women moves into the assembled throng carrying pots shaped like large metallic gongs, and in unison they hit these massive props to a beat provided by the large stationary percussion section on the side of the central playing area. As in the local legend, the clamor of the banging of the pots causes the *Bakunawa* to spit out its victim, the moon, and she flies back onto a raised platform, reassuming the rounded pattern of movement seen earlier, suggesting that she has been returned to the sky.

As the monster and moon-*bakla* disappear stage right, a full contingent of tribal men moves out toward the audience, now wearing massive orange and yellow headdresses that add nearly two feet to their height, while carrying enormous drums. Joining the village women, the two formations merge and the men place their drums on the ground, dancing around the women as together they celebrate the defeat of the *Bakunawa*. The final obligatory reveal is of the Santo Niño, in whose honor the Dinagyang Festival is held. Suddenly about a dozen, four-foot tall, one-dimensional pictorial representations of the Santo Niño emerge from upstage while some of the tribal men, faces and bodies still blackened to represent the indigenous Ati and resplendent in their orange and yellow costumes and massive headpieces, step from behind this crowded stage of Niños. The men and their Niños quickly run off to the side as the backdrop parts, again revealing a large group of tribal men. They race toward the audience, high-kicking and raising their arms to the beat of the drum, while the *bakla* moon-maidens again reappear on the shoulders of the men, raising effigies of the Santo Niño aloft as a large float carrying more than two dozen little Niños and crowned by a much larger Niño, all clad in identical clothing, assumes the center-stage position. A giant one-dimensional painted Niño is raced into the forward position and in unison all dancers shout the traditional cry associated with this and other Santo Niño festivals, "Viva Santo Niño, Viva!" in a final display of exuberance and visual splendor. Then, in less than thirty seconds, approximately two hundred people, including dancers, scene movers, and musicians speed off to the audience's right in a tightly choreographed exit, leaving the street in front of the viewing area empty, ready for the next dance group. While many dance groups achieved a level of technical precision similar to this group, in addition to excelling in all of the formal judging elements, Tribu Panayanon evinced a near-manic intensity, and the spectacle created by the gigantic *Bakunawa* weaving its way across the playing area was unparalleled.

As this account suggests, street dancing is even further removed from actual folk dancing than Bayanihan's work. Fundamentally, it is less about actual dancing bodies and more about display and rapid transformation of all visual elements, from costuming and props to the overall mise-en-scène, all activated by human movement and labor and supported by clever design. When watching these routines online with the sound off, both dancers and set movers appear as if on some amphetamine-like drug, as scenic elements are raced and perfectly positioned into place, while dancers appear seemingly from nowhere, flapping their arms and fluttering their hands, activating visual transformations with costumes and headpieces that cause the overall color palate and visual field to shift many times per minute. The viewer is compelled to respond to the power of movement when it is

Figure 7. The movements of the giant sea monster or *Bakunawa* are integrated into the dance in the 2013 Aliwan winning entry of the Tribu Panayanon from Iloilo City. Photo by author.

amplified by the number of bodies onstage as, for instance, when dozens of dancers raise their arms in unison while swaying in the same direction. The set-up for each successive segment of the dance routine is effectively masked as the audience's gaze is continually drawn to large patterns of group movement and visual explosions created through shifting scenic elements, costume transformations, or by moving dancers up, down, and across the playing area on platforms. Choreography is largely executed in groups and lines, allowing for rapid shifts as an army of dancers suddenly parts or steps back, revealing another group that constitutes the new visual focus. Movable scenic elements along both the back and the sides of the playing area also serve to mask the exits and dramatically highlight the entrances of lines of dancers who may also enter the space at a diagonal.

This is complex, crowd-control choreography on a grand scale where even the slightest errors in timing could result in serious injuries to dancers and scene shifters. No one image lingers insofar as the pace is relentless while images communicating the basic storyline are thrown outward at the eyes of the viewer in a kaleidoscopic fashion. To see this form live from a frontal position is akin to watching a bottle rocket going off as it endlessly reveals new combinations of color and movement. As Sally Ann Ness observes about the then-emergent street dancing practice at Sinulog in the mid-1980s, "parade choreography was directed toward inspiring an audience who, if they had nothing else in common with the performers, all had human eyes, eyes sensitive to color, spatial design, synchrony of movement, and visual suggestions of 'The Exotic'" (Ness 1995, 11). Significantly, the speed of visual transformation and its frontal orientation is natural for transmission via television or as YouTube videos, where even the routines of companies that do not win the top prizes are endlessly replicated on blogs and other Web sites.

This is the type of dance that Basilio Villaruz has critiqued for its "confused mixed bayanihan bag of tribal-cum-regional-cum-pseudo-European-cum-Moslem-Malay choreography" (Villaruz 2006, 196). As he observes, "Spectacular as these dances may be on their own, the idea of spectacle is really about dazzling speed, sequencing, and sequins. This is proof of how even the communal rituals in the provinces are being commercialized" (188). In the case of the 2013 winning Aliwan entry, a local legend is woven into and around a frantically paced theatrical routine that involves very little in the way of complex dance movements, but that, in its execution, looks much like winning entries from other parts of the country, with one spectacular transformation after another and one or two pivotal, show-stopping moments, such as when the dragon swallows and later expels from its mouth at great height a dancer in a white, sequined costume representing the moon.

A feature of regional festivals in the Philippines, whether the focus is on a local patron saint, a foundational event of historical or cultural import, a local or animist myth, or the celebration of a local product, is that they all contain much more than street dancing alone, and as noted earlier, Aliwan is no exception. The final dance competition, which also features the float parade and competition, is preceded by two nights devoted to the Reyna ng Aliwan (Queen of Aliwan/Miss Aliwan) Competition.[15] As has been the case for much of its history, the 2013 winner was Miss Cebu,[16] well-represented by the articulate and poised Jaime Ferrell. Susan Isorena-Arcega observes that this pairing of events is natural, "Because Filipinos love beauty pageants . . . [E]very barrio fiesta has always had a beauty pageant. . . . So it just had to be part of Aliwan" (Isorena-Arcega 2013).[17] In addition to the evening wear and swimsuit competitions and the obligatory question-and-answer segment, the Aliwan version includes a native costume segment, where each contestant embodies her place of origin with spectacular neoethnic costumes that offer up considerable scenic spectacle, much as street dance competitions do. Audiences appear to take special delight when mistakes are made in the question-and-answer competition, as contestants are generally expected to answer all questions in English and some are clearly far from fluent in the language.[18] The beauty pageant is broken up with song and dance acts by teen heartthrobs and popular singers, as well as games that require audience participation onstage. This attracts a largely youthful audience of thousands who stand around the massive outdoor stage in front of the Aliw Theatre or who sit with family and friends in bleachers at some remove from the stage. As with many festival events around the country, a large area—in this case a block-long row behind the seating bank—was given over to the sale of handmade goods and crafts from around the Philippines.

This glut of activities marks all festivals in the Philippines and has a long history in religious festivals where a wide range of events has been present from the earliest days of Spanish colonization, as we have seen. From the spectatorial, experiential point of view this too-muchness is both a blessing and a curse, a condition that is well expressed in the Tagalog word *grabe,* which can mean "fantastic," or "really great," but in its current use by Manileños may also suggest too much—an excess.[19] As a concept, *grabe* has application to this event, where no one thing is ever enough. No fees are charged for any segment of the festival and people are free to come and go as they please. By the end of three nights, with the final day starting at 3:00 p.m.—assuming one wants a good seat from which to view the dance competition—and ending with fireworks around 11:00 p.m., the spectator who attempts to take it all in is well and truly spent, with a body attesting to the meaning of *grabe.*

Street Dancing, Cultural Tourism, and the Creative Industries

The other *grabe* factor is the time, expense, and financial resources it takes in one of Asia's poorest countries to bring one hundred dancers and an equal or greater number of set movers, musicians, and adult chaperones from some of the vast archipelago's most distant islands to Manila. While a prize of 1 million pesos (US$23,000) to the winning group might sound like a princely sum, it only amounts to US$115 per participant for a group of two hundred, hardly enough to cover the cost of moving people, props, and massive sets on huge, sturdy, welded metal frames on wheels across the country on boats and trucks, much less pay the fees of a professional choreographer, scenic artist, and the cost of putting the group up over a period of three to five nights. Typically, local governments, youth organizations, and in the case of Sinulog and Dinagyang, foundations supported by local businesses, provide financial assistance for dance presentations at local festivals and the trips of winning contingents to Aliwan.[20] Throughout the country, festivals are seen as cornerstones in the local and regional strategies for expanding tourism by expressing a distinctive local identity, with street dance increasingly taking the leading role at these events and in their promotion.

Tribu Panayanon's 2013 choreographer, Rommel Flogen,[21] trained in dance as a physical education major at a regional university, has choreographed many winning groups and is much in demand elsewhere (Isorena-Arcega 2013). So important is "winning choreography" to the country's most high-profile festivals such as Dinagyang, that in 2012 the local Iloilo City Tourism Office announced that it was setting up a "retraining course" for choreographers to "make them more globally competitive" (Montesa 2012). The fifth win at Aliwan by a group from Dinagyang in 2013 was hailed by the city's mayor, Jed Patrick Mabilog, as having the potential to "help catapult Iloilo City as the premier festival capital of the Philippines" (Pendon 2013), a position that would mean much for the many local businesses that would benefit from a spike in tourism. Villaruz expresses concerns about how such groups can become pawns in the hands of the local political elite:

> Also, street-dance groups gain attention for their ranks or prizes in competitions rather than for their role in the evolution of a contemporary folklore in dance. They easily become instruments in political, promotional, or commercial agenda. They are viewed less as laboratories of cultural expressions than as products to prove a municipality's or a market's stage management of a state/product image. The support they receive is both tendentious and intermittent, a showcase of prestige and power rather than a genuine effort to nurture culture in general. (Villaruz 2006, 10)

Writing about dance at the Sinulog Festival, Sally Ann Ness observes that what had originally been a healing ritual conducted outside the Basilica Minore del Santo Niño in Cebu City by middle-aged and elderly women selling devotional candles was consciously reenvisioned in the early 1980s as the basis for a competitive dance form (1995). Within a few short years, by 1985, the parade had developed a national reputation and was drawing over one million spectators. The consequences, she notes, were significant:

> In the new context, the sinulog became a means of representing the ideal self-image of the city and its region to the world at large. . . . This was a sinulog style meant to be looked at by a variety of audiences simultaneously: contest judges, local friends and family of the participants, TV cameras from Manila, devotees of the Santo Niño from all over the archipelago, and tourists being flown in from Japan, the U.S. and other overseas locations. The performances now sought to speak a universal visual language, to transcend or translate a variety of cultural systems of

> interpretation, and to represent a number of largely unrelated themes: the natural beauty of Cebu and the Philippines, the graciousness and hospitality of the local culture, the history of the archipelago, the traditional material culture of the region, and, of course, the local experience of devotion to the Santo Niño. (Ness 1995, 5–6)

Though Sinulog provides possibly a singular contemporary example of a small, localized ritual form being transformed in a single generation, virtually all of the country's festivals today, regardless of their origins, incorporate street dancing in a way that can and often does serve political masters.

In Cebu, for instance, the use of street dancing as a rehabilitation tool in the state prison is identified with the Reyes family, the political dynasty that held key political positions in the province for over a generation (see also Peterson 2012). Noteworthy was the presence at Aliwan 2010 of street-dance contingents from two major festivals (Buklod and Padang-Padang) in the province of Maguindanao in the Autonomous Region in Muslim Mindanao, just months after the November 2009 summary execution of fifty-eight people accompanying a local politician as he sought to file papers to run for office, setting himself in opposition to the incumbent mayor, a member of the legendary Ampatuan clan that had long run the province. The Ampatuan massacre, as it has come to be known, has the distinction of being the world's worst single massacre of journalists in history. At a time when legal proceedings against the Ampatuan family were dominating the front pages of the national newspapers, there was no sense in the reporting on Aliwan or the running commentary offered by emcees during the dance competition that this year was different from any other. Indeed, so called extra-judicial killings are common in the Philippines in the run-up to elections, so while the scale of the Ampatuan massacre set it apart from the usual preelection execution of political opponents of powerful clans, there was nothing unusual about the presence of these companies, even in the wake of this extraordinary act of violence.

The development of tourism is inevitably on the agenda of all festival organizers, including Aliwan's. The national tourism infrastructure in the Philippines is among the most sophisticated and unitary in the world and virtually all major regional festivals are packaged in a remarkably similar fashion. Until recently, all of the country's major festivals were listed and described on the Department of Tourism's Web site, while speeches at the start of all festivals by local politicians and tourism officials typically repeat the rhetoric that links tourism with economic development. At regional festivals, the growth of tourism is often put forth as an answer to local or regional poverty, whereas culture is positioned not only as the foundation for a stronger individual and regional identity but also as the basis for the expanded interest of domestic and international tourists in the region. Moreover, such rhetoric serves the interests of the oligarchs and ruling elites to the extent that it absolves them of any further responsibility for dealing with poverty, particularly, in the parts of the archipelago far from Manila. The belief that cultural tourism can combat poverty extends back to the Marcos years when a vast, centrally controlled national tourism bureaucracy was assembled at the very time martial law was imposed on the country in 1972 (Richter 1980, 1989). In 2013 the national Department of Tourism teamed up with Aliwan as an active sponsor insofar as the event fit squarely within the framework of their new international branding exercise, the "It's more fun in the Philippines" campaign (Isorena-Arcega 2013).

Susan Isorena-Arcega and Nestor Jardin, two informants with long histories of involvement with Aliwan as publicist and judge, respectively, both evoked the potential of street dancing to contribute to the development of the "creative industries," a term that the government agency, Invest Philippines (2010b), uses on its Web site, borrowing language from a report titled *Arangkada Philippines 2010,* created by the Joint Foreign Chambers of the Philippines, and largely authored by American Chamber of Commerce senior adviser John Forbes (2010, 91). *Arangkada,* a word that translates as "accelerating" or "pulling ahead," is precisely what the report argues that the Philippines must do if it is to catch up with other Southeast Asian countries that have left it in the dust economically. The report, which appears to have been adopted virtually as policy by the government of the Philippines, identifies the creative industries as one of the seven "Big Winner Sectors" (Forbes 2010, 57), where rapid economic growth can occur with the right policies in place. According to both the report and the Invest Philippines Web site: "The Creative Economy is defined as industries which have their origin in individual creativity, skill, and talent and which have potential for wealth and job creation through the generation and exploitation of intellectual property" (Forbes 2010, 91; Invest Philippines 2010b). Included in the category are "a wide array of subsectors including advertising, animation, architecture, broadcast arts, crafts, culinary arts, cultural/heritage activities, design, film, literature, music, new media, performing arts, publishing, and visual arts" (Forbes 2010, 91; Invest Philippines 2010b). Isorena-Arcega observed that this new push picks up from the legacy of Imelda Marcos, who "really was ahead of her time" in seeing the arts as a potential generator of economic growth nearly thirty years before the concept of the "creative industries" caught hold: "She had a vision of getting education involved with tourism, with trade and industry, and with the export center. And she had a master plan." Marcos' strategy worked, she argued, "because she held on to everything, because she supervised everything," noting that in the intervening years as the center has been less strong, each region has sought to reproduce a "mini-version of what she had done" (Isorena-Arcega 2013).

More recently, Invest Philippines appears to have at least tacitly adopted the recommendations of the *Arangkada* report, which sets out an ambitious plan for economic growth where the creative industries, along with the other six sectors, will potentially add US$75 billion in foreign investment and create ten million new jobs within the decade (Invest Philippines 2010a). Since it came to power in 2010, the Aquino government has strongly supported the expansion of the sector. In a paper delivered at a national tourism conference, Nestor Jardin makes the case for festivals featuring street dance as a source of significant economic activity, placing it within a creative industries framework:

> As a creative industry event, the economic activity that street dance festivals generate can be phenomenal. Let's take the example of Cebu's Sinulog. I am a veteran judge of the Sinulog and every time I go to Cebu, all planes are fully booked, hotels are turning away guests, restaurants are packed, the streets are crammed with vendors, the resorts are enjoying brick business, and the malls are having a heyday with their sales. On top of this, people engaged in mounting the productions such as costume makers, choreographers, props makers, providers of *meriendas* [snacks], are all busy and are therefore earning from the services that they provide. If we find a way to compute the economic returns of these festivals and compare it to the amount spent in mounting the festivals, I'm sure we will all be pleasantly surprised. (Jardin 2009, 2)

Jardin here sets out a core argument used to support the creative industries concept globally: that it returns many times the initial investment and that the income it generates flows across a range of businesses, particularly in the transportation, hospitality, and service sectors, where reliable mechanisms generally do not yet exist for tracking the additional income generated by creative industries events. Testing and proving this claim with reliable quantitative data would greatly benefit those working in this and related fields.

My experience as a spectator at Aliwan over an eight-year period suggests that very few foreigners attend this event, while Manileños from comfortable, middle-class backgrounds who live far from where the event is held along Manila Bay know nothing about it. The economic spin-offs that Jardin associates with Sinulog extend largely either from a public that is returning to their home region on an annual trip or from local residents. Further, Manila at the time of Aliwan is no Rio at Mardi Gras. Planeloads of international tourists are unlikely to decamp on the nonexistent beaches of Manila Bay anytime soon, in spite of the dreams that Imelda Marcos had in the 1970s when in a single year (1975–1976) as mayor of Metro Manila she spent as much as 20 percent of the government's total annual expenditures on building luxury hotels along the bay to accommodate the spike in anticipated well-heeled foreign arrivals (Richter 1989, 57). Ironically, the Aliwan Fiesta takes place virtually in the geographic center of this area that was once seen has having the potential to become a kind of Southeast Asian Monte Carlo, a vision that, sadly, falls short of today's reality.

Dancers and the Inner Experience of Dance

Aliwan coincides with the hot, dry season, a time of year in which school-aged youth who participate in this festival are on vacation and have a good deal of free time. While for some, enforced participation in group dance at school may be one of their least favorite activities, many youth choose to invest considerable additional time and energy in this form, taking it beyond the schoolyard and placing it at the center of their lives. As Alexander Cortez observes of these kids who choose to come together, "They're dancing. They have the energy. They're with their friends there." The social dimension of participating with friends, neighbors, and schoolmates cannot be underrated. As one walks through the backstage area where these groups congregate for hours prior to performing, one takes in the energy of young people who clearly enjoy being in the company of their peers. For many of the youth who come to Aliwan during their summer vacation, it is their first time traveling outside of their home province, and coming to Manila is a once-in-a-lifetime experience that will be part of their shared experience with their peer group for the rest of their lives. Though describing his own experience of participating in a ritual dance form from Mindanao known as *buklog*, Villaruz's comments speak to the pleasure derived from dancing, and why so many are willing to devote so much time to it:

> As children, we have all felt the thrill of swinging up and down. It's a transcendent feeling that allows us to forget the mundane, as we lose ourselves in the rhythm of going up and down, in the wind, and in the dramatic beating of our heart—our total being. . . . Its rhythm, created by everyone involved, allows for utter abandonment. A taste of ecstasy is reached through the act of dance, and there is that unexpected surge of energy in the act of abandonment. And in the *buklog* these emotions are very much a product of the whole community's effort. (Villaruz 2006, 40)

It is the effort of the "whole community" that marks off participating as a dancer in these events. No young person is alone, all are watched by one another, and the palpable intensity of the peer-group bonding results in a shared experience as they create a collective cultural identity in the present moment.

The collective expression of these acts of pleasure, created and expressed through a disciplined artistic framework, is especially important for Filipinos. If this is the larger, foundational cultural frame, then Mihaly Csikszentmihalyi's detailed inquiry into what he terms "the phenomenology of enjoyment" may point to the way in which happiness is situated inside the dancer's body. Csikszentmihalyi's rigorously cross-cultural research sought to identify and map out the components of *flow*, "the state in which people are so involved in an activity that nothing else seems to matter; the experience itself is so enjoyable that people will do it even at great cost, for the sheer sake of doing it" (Csikszentmihalyi 1992, 4). Though Csikszentmihalyi sets out these states in relation to the individual's experience, I would assert that the inner experience is enhanced and set off by the communal framework in which the Filipino street dancer is situated. The eight components within a larger phenomenology of enjoyment were drawn from extensive reflections by participants "on how it feels when their experience is most positive" (49). The research of his team, working in various parts of the world, including Asia, identified the following eight features of the experience, of which people consistently mentioned at least one, and often all of the following:

> First the experience usually occurs when we confront tasks we have a chance of completing. Second, we must be able to concentrate on what we are doing. Third and fourth, the concentration is usually possible because the task undertaken has clear goals and provides immediate feedback. Fifth, one acts with a deep but effortless involvement that removes from awareness the worries and frustrations of everyday life. Sixth, enjoyable experiences allow people to exercise a sense of control over their actions. Seventh, concern for the self disappears, yet paradoxically the sense of self emerges stronger after the flow experience is over. Finally, the sense of the duration of time is altered; hours pass by in minutes, and minutes can stretch out to seem like hours. The combination of all these elements causes a sense of deep enjoyment that is so rewarding people feel that expending a great deal of energy is worthwhile simply to be able to feel it. (Csikszentmihalyi 1992, 49)

The first four elements are virtual requirements for this form of dance: Dancers are given the time and opportunity to master tasks that are within their range of capabilities executed in a very clearly delineated framework, one that offers and may well even require immediate feedback in order to simply stay safe, whereas the actions are complex and so interconnected with the actions of other dancers and the movement of scenic elements and use of props that strict concentration is a formal requirement.

The fifth element, that sense of "effortless involvement" where the "worries and frustrations of everyday life" vanish are possibly what Aliwan judge Lisa Macuja-Elizalde was referring to when she spoke of dancers being *ganado,* that it was not enough to simply look as though they were enjoying themselves, but rather that "they have to be enjoying themselves" and that this quality was something that presumably the judges should be able to feel. This sense of fully inhabiting this state of joy links up with the cultural value of uniting *sa loób* with *sa labas;* dancers should be able to achieve this union and share it with the audience. It must be felt to be communicated because it is not enough to merely "show" it—otherwise the circuit of emotional health is incomplete. Feeling that one has control over one's actions is also important, and without the preceding elements one would not feel that sense of mastery. The addition of "effortless involvement" that comes from mastering the tasks involved in a pleasurable activity heightens the sense that one has complete control over one's organism. The final two states, where concern for self disappears, though "paradoxically" it is "stronger after the flow experience is over," and where one's temporal sense is altered, are more difficult to track and measure without reference to specific examples. While the six initial states identified by Csikszentmihalyi's researchers are virtual requirements for a precise form of dance such as street dancing, and there is an extent to which the sensitive viewer can not only see but also feel them when they are present, the final two states are not ones that can be easily verified without seeking to get inside the inner experience of the dancer at these events. My experience of dancing at the Ati-atihan Festival suggests that these final two states are present, at least potentially; my body retains that feeling of merging with others while dancing, and in the memory of the experience, I can see myself individually and in relation to the other; further, my sense of an altered temporality is one of the key elements that imprints most fully on the body and compels me to return every year.

Bayan and Dance

Bayan, as we have seen, is built on "sets of definable loyalties that could be mobilized for common enterprises" (Woods 2005, 7) and is largely determined by how people feel in relation to one another and the extent to which they identify as a group. Because the individual "is not the irreducible unit of being for the Filipino" inasmuch as "the Filipino understanding of the human being is still conditioned primarily by the idea of being-in-relation" (Beltran 1987, 226), *bayan* is necessarily the foundational concept in terms of how a Filipino expresses his or her identity in relation to others. As the expressive, embodied performance form shared by the greatest numbers of Filipinos, it is through dance that the many strands of *bayan* are most evident and most complex in their operation. In an effort to unpack *bayan* through dance, I propose a *bayan* action model (see figure 8) in which the larger circle of *bayan*-as-people (B4) contains three interlocking, overlapping circles: the physical place of the archipelago that constitutes the Philippines (B1); *bayan*-as-nation, the country of the Philippines, a constructed set of loyalties toward the larger whole of the country that reflects the nationalist project that started well before the end of the American colonial period (B2); and the cultural imaginary of what it means to be Filipino, one that, as we have seen, has been largely the creation of Tagalog-speaking elites in the capital, but which in its felt and embodied expression is rarely problematized, except by educated elites themselves (B3). An infinite number of smaller communities that self-define by location, religion, shared cultural practices, language/dialect, and kinship ties are situated in place (B1), but can also be appropriated by *bayan*-as-nation (B2) and *bayan*-as-cultural imaginary (B3), thus occupying the shared spaces. Those small "b" *bayan* groupings that collectively constitute those communities that are invested in the project of nation (B2) sit within the shared circle of both place and nation, while those less invested in nation, but that exist largely as constituents of the cultural imaginary, are sited in the area shared by B1 and B3. I have acknowledged from the start that this book cannot claim to cover performance practices across the whole of the archipelago. Thus without years of fieldwork in the various regions, the ways in which localized populations respond to this larger cultural imaginary that I am setting out here cannot be fully assessed. Though I will provide examples of ways in which individual forms relate to these three frames, I leave it to others to test their applicability to cultural understandings embedded in the various regions of the country.

Also, as we can see in the model, those communities with surviving dance practices that have efficacy as ritual (e.g., the examples I gave of the *tayaw* and *bendian* at a traditional *canao* in the Cordillera) and are not invested in the cultural imaginary or nation at all, are represented as remaining entirely within the confines of place (B1) and are not shared with other circles. My experience with dances within this region also suggests that there is very little flowing back to the region from the cultural imaginary or nation inasmuch as the indigenous people of that region seem to have a strong sense of who they are and their dance traditions largely circulate internally and are not returned to them in a mediated fashion. To put it another way, few if anyone from tribes in the Cordillera would need to watch a Bayanihan production, look up videos online, or study the how-to manuals of Reyes-Aquino or, in more recent compendiums (Guillen 1999–2004), fig-

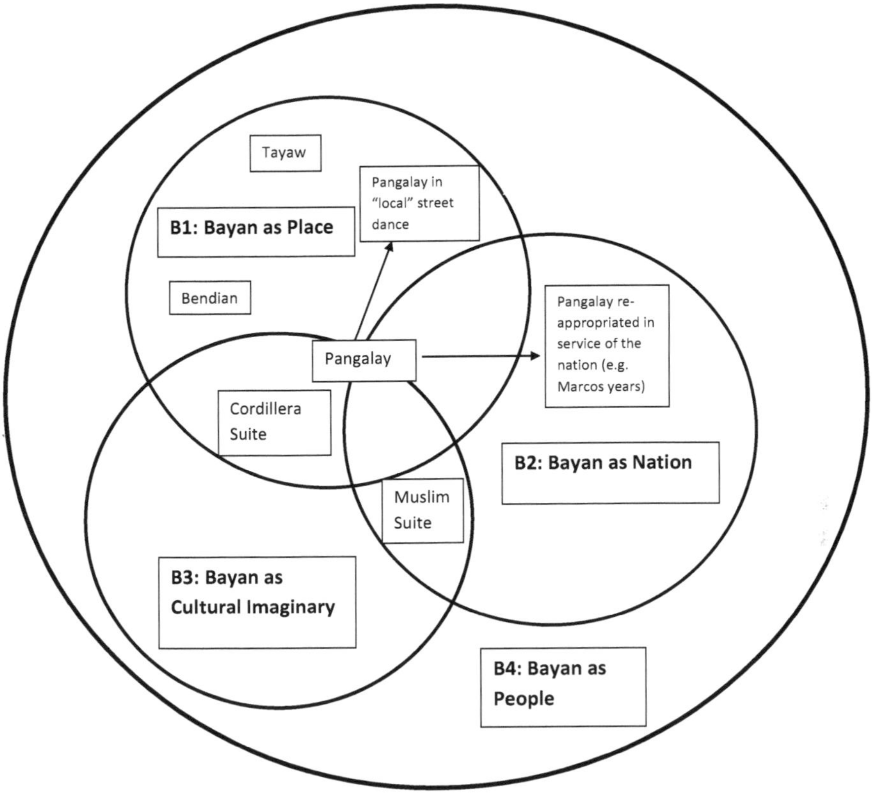

Figure 8. *Bayan* action model #1.

ure out the steps to local ritual dances such as the *tayaw* or *bendian* because these dances and what they mean are in their bodies. The "Muslim Suite," adopted by the state as an emblem of Filipino-ness, particularly during the Marcos era, exists within the frames of *bayan*-as-nation (B2) and *bayan*-as-cultural imaginary (B3), while the "Cordillera Suite," though remaining deeply emplaced in its indigenous *(katutubong)* context (B1), in its expression and distribution is equally situated within the field of *bayan*-as-cultural imaginary (B3).

Some communities only marginally invested in the idea of a Filipino cultural imaginary or nation can be represented by having most of their mass inside B1 and only marginally resting over the boundaries of B2 and/or B3. Also in figure 8, the form of *pangalay,* which no longer exists as a significant cultural force on its home ground in the Sulu Archipelago, is represented as being largely inside B2 and B3 inasmuch as it is part of the Filipino cultural imaginary (indeed, it circulates widely both within Mindanao and Manila dance circles) and has also been appropriated in the service as *bayan*-as-nation through Bayanihan's global reach. Such a form can in turn return to another "place," repackaged as a signature, "local" form, as is the case with *pangalay* where its external trappings are reworked into popular expressions of contemporary "street dancing" emanating from Mindanao. Thus here there is a line that reconnects this form from its displaced original position within the Sulu archipelago, and reemplaces it back into another place entirely—even though it is nominally part of the same region. This reworked, reemplaced form may be experienced as a celebration of an authentic local culture, for instance, as in the example given of Maranao dance that becomes reappropriated after an earlier appropriation in the service of a national Filipino culture. Thus, in the Marcos years, the form became a symbol of the nation, of strength in diversity.

Bayan-as-people (B4) necessarily incorporates all three circles, B1, B2, and B3, inasmuch as people are constituted by place but may have different points of identification with nation (B2) and the larger Filipino cultural imaginary (B3). Filipino friends who return with me each year to dance through the streets with the Santo Niño at the Ati-atihan Festival are constituted by the place where the experience of connecting with one another by and through the Santo Niño takes place. The embodied, localized experience has everything to do with what happens in Kalibo, and what does not happen in other places. Thus, even though its external trappings are symbolically appropriated by the state, dancing to the Santo Niño becomes what people do. In point of fact, however, historically, dancing to the Santo Niño is what Cebuanos and Visayan people do. Where it is an invented tradition—as it largely is in the Tagalog region, for instance—or where it is reinvigorated or transplanted elsewhere in the region, as with the Dinagyang and Sinulog Festivals, for instance, it occupies the coordinates of place, nation, and cultural imaginary. Figure 9 sets out this triangulation between how it is still expressed in place (what we do in Kalibo every year), how it serves the nation, and how it is extended to other, invented or newer Santo Niño festivals, in this final instance straddling place, nation, and cultural imaginary.

For Filipino-Americans who participate in Pilipino Cultural Nights (PCNs), through the act of performing they are entering into shared sphere of *bayan*-as-people; by dancing the displaced *singkil* from the "Muslim Suite" or appearing as Igorot warriors of the "Cordillera Suite," they are connecting with a larger local and global community of Pinoys as well as with their families and long-dead ancestors who may have come from a range of places in the Philippines a generation or more ago. As Theodore Gonzalves observes,

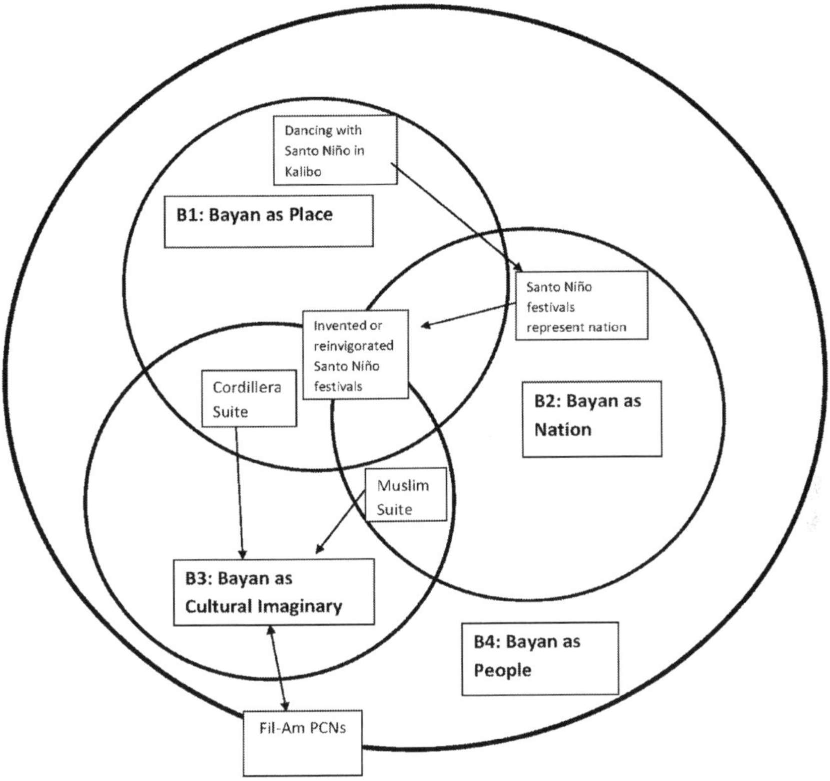

Figure 9. *Bayan* action model #2.

> For PCN performers, "Filipino culture," rendered through the show's dances, seems to be a timeless thing—as if it has always existed; as if performing the movements, donning the costumes, and playing the native instruments in the present gives the performer a simultaneity with an unchanged past. (Gonzalves 2010, loc. 192)

These foundational Bayanihan suites now exist in the cultural imaginary and have taken on lives of their own. In figure 9, the point of entry for those participating in PCNs is largely through the Filipino cultural imaginary—thus, the line connecting Filipino-Americans with B3. The arrow moves in both directions in that because of their significant presence in the global diaspora, they contribute meaningfully to *bayan*-as-imaginary. Their need to be a part of that larger circle (B4) of *bayan*-as-people is no less significant and pressing, and their motivations for participating are no less valid than they would be for any other group; indeed, their need for participation may be even greater if in their lived experience they feel marginalized by mainstream American culture. Depending on their degree of identification with what it means to be American or a hyphenated American, they may be situated both partially within the circle of *bayan*-as-people and outside it, also living in the circle that constitutes their other *bayan*.

Many well-heeled cosmopolitan Filipinos whom I have met lament the absence in the Philippines of the kind of iconic national performance forms extending from a centralized court culture such as is found in Bali, Java (particularly Yogyakarta and Solo), and Thailand. Given the length of colonial rule, it is especially difficult to find performance forms that reach back to a time before Catholicism and contact with Spanish and American culture and that offer up this kind of precontact "purity" in terms of the functions for dance. In this context, the dance forms from the remote Cordillera and resistant Muslim south serve as bookends on a continuum in the search for cultural authenticity through dance. In the period since it achieved its independence from the United States, a national culture has been created through dance where it was previously perceived as being absent, though this contemporary creation is often disconnected from the roots of traditions in the *bayan* of *barangays,* towns, and regions, existing only within the frames of nation and the cultural imaginary. Instead, it may well be that cultural identity, rather than being compartmentalized into what often seems like an unending genealogical regression of forms back to some imagined past point, lives on in the interstitial spaces, in the capacity to adapt, change, and even appropriate and commercialize. As Sally Ann Ness observes about the way dance circulates at cultural villages in Mindanao:

> Cultural identity, in particular, is made evident at present, not simply by participation or lack thereof in an established tradition of some kind, whose ever-stable enactments allow for such "in" or "out" commitments to be made. Rather, cultural identity emerges in the way in which participation is *qualified* by some factor or set thereof in a whole variety of practices—not all of them having cultural, or the same cultural sources. (Ness 2003, 243)

My concern throughout this book has not been with imagined and contesting notions of "authenticity," but rather with what benefits individuals and communities derive by participating in the mass performance forms of *sinakulo* and folk-inflected dance. That through their participation in PNCs, Filipino-American students "demonstrate that Filipinos do have a culture" (Gonzalves 2005, 37), is an important achievement for those who are physically removed from the culture of their parents and grandparents and marginalized in the country of their birth. And for the Bayanihan dancers who exploded onto the world stage in Brussels in 1958, the sources of their cultural expressions onstage and how they were manipulated are ultimately less significant than what started at that moment. With its legendary status, it is the fixed point from which both the Filipino cultural imaginary and *bayan*-as-nation received external validation. Whether or not celebrating such validation was a good thing I leave to others to debate. Culture is and has often been determined by forces that are not cultural but rather extracultural, as we have seen with street dancing. Yet in spite of or perhaps because of this, participants find meaning in participation, their experiences contribute to their understanding of their cultural identity as Filipinos, and as a collective group of people from a particular region, city, town, or *barangay*, the bonds that they share, create, and celebrate through participation contribute greatly to individual and collective happiness.

CHAPTER 7

Juana Change

Performing the Personal and the Political

In any big Asian city, you can learn a lot by talking to taxi drivers. In Manila, where many drivers listen to the radio for twelve hours or more every day, it has been my experience that their comments frequently represent a kind of bellwether of what the future may hold. Their sufferings, their hardships, and their political apathy often reflect the sufferings, hardships, and political apathy of the masses; when they express hope for the future, one should sit up and take notice. Thus I want to start this chapter with two taxi-driver anecdotes, set precisely three years apart, in the lead up to the 2010 general election in which Benigno "Noynoy" Aquino III became president of the Philippines, and the following general election three years later. In 2010 I spent nearly six months based in Manila during the period that included the election, a time that is traditionally marked by empty promises of the sons and daughters of the hereditary oligarchy that dominates the country's political and economic life and marred by extrajudicial killings and massive vote-buying, widely known as running a "traditional campaign." By the last few weeks of the 2010 campaign, the four viable candidates were "Noynoy" Aquino, the son of Cory Aquino, the country's first post-Marcos president and her martyred husband, and descended from one of the country's wealthiest and most-powerful families; Joseph Estrada, the movie star ex-president who was convicted of plunder and famously booted out of office after massive street rallies; Manny Villar, one of the nation's wealthiest real estate tycoons, who misleadingly painted himself as having come from humble roots; and the brainy former secretary of defense, Gilberto "Gibo" Teodoro, second cousin of Noynoy, and from a branch of the Cojuangco family long at odds with the Aquinos. This was the context in which I found myself in a taxi stuck in hopelessly congested Manila traffic, asking the driver what he thought of the choices in the presidential election, a contest that seemed more open than it had ever been. His response rendered me speechless: "Whoever is president, I'm still driver." There was a resigned quality in his voice, suggesting that there was no point in caring about the outcome. In spite of the grand promises of politicians over the past three decades, the working poor of the country have seen no economic progress since the fall of the Marcos regime in 1986. For taxi drivers the situation is particularly acute; their operating costs have gone up, but fares have not. Each passing year they earn less and less and they struggle harder and harder.

Fast-forward to the 2013 election and I again found myself in a taxi in impossible traffic. I was on my way to interview performer and social activist Mae Paner, better known as Juana Change, when our progress came to a halt in Makati, a city that constitutes part of Metro Manila that is half mini-Singapore with gleaming office towers and exclusive gated communities, and half working and middle-class families living in older, two- and three-story structures. A road detour forced us around an area where a massive stage was being set up for a campaign rally for Jejomar "JunJun" Binay Jr., the son of the former mayor of Makati and the country's vice president, who was staking his claim on the country's richest city on the basis of the family name. His sister, Abigail "Abby" Binay, was simultaneously running for congressional representative of the district. Both later won their respective campaigns. The taxi driver, realizing that our progress was slowed by preparations for a Binay rally volunteered: "Political dynasties, bad!" Again, I was speechless, only this time for entirely different reasons. First of all, never, in my years in the Philippines, in any of hundreds of taxi rides I have taken since 2001, has any taxi driver articulated a political view without first being queried or gently prodded for a response. And second, there was the substance of the statement, which suggested to me that something significant had begun to shift in the consciousness of urban Manileños to enable them to recognize that dynastic politics are at the root of much of what is wrong with the Philippines politically, economically, and socially, and that ordinary citizens might well have the capacity to do something to end the practice.

I would assert that something has been changing in the consciousness of Filipinos in the years since 2010—at least in Metro Manila—and that the social activist performance work of Mae Paner (aka "Juana Change") reflects this shift. Her work, created largely with writer Rody Vera, has reached an ever-widening audience since 2009 when her "Juana Change" and "Convergence Team" videos playfully and unflinchingly took on the corruption of the government led by former president Gloria Macapagal-Arroyo. The work of Paner and Vera is situated within the long tradition of socially conscious theatre in the Philippines, most famously associated with the People's Educational Theatre Association (PETA), which sought to "conscientize" or infuse consciousness into the disenfranchised masses of Filipino citizens. This spirit has been present as Paner's alter ego Juana Change helped usher out Arroyo, as she stood on the stage introducing Noynoy Aquino at campaign rallies, as she criticized and later called for the resignation of the president she helped elect, and perhaps even more significantly, as she, along with performance artist and tour guide Carlos Celdran, ridiculed politicians for filling the public space with billboards and campaign posters in which they took personal credit for taxpayer-financed projects, and took on the poison of dynastic politics. This process of empowering the individual through theatre so that the conscience is activated and the individual becomes personally committed to taking social action was the basis for the pioneering work of PETA from the time it was formed in 1967, and especially later as it attacked the political, social, and economic ills during the period of the Marcos dictatorship. By the time I arrived in the Philippines in 2001, PETA's influence had diminished considerably. It was in the process of fundraising for a permanent theatre building, and in the years that followed its shift in focus effectively put an end to its national "informance" tours,[1] which went out into the poorer urban *barangays* and regions and dealt with issues such as violence against women and reproductive rights.[2] Paner herself was associated with PETA in her early years, as was Rody Vera, an important theatre activist and playwright in those heady days of anti-Marcos activism.[3] Together they extended through other means PETA's social-activism, a force in theatre that has been influential throughout the region.[4] In this final chapter we are reversing the inquiry by shifting from community-based performance to performance that mobilizes a community and brings it into being in ways that Catherine Diamond has termed "communities of imagination" (2012).

This chapter also suggests the possibility of switching the relative power positions of theatre and politics, showing how in the case of Paner and Vera in particular, street theatre, agitprop performance, performance at campaign rallies, YouTube videos, and even a major-release movie,[5] have repositioned theatre as a force capable of fighting back against a political and economic elite under whose watch the country has shifted from being the richest country in Asia after Japan in the late 1950s, to among the very poorest. As we saw most spectacularly with the example of the Reyes family in Marinduque, those who wield political and economic power have long been able to shape and contain the frameworks in which large-scale community events featuring performance operate. We have also seen how the selection and national and international circulation of certain exemplary forms of dance also owe much to politics, both locally and nationally, as highly mediated practices become the new "norm" for a performance form or style that circulates back to local regions as "authentic." In this chapter community-building through performance goes full circle. If throughout much of this book the suggestion has been that communities self-define and are reinforced through performance practices they participate in that are situated in a particular place, here we will see that new ways of configuring a relationship to a larger circle of *bayan* can be created through activist performance, which Paner terms "advocacy," that seeks to connect ever-expanding communities of individuals to an alternative vision of *bayan*-as-nation.

We also return here to the matter of happiness through performance. Throughout this book I have asserted that participating in community-based performance such as the *sinakulo* or street dancing fulfills needs beyond or in addition to those of *panata*—that the act of doing these things brings pleasure, that it has the capacity to place us in what Mihaly Csikszentmihalyi has described as "flow" states in which the one merges with the many, and that we emerge after the experience with a stronger sense of personal empowerment and sometimes—as was the case with Ati-atihan—with memories that imprint on our bodies and alter our experience of temporality. However, here we will not map out the internal state of the performer-participant, but consider how the impulse toward the performative is expressed through political performance. And here I mean not only the performance of politicians, but the ways in which performance has more recently been reactivated to reshape the national political field. As we have seen in the numerous sites examined in this book, many—and I would assert most—Filipinos connect with one another in communities through the performative, by emplacing fun and celebration into the major shared communal experiences around which much of the rest of their lives are organized. Thus it is hardly surprising that Filipino politicians and those seeking to effect political change can maximize their effectiveness and draw in the largest potential audience by offering performances that are enjoyable and entertaining, and that bring all individuals into the collective whole through performance, even offering them an opening to perform as well. We shall see that the final Manila rally in the 2010 presidential campaign of Noynoy Aquino largely featured performers rather than politicians making speeches, and invited the audience to sing along, joining, if only for a brief moment, a diverse and united community of individuals committed to a *bayan* that does not yet exist, one that remained (and remains) aspirational. As I suggested in the introduction, the need to infuse life with pleasure through group activities that involve performance is especially welcome and even necessary in a country where social, political, and economic forces conspire against the individual and divide communities. And in the Philippines, as we have seen, performance has long been used in ways that ultimately exploit the masses and divert their attention from poverty, injustice, and the social and economic order that serves the interest of the ruling elite. Thus it is appropriate to start by briefly setting out those powerful, seemingly intractable forces that would seem to stand in the way of happiness in the Philippines.

Happiness and the "Trapo" Politician

When it comes to happiness, most Filipinos have much to be unhappy about. Saddled with a system of comprador capitalism where the so-called "trapo" political class represents the interests of a small political and economic oligarchy while offering table crumbs or empty promises to the poor, the Philippines is one of many countries in the world where the masses clearly deserve a better government. Derived from the Spanish word for "rag," a "trapo" is a "traditional politician" who conducts a "traditional campaign," which inevitably involves vote-buying, using personal or family financial resources. Colonized economically by the United States well after independence in 1946, for over a hundred years the Philippines has been a country where a small number of dominant mestizo families own and control much of the land and means of production. Benedict Anderson, in an influential 1988 article, cut through the historical myths that many Filipinos perpetuate about themselves, observing, as historical fact bears out, that the class of the "Mestizo Filipino" out of which the economic and political elite of the country emerged was composed largely of descendants from mixed Chinese-Filipino Catholic families. Anderson traces out the genealogies of a few key families that have been at the center of political and economic life since the end of Spanish rule and the early days of American colonial administration. Only those Hispanized Chinese-Filipino families already in possession of considerable financial assets were in a position to purchase the vast land holdings of the religious orders when the Americans sold them off into private hands (Anderson 1988, 11). The wealth and status of the Cojuanco family, from which Noynoy's mother Cory descends, extends from this period, and some family members have a less than distinguished political pedigree, most notably her cousin Eduardo "Danding" Cojuanco, who "became Governor of Tarlac [Province] with Ferdinand Marcos's backing, and went on to count among the most notorious of the Marcos cronies" (4). Like many from such a class background, when she married Benigno Aquino Jr., she became part of another prominent family in the region, one that was equally blemished. Anderson observes that Benigno Aquino Sr., Cory's father-in-law, "won lasting notoriety for his active collaboration with the Japanese Occupation regime" (ibid.), having served as speaker of the National Assembly under the Japanese. In the last days of the war he was flown to Tokyo, presumably for his own safety, and after returning to the Philippines in 1946 he was released on bail. He never stood trial for the crime of treason, which elsewhere in the world would surely have brought the death penalty had he been convicted. While Anderson asserts that the "heyday" of this form of government was the period 1954–1972, its features remain a legacy in today's underdeveloped economic landscape, which is plundered by the oligarchs:

> Under the guise of promoting economic independence and import-substitution industrialization, exchange rates were manipulated, monopolistic licences parcelled out, huge, cheap, often unrepaid bank loans passed around, and the national budget frittered away in pork barrel legislation. (Anderson 1988, 16)

As we will see later in this chapter, by attacking the long-standing practice of rewarding political cronies through "pork-barrel legislation," Juana Change helped ignite a national movement that may well ultimately lead to a more full-scale frontal attack on the power of the oligarchy.

Dante Simbulan (2005) calls this system, which dates back to Spanish rule administered through Mexico, "the modern principalia," a mode of social, political, economic, and cultural ordering of society where power is concentrated in an elite—the *principalia*—a group that served its Spanish and American masters well in extracting labor, taxes, and wealth from the local population while lording over them. Though Simbulan's study covers the immediate postindependence era, it remains relevant; he notes that colleagues have continued to observe "the striking similarity of the description, events, and behaviour patterns of the elite—*then* and *now.* Just change the dates and the personnel involved, they said, and you are practically describing the happening and the behaviour of the Philippine elite today" (Simbulan 2005, xviii). He describes the virtual hereditary transfer of power that still exists, and the practice of vote-buying and shoring up one's positions through "the liberal use of guns, goons, and gold (or the three G's as the common people now say)" (xix).[6]

> This is the kind of "democracy" that the oligarchy and their apologists often say we have in the Philippines. It is a "democracy" devoid of substance, a facade conveniently used by the elite to camouflage their monopoly of power, a democracy of the plutocrats or the wealthy few. . . . These are the people who have monopolized political power in the Philippines ever since the nation-state was formed. They are the people who comprise the *modern principalia.* (Simbulan 2005, xix)

Simbulan invokes Anderson's use of the term "Caciquism," noting that as it is practiced in the Philippines it "broadly means boss rule" (30), citing a late nineteenth-century source that characterizes the cacique as follows:

> In all the details of public life, you will see him interfering, either directly or indirectly, by means of his agent, in order to further his own personal interests and swell his pockets. During election time, he does a great deal

of manipulating, making justice conform to his personal whims. (cited in Simbulan 2005, 30)

Though not descended from the *principalia* class, the ultimate leader of this type was Ferdinand Marcos, who played to the masses with his "strongman" rhetoric and the fictional stories of his humble background and heroic exploits during World War II.[7] His wife performed an identity not unlike that of Eva Peron, in which her glamour and financial excesses were geared to putting on a show for the poor and enabling her to appear as the "shining star" to which they might look, thus deflecting them away from the drudgery and grinding poverty of their daily lives. They were a terrifyingly brilliant duo, with Imelda offering herself as a vision of "the true, the good and the beautiful" (Diaz 2003),[8] while Ferdinand used fiercely nationalist rhetoric and the need to protect the country from internal enemies as the justification for the imposition of martial law. It was rule by the strongman and the iron maiden, who both famously lined their pockets and protected those in the inner circle. By the 1960s power was not in owning vast tracts of agricultural land, epitomized by the old hacienda system that had supported families such as the Cojuancos and Aquinos, but in possessing the huge financial monetarized resources that can be controlled by the state. And it was here that Marcos and his wife, both from families on the "lower fringes of the oligarchy," departed from the upper orders. As Anderson observes, "almost from the beginning of his presidency in 1965, Marcos had moved mentally out of the nineteenth century, and understood that in our time wealth serves power, and that the key card is the state. Manila's Louis Napoleon" (Anderson 1988, 20). As Richard Holbrooke, U.S. assistant secretary of state during the first term of the Reagan administration (1981–1984), observed about the First Lady: "For her it was about personal power, not about leadership. Even her good works projects, like cleaning up metro Manila were just cosmetics. To Imelda Marcos, everything is personal. Everything" (Diaz 2003). And it is precisely because it was always about amassing, maintaining, and displaying personal power that by the early 1980s, after a decade of rule under martial law and after alienating virtually all classes in society, and even with the enthusiastic support of the Reagan administration, the center was vulnerable.

Theatre and the "People Power Revolution"

The singular event that marked the beginning of the end for the regime was the assassination of Benigno "Ninoy" Aquino Jr., father of the current president. The senior Aquino had served in the Senate of the Philippines prior to the imposition of martial law in 1972, at which time he was arrested and imprisoned for seven years. Returning from a lengthy period of medical treatment and de facto political exile in the United States, he was killed—most people believe at the hands of Marcos thugs—on August 21, 1983, on the tarmac at the international airport that now bears his name. Steven Shirley sets out the drama of the martyred Ninoy and the suffering Cory in a framework that parallels the story of the *pasyon:*

> His Golgotha was the Manila airport and his cross was the tarmac where he, like Jesus, was betrayed by his own people and executed by their corrupt government. Cory was portrayed as the suffering Mary. Mary the mother and Mary Magdalene, who wept at the death of the fallen savior. (Shirley 2004, 71)

Ninoy's martyrdom was the match that lit the fuse of the so-called EDSA or People Power Revolution, and one might rightfully conclude that Marcos could have held out much longer had the country not turned against him for appearing to be behind such a brazenly thuggish and immoral act. The Philippines is noted for being the only government in Asia where in contemporary times an oppressive regime was overthrown by so-called people power. In February 1986 hundreds of thousands of Filipinos brought the country to a standstill by occupying the arterial road known as EDSA (Epifanio de los Santos, or, rather auspiciously, "Epiphany of the Saints"), and standing up against the forces and military might of the state. When the Marcoses fled, along with significant sums of cash and jewels (though without Imelda's famous cache of shoes), the country seemed to unite politically around a progressive center, embodied by Corazon Aquino, the self-proclaimed "plain housewife" president, and wife of the slain political martyr. As her very name—Corazon, Spanish for heart—suggests, she at least initially embodied all that was brave, heroic, and good in this new Filipino order, and the progressive forces of the left rallied behind her as did the masses due to the high moral position she occupied.

Theatre had already played a significant role in "conscientizing" the masses during the period of martial law, as activist artists staged "'lightning performances' . . . where people usually converged, like market places and churchyards. In a flash, a team of three or four activists acted out a scene that denounced the dictatorship and exhorted the people to reject and fight it" (Ilagan 2010, 118). These agitprop theatrical skits, characterized as "hit and run" performances (van Erven 1992, 46), popped up randomly around Metro Manila, parodying the excesses of the Marcos regime, highlighting their inhumanity and excesses, and drawing attention to illegal detentions and disappearances of thousands of people deemed to be threats to the regime. Tiongson (1994b, 128) observes that from 1972 onward, many theatre artists who engaged in such activity were arrested and detained. Works by PETA playwrights, staged in the final years of the regime, used humor and parody to respond to the political crisis. Among the best-known of these was Chris Millado's *Buwan at Baril sa E♭ Major* (Moon and Gun in E♭ Major), which features the First Lady trying to revive her vampire husband, Ilocula—a name that conflates Dracula with Ilocos Norte, Marcos' home region.[9]

As street theatre and the occasional brave stage play was "conscientizing" the masses, popular music was providing the sound track and inspiration lyrics for a brighter tomorrow. Songs by the folk singer Noel Cabangon and the then-youthful group Apo Hiking Society became hugely popular, some serving as anthems for the impending revolution. Cabangon's "Ako'y Isang Mabuting Pilipino" (I Am a Good Filipino) spoke to the duties of a citizen who respects the rights of others and contributes to the civic good:

Ako'y isang mabuting Pilipino
Minamahal ko ang bayan ko
Tinutupad ko ang aking mga tungkulin
Sinusunod ko ang kanyang mga alituntunin[10]

I am a good Filipino
My country is dear to my heart
I fulfill my obligations
I follow our rules

The lyrics that follow articulate the specific obligations of citizens ("I do not give or take bribes," "I do not throw garbage on the street"), setting their actions in stark contrast to the criminal plundering of state coffers by the Marcoses.

"Handog ng Pilipino sa Mundo" (The Gift of the Philippines to the World), written just after the EDSA Revolution in 1986, has long been regarded as the "People Power" anthem. Reputedly composed in a flash of inspiration in a mere twenty minutes by singer-songwriter Jim Paredes, its powerfully emotional lyrics offered hope for a brighter tomorrow at a time when the country was still under the grip of an increasingly brutal and ultimately illegal government, which ultimately refused to honor the results of legally constituted elections. The song's refrain points to an outside world watching this moment, suggesting that Filipinos should be proud of having overthrown a corrupt and illegal government without violence:

Handog ng Pilipino sa mundo,
Mapayapang paraang pagbabago.

> *Katotohanan, kalayaan, katarungan*
> *Ay kayang makamit na walang dahas.*
> *Basta't magkaisa tayong lahat.*[11]
>
> The gift Filipinos offer to the world,
> Change in a peaceful manner.
> Truth, freedom, justice
> can be achieved without violence.
> Provided we are all united together.

Theirs was an extraordinarily theatrical revolution, in which nuns literally stepped into the streets and stopped the tanks, and where Corazon Aquino spent her final nights before assuming the presidency in a convent protected by Carmelite nuns. Rich in visual iconography, this is a revolution that lives on in the many powerful photographic images of ordinary people taking to the streets, supported by the moral authority of the Catholic Church. And as the meeting place of the revolution, its ground zero, is the country's most heavily trafficked roads—the literal lifeline of Metro Manila—one can never escape the living presence of the EDSA Revolution.

This great opening in the firmament of Filipino political life of which EDSA was the symbol was to prove short-lived. It soon became clear that Cory Aquino was no match for the powerfully entrenched forces unwilling to give up their stranglehold on the nation's political and economic resources. It was particularly difficult to enact legislation that would lead to agrarian reform because the wealthy families, including Aquino's own, who controlled the vast estates on which the rural poor labored resisted progressive change. Writing just two years after the revolution, Anderson observes that the allies on the right and left had already deserted the coalition that brought Aquino to power:

> From the right, ambitious middle-ranking and junior officers of the National Army, frustrated finally by the old regime's visible decay and the ethnic nepotism of its premier danseur; the ever-hopeful technocracy and the non-crony segments of Manila's business community; almost all factions of the Church; the middle class; the non-NPA [New People's Army] sectors of the intelligentsia; sundry self-described "cause-oriented groups" which regarded themselves as the vanguard of a newly-legal Left; and the oligarchs (Anderson 1988, 24).

Anderson observes that even by the so-called restoration of democracy elections in May 1987, the larger political battle was already lost, as "traditional political families" were overwhelmingly returned to the reconstituted House of Representatives and Senate.[12]

If one were to fast-forward a generation to 2009, it would have been difficult indeed to find a single person in the middle or poorer classes who believed that the quality of life for most Filipinos was any better than it had been at the end of the Marcos era. When I first started coming to the Philippines in 2001, one highly respected figure in the arts noted wistfully that at least under the Marcoses the infrastructure was not completely collapsing, unlike at the then-present moment, where chunks of city sidewalks were giving way to open sewers, and the inefficient engines of jeepneys and motorbikes were belching toxic smoke out into traffic-clogged streets, some of which were virtual brown canyons of soot and emphysema-inducing poisons. There had been no meaningful land reform, the poor were poorer than ever, educational standards and completion rates had fallen, and the country was run by the much-hated Gloria Macapagal Arroyo (then known as "GMA"), who by 2009 was widely believed to have rigged the latest set of elections that kept her in power. There were stories of brown paper bags of money leaving Malacañang, the presidential palace, and to make matters worse, in the run-up to the election season it appeared that the heir apparent to the presidency after her term expired in 2010 was to be Manny Villar, a real estate tycoon, and one of the country's richest men. Under such circumstances, voter apathy was more the rule than the exception.

Saint Cory, the Martyr, and the Son

Then, on August 1, 2009, everything suddenly seemed to change. Corazon Aquino died after a long bout with cancer. From the beginning, the public outpouring of grief was epic. In the most theatrical of all send-offs, singer Lea Salonga, herself a national icon of Filipino pride after her international success in the hit musical, *Miss Saigon,* crooned "Bayan Ko" (My Country) accompanied by a full orchestra, at the conclusion of the Requiem Mass for Aquino as her coffin was carried out of the Manila Cathedral on August 5. With "Bayan Ko," the Philippines is perhaps the only country in the world with an unofficial second national anthem whose lyrics, melody line, and emotional tone speak not to the greatness of nation, but rather to its unfulfilled potential, to the hope for a better tomorrow. Written in 1898 to protest continuing American occupation of the Philippines, "Bayan Ko" was incorporated into a popular Spanish-language *zarzuela* (musical), *Walang Sugat* (No Wound). During the Marcos years, the Tagalog version of the song with lyrics by José Corazón de Jesús and music by Constancio de Guzmán became a popular protest song, and later, after the EDSA Revolution of 1986, it became associated with Cory Aquino, as she came to embody the hopes of the nation for a better future. The lyrics in Tagalog and English bear setting out here in full:

Ang bayan kong Pilipinas,
Lupain ng ginto't bulaklak.
Pag-ibig na sa kanyang palad,
Nag-alay ng ganda't dilag.

My country, the Philippines,
Land of gold and flowers.
With love in the palm of her hands,
She offered beauty and splendor.

At sa kanyang yumi at ganda,
Dayuhan ay nahalina.
Bayan ko, binihag ka.
Nasadlak sa dusa.

And by her modesty and beauty,
Foreigners were charmed.
My country, you were made captive.
Plunged into despair.

Chorus

Ibon mang may layang lumipad,
Kulungin mo at umiiyak.
Bayan pa kayang sakdal-dilag,
Ang 'di magnasang makaalpas?

Birds that fly freely,
Cage them and they will cry.
How much more a beautiful nation,
Shall long to break free?

Pilipinas kong minumutya,
Pugad ng luha at dalita.
Aking adhika,
Makita kang sakdal laya!

The Philippines, my beloved,
Cradle of tears and misery.

My wish,
Is to see you truly free![13]

In stark contrast to the official national anthem, which sounds uncannily like an inverted version of "La Marseillaise," "Bayan Ko" is a soaring, emotive, plaintive folk song that points to the country's colonial past while suggesting that it continues to live as a captive nation. As we have seen, *bayan* is not just nation, it is personal; it is how one chooses to identify oneself and to live and be with others. A *bayan* that is not free are a people who are not free. Salonga's highly emotional rendering of "Bayan Ko" was broadcast live on national television on August 5, cutting between close-ups of her quivering face and shots of the cathedral packed with mourners, the family—including a shot that lingered on Noynoy—and those gathered outside the cathedral in the rain, notably military officers and legions of enthusiastic, flag-waving Filipinos. Her "Bayan Ko" was part lament, part love song, infused with a deep sense of longing for a better future, reflecting the mood of the nation. In spite of the hope of the EDSA Revolution embodied by this woman, Cory Aquino, the country remained enslaved to those who exploit it for their own profit. It was as if the nation were mourning for itself as well as Cory.

That the death of Cory Aquino could or would be a game-changer in the political campaign makes sense only if one considers that the promise and spirit of the EDSA Revolution, dormant since the heady, optimistic days immediately after she came to power in 1986, remained beneath the surface, waiting to be unleashed. And as was the case with anti-Marcos activism, the power of both theatre and music played a key role in fueling the public face of the movement that led to the election of Noynoy to the presidency less than a year later, in May 2010. That this constitutionally shy, awkward only son of Cory and Ninoy would ever be president was something no one could have predicted, that is unless one takes into account the moral authority of Corazon Aquino and his martyred father, now exerted from beyond the grave. To some extent it was inevitable that the family would be in the media spotlight in the days and weeks following Cory's death, though this was largely due to the profile of Noynoy's sister Kris Aquino, an attractive television star and talk-show host, and her handsome then-husband James Yap,[14] a professional basketball player. Yet more than his telegenic sister and brother-in-law, it was the feeling that the revolution was never completed, that the promise of EDSA had never been fully realized, that enabled the moral authority of the mother to be transferred, somewhat unwittingly—at least initially—to the son.

At the time of Cory's death, the 2010 election was shaping up along predictable lines, with the GMA-supported candidate Villar championing the poor while doing the bidding of the rich and engaged in a "traditional campaign."[15] The front-runner for the Liberal Party was Mar Roxas, descended from a famous political dynasty and grandson of the first president of the Philippines. Unlike the good-looking and smoothly patrician Senator Roxas, Noynoy was relatively undistinguished looking and in possession of an unspectacular record in the Senate of the Philippines; yet in spite of these obstacles, within a single month after his mother's death the Liberal Party had a ticket headed by him and former front-runner Roxas as the vice-presidential candidate. Support for an Aquino campaign came together so rapidly not because Noynoy was an accomplished politician—indeed he had a reputation for being a bit of a slacker—but because in many respects he was an empty vessel around which the forces of a progressive left could coalesce, much as they did in 1987. Mae Paner's videos as Juana Change had sent up the illegal practices and backroom deals of the GMA administration, and by mid-2009 she already had a history of actively campaigning for "None of the above," the tagline for one of her well-known videos. Paner (2010) recalls that when Noynoy finally relented and agreed to run, after much pressure was put on him, she and other activists felt "a collective intelligence there" that made supporting him a necessity. Another informant, Marian Pastor Roces, an independent curator and self-defined "political animal" who worked on the campaign behind the scenes, recalls this period: "Immediately after the announcement there were just group meetings everywhere. The whole city was just full of meetings. And it was just happening simultaneously. Then it coalesced. Groups coalesced" (Pastor Roces 2010). Pastor Roces recalled that the nascent campaign mobilized major figures on the left, including one person who served the de facto "power center," noting that people like herself and Paner were "very much at the fringes." Yet from that position on the fringes, Paner had a significant influence on the campaign, so much so that Noynoy himself later came to view her as the "moral force" of the campaign (Paner 2011, 2013). How PETA-trained Paner, a former producer of television advertising, came to be associated with Noynoy's ascendency to the presidency is the subject to which we now turn.

Juana Change and the Election of Noynoy Aquino

At the outset of the 2010 presidential campaign, Noynoy's ascent to the top spot on the Liberal Party ticket was largely a matter of political expediency. Like most political parties in the Philippines, the Liberal Party has no clear platform or ideological position and is largely identified with the individuals who lead it. Because the party orientation of a candidate is largely determined by family allegiances and alliances with other powerbrokers, the party from which an individual is running tells us who his or her allies are, and often little else. What really matters is who is backing the candidate and whether or not they can mobilize the financial resources to conduct a "traditional campaign," which necessitates vote-buying. When it became clear by late August that the moral authority of the mother was being transferred to the son, it was hardly surprising that the powerbrokers in the Liberal Party began to ask themselves whether or not it might be more expedient to push the patrician Mar Roxas aside in favor of the son of a martyr who had the potential to reactivate the masses. By all accounts, the elevation of Noynoy involved the kinds of activist meetings described by Pastor Roces as well as intense discussions with the two powerful camps in the Liberal Party, the so-called Hyatt 10 reformist group,[16] and the entrenched, conservative forces within the party, which largely reflects the interests of the "trapos."

A number of smaller, progressive forces and an army of volunteers came together collectively believing, for the first time since the 1986 EDSA Revolution that brought down Ferdinand Marcos, that real political change was possible. By the time of Cory's death, Juana Change had already come to serve as a symbol of the desire for political change, through her videos critiquing the entrenched corruption of the Arroyo regime and the forces that held the country and its people back. The name of her "Everywoman" character signifies both the opportunity for change ("Wanna Change?") and its negative in that *Wa na* in Tagalog, when placed before the word "change," becomes *wala nang* change, conveying a sense of resigning oneself to the current situation, the belief that change is hopeless. This, according to Rody Vera (2011), is a "dichotomy that reflects the apathy and sincere hope of a divided nation." The lyrics to her tuneful song "Juana Change," distributed in video through social media, lamented the state of affairs as the country headed toward the 2010 election:

> *Kawawa naman itong bayan natin.*
> *Hindi makaahon itong bayan natin*
>
> Woe to this country of ours.
> We cannot rise above this country.

Followed by the refrain:

> I Juana Juana Change Change
> I Juana Juana Juana Change Change Change Juana.[17]

Equally worn down by the lack of political change was influential political commentator Conrado de Quiros of the *Philippines Daily Inquirer*, who here reflects back on this critical moment when he, like Juana Change and other progressives, decided to step into the political fray and actively support Noynoy:

> I saw myself as participating in a very partisan way in a project vaster and grander than an election. That was the project of ending nine years of misrule, or indeed illegitimate rule, and ushering in the hope or possibility of a better world. From the start I kept saying that Noynoy was more than an ordinary candidate—no one comes from out of the blue to get the numbers that he did in an ordinary election—and this was more than an ordinary election. His mandate was not to win for himself the presidency but to win for the people their liberty. (de Quiros 2010)

For de Quiros, Noynoy's campaign "was an EDSA masquerading as an election, which was proven by the people massing to the elementary public schools even as an angry sun beat upon the earth, as they massed during Cory's funeral even as a grieving sky let fall its tears upon the earth." Here de Quiros conjures up the visual iconography of the EDSA Revolution, with the masses in the streets, now newly reunited in their grief, braving the elements and putting up with extremes of discomfort in order to stand up for a brighter tomorrow.

Rather than shaping up as a battle between the reformist and "trapo" elements within the Liberal Party, the rift in the campaign, "from the start . . . was between the reformist volunteer groups and the trapo political party" (de Quiros 2010). Indeed, the campaign, and Juana Change's position within it as a key volunteer mobilizing the left, supports his observation. Mae Paner recalls her involvement in the campaign as often having been fraught with difficulties, chiefly because the "trapo" politicians who campaigned under the banner of the Liberal Party distrusted her as well as the other volunteers who took to the road and toured the country with the "Rock the Vote" campaign, sharing the stage with the politicians at rallies. She pulled her character Juana Change out of these stage presentations in March 2010, just months before the election, though the following month Juana Change was on the road again in the United States for eleven "Noy-Mar" campaign fundraising events in cities with large Filipino-American populations.[18] She recalls one of her routines before such an audience in which she enacted a young woman living in the slums on a few hundred pesos a day, observing that "People were emotional about this, reminding them of things they wanted to forget about their country."

Paner's act was no doubt a difficult one for the "trapo" politicians to swallow, and indeed her onstage presence at rallies at times overshadowed that of the politicians. As for Noynoy, Paner recalls his having said of her stage routine, "I don't want Juana to crush my balls" (2010). There is no doubt that Juana Change's act was big, very big. First of all, there is her size. Though she has dropped about a hundred pounds since the end of the campaign, at the time of the rallies, it is not much of an exaggeration to suggest she was among the biggest, fattest women in the Philippines, certainly of those in the public spotlight. And in a country where the women presented in the media and in film and television are routinely slender, small framed, light-skinned, and delicately boned, Paner is none of these things. She has the wide nose bridge that, although common at street level, is absent on the faces of men and women in the entertainment industry, and she does not have the prized, milky white skin of the women who look down on urban Manila from the advertisements on billboards that are as large as football fields. In her onstage persona at the "Rock the Vote" rallies, Paner wore a spangled, tight-fitting dress with classic Imelda butterfly sleeves and an iridescent blue tinsel wig, which had the effect of making her appear even larger and scarier than she was in real life. At moments when she turned her back to the audience, one caught a glimpse of a skull-and-crossbones design that covered the entire back of the dress. Were she to perform on the stage of a gay bar in Sydney or San Francisco, one might mistake her for a very large, square-framed man in drag with enormous breasts, an impression her boisterous, campy presentational style and raspy stage voice might well reinforce.

What follows is an account of Juana Change's stage routine near the end of a six-hour "Rock the Vote" rally held a week before the election. Presented on a temporary raised stage on the backside of the massive EDSA monument, which immortalizes those who took to the streets in 1986, depicting them in heroic scale as they lead a forward charge carrying flags and banners, Juana Change appeared after many hours of opening musical acts, yet well before the politicians appeared. If it were a television sitcom filmed before a live audience, one might characterize Paner's Juana Change as the "warm-up act" designed to whip the audience into a heightened emotional state, preparing them for the big entrance of the big guy and others who joined him onstage as part of the Liberal Party ticket, which included not only vice-presidential candidate Roxas, who would later lose to Jejomar Binay on the basis of the popular vote, but also candidates for the Senate and House of Representatives. Comic entertainers at such a function might tell a few lighthearted jokes at the expense of the candidate, but Juana Change put the audience in the middle of the exchange, subverting their expectations, and putting them in the defensive position. The following interactive exchange with the audience,[19] set out below in translation, reflects a tactic that many of the paid campaign staff might have regarded as too risky and unconventional:

> *JC:* Do you think Mar Roxas will save you?
>
> *Aud:* Yeahhhhh!
>
> *JC:* What is hard to do, you have already done. You are already here. You are already celebrating as if you were sure there's going to be change. Are you willing to bet on it?
>
> *Aud:* Yeahhhh!
>
> *JC:* How about you? *(directed at an audience member)* And you? *(directed at another audience member)*
>
> *Aud: (enthusiastic response from audience)*
>
> *JC:* NO! At this time who will win? Do you think Noynoy will?
>
> *Aud:* Yeahhhh!
>
> *JC:* If you think he is different from the others you are mistaken! *(directed at audience)* Friend, will you fight [for this]?
>
> *Aud:* Yeahhhh!
>
> *JC:* OK, fight if you're really for Noynoy. *(She makes moves as if she's going to fight with audience members, which given her size is both funny and slightly threatening.)*

At this point, further banter ensues and she picks up on the theme of their empowerment, reminding them that they, the masses in attendance, possess the real power, and that they must remain vigilant and not trust the promises of anyone, least of all Noynoy and Mar Roxas. She continues: "We are the ones to save ourselves, we are the ones to save our lives. The success is not with Noynoy, but with the whole of the Philippines. We cannot win this alone!"

For those overseeing a typical campaign, the risks behind such a tactic were considerable, especially as it plays against what everyone is taught to believe about the way politics functions in the Philippines. Juana Change's suggestion that things will not magically improve with the election of Noynoy, that they need to fight, that only they can change the political landscape of the country, is in many respects contrary to the lived experience of those hearing these words who expect elected politicians to "give them" tangible things both in order to be elected and after the election. In a political framework where most individuals are powerless

Figure 10. Juana Change (Mae Paner) inciting the audience at the "Rock the Vote" rally, Manila, May 2, 2010. Photo by author.

and dependent on the state through their local elected representative, Juana Change's exhortation that "We are the ones to save ourselves" is a deeply radical statement.

Juana Change was able to get away with this only because even before Noynoy fever swept the country, she was already identified with change. As Paner put it, in the eyes of many, "It's better to be on the side of Juana." But even so, Juana did the opposite of what one would ordinarily expect at a rally; she openly sought to antagonize the audience. Paner recalls the impulse behind this oppositional mode of expression:

> Juana Change is not there to make you feel or feel comfortable, in fact the opposite of that. [So I] banter about you think this guy will win, come on? I think they were a bit too *mayabang* [arrogant], complacent. So I had to display this attitude that, so you think you've won already, watch out! Continue until D-day and beyond. We knew there was going to be cheating. Because everybody was happy. (Paner 2010)

Paner's final caveat is an acknowledgment that even though by all accounts "Noy-Mar" did not undertake a "traditional campaign," it would have been impossible to guarantee that all others from the Liberal Party who graced the stage at these "Rock the Vote" rallies were running unblemished campaigns. In these final days of the campaign there was much enthusiasm as it appeared that in a mere nine months Noynoy had come from nowhere to overtake the early front-runners, Villar and his own running mate, Roxas. Juana Change responded to the crowd's exuberance, further pumped up by hours of high-octane music acts, exhorting them to curb their enthusiasm, challenging their unquestioning faith in the power of political leaders to magically effect change, taking it a step further by suggesting that real political change was an impossibility as long as they held such a view.

The slogan of the Noy-Mar campaign in this final push prior to the election was the simplistic *Kung Walang Korupt, Walang Mahirap,* which conveys the meaning, "Without corruption, there will be no difficulties," or, even more simply, "No corruption, [then] no difficulties." That Juana was "conscientizing" the audience in good, old-fashioned PETA style while the public rhetoric of the campaign remained so utterly reductive reflects the disjunction between the continuing realities of political life in the Philippines and what Juana Change and the forces of the progressive left sought for Filipinos. While she was exhorting voters to maintain a critical eye, even a slightly jaundiced one, banners on the stage and throughout the vast area surrounding the audience proclaimed a very simple equation, one as old and tired as any that might underlie a political campaign. The logic behind the slogan goes something like this: (1) Our country is famously corrupt; (2) Corruption is the root of all evil in our country; (3) If elected, Noy-Mar will eliminate corruption; and (4) When they eliminate corruption, all of our difficulties, including poverty, economic inequality, lack of access to medical care, and the exploitation of Filipino labor overseas, will end. Corruption has long been the bogeyman used in political rhetoric, and one can argue that by focusing on corruption rather than the systemic forces that make corruption both possible and necessary, the slogan of the Noy-Mar campaign was not only empty of meaning, but in fact a pledge to continue with business as usual after the election. Indeed, as has been noted earlier in this chapter, Aquino comes from one of the landowning first families of the nation, and presumably someone in his family authorized the coldblooded murder of twelve impoverished landless farmers and two children as they protested on his family's vast estate, Hacienda Luisita, in 2004.[20] Thus the obvious question is, as it has long been: How can anyone from one of these families with relatives who have engaged in corruption, intimidation, vote-buying, and even murder in order to maintain their wealth and position possibly go against the long-term interests of their clan and carry out the structural reform necessary to ensure that the conditions for *walang korupt* are possible?

Mindful of this, Juana Change urged vigilance, even on the eve of what many were beginning to believe would be a historic victory, in which a broad coalition, supported by a vast youth vote mobilized through the "Rock the Vote" campaign, would remove a much-despised government through democratic means and replace it with one that would set a new course for the country. The emotional structure and logic of that penultimate Manila rally was brilliant in terms of its ability to mobilize and activate the assembled crowd. A series of dynamic and diverse song and dance numbers, primarily by young artists, occupied the first four hours of the event. Juana Change then jolted the already pumped-up audience by placing them in the center of the equation, which served as the prelude for a short but stirring campaign speech by Noynoy, while the evening concluded with songs by Jim Paredes and the Apo Hiking Society, essentially wrapping up the entire event in the spirit of the EDSA Revolution. Many Filipinos felt genuine joy when he won on May 10, and great hope that this hideously corrupt nation, in many respects run as a feudal oligarchy, would and could be turned around. The spirit of the EDSA Revolution had been revived, and was channeled by the Noy-Mar campaign in the shadow of the EDSA monument, part of an emotional arc that started with the outpouring of public grief on the death of Noynoy's mother Cory. The hopes and dreams of so many, particularly the generation of Filipino activists who came of age in the late 1970s and early 1980s, including even those on the left, were rekindled in this one brief interlude that started in August 2009 and led to the election of Noynoy in May 2010. But for many, this hope was short-lived.

Taking on the Dynasties

Upon assuming office, the new administration vigorously responded to the corruption of the previous administration, made a number of progressive appointments to key departments, and built the foundation for a more principled, less corrupt government in which even those at the very top, including former presidents and Supreme Court judges, are subject to the rule of law. Yet the "dream team" of Noy-Mar never materialized. Because the office of vice president is elected in a separate popular vote, in the end Noynoy's vice president was not Roxas but rather Jojo Binay, the feisty, former mayor of Makati. Although Noynoy has at times attempted to sideline Binay, his power base is strong by virtue of having run Manila's wealthiest city, one with a sizable enclave full of fine restaurants, fancy shopping malls, and high-rise office buildings for expatriates and wealthy locals.

But within a year of the election, Juana Change and Noynoy parted company, not over politics but over style. Rebranded as "PNoy" (a play on *Pinoy,* slang for a Filipino) after he took office as president, for many, Noynoy's moral strength was his willingness to shun the extravagant trappings of life as president of the republic. My Tagalog teacher told me that she decided to vote for him on election day when she saw him on television, patiently standing in line to vote in his home electorate north of Manila. She said it moved her almost to tears that he did not behave like a "normal" politician requiring special treatment, and that what prompted her to change her mind at the last minute was her belief that he was temperamentally different from the others. The bachelor president chose to live in the relatively modest guesthouse, the Bahay Pangarap on the grounds of Malacañang, rather than in the former Spanish governor-general's palace occupied by most heads of state, including his predecessor, GMA. And as a further marker of his humility, he honored his campaign pledge to eliminate "wang-wang," the long-standing practice in which presidential motorcades raced through the streets with lights flashing and sirens blaring, forcing other cars off the road. PNoy, unlike some of his famously flashy predecessors in the top job, appears to be a fundamentally decent, constitutionally shy guy, who does not wish his life to be complicated by the external trappings of power.

Thus it came as a bit of a shock to some when in January 2011, presidential spokesman Edwin Lacierda confirmed the rumor that the fifty-year-old PNoy had purchased a Porsche. It was pointed out that the Porsche was a "third-hand" 2007 model bought with his private funds. Yet given that he had just a month earlier issued a memorandum requiring government agencies "to be more prudent in spending government funds, especially in the acquisition of motor vehicles" (Sisante 2011), the timing of this midlife-crisis purchase raised some eyebrows, including those of Mae Paner and her collaborator Rody Vera. They quickly created a video that was much circulated and resulted in a national news story covered by the major networks and newspapers. The wickedly clever video starts as Juana Change, assuming her "Everywoman" character as the voice of reason, happens upon four people huddled inside a small shelter by the side of the road in a rural area. Each of them—nurse, student, man with crutch, and old woman—are awaiting the arrival of PNoy's Porsche in the hopes of hitching a ride. While the male student enthuses that "the car of progress is on its way," Juana Change points out that the Porsche cost 4.5 million pesos (approximately US$100,000), an astronomical sum of money for most Filipinos.[21] More than the lighthearted banter, what probably did not sit well with the new administration was the suggestion that they had accomplished nothing, as the following exchange suggests:

Nurse: But he said he bought the car to relieve his stress. It's really stressful to run a government.

JC: What has his government done so far?

(They all look at each other in a moment of awkward silence.)

Student: Come on, you should understand. It's so stressful having done nothing when there is much to be done.

The student later reads from Republic Act No. 6713, the Code of Conduct and Ethical Standards for Public Officials and Employees, passed while Noynoy's mother served as president, citing section 4(h), "simple living," which states that "Public officials and employees and their families shall lead modest lives appropriate to their positions and income. They shall not indulge in extravagant or ostentatious display of wealth in any form" (Philippines Civil Service Commission 1989). After a cartoonish-looking PNoy speeds by, drenching them with a pool of standing water, they pledge solidarity to one another and take to the road. Although the telling of jokes can offer an escape valve that enables the poor to endure rather than act, there is no doubt that Paner and Vera's video was designed to mobilize their audience to engage in the very kind of policing of the new administration that Juana Change had called for at the penultimate campaign rally in Manila less than a year earlier.

The official response to the video from the president's communications development and strategic planning secretary, Ricky Carandang, was that the government had chosen to ignore it (Cheng 2011), but Paner recalls a quite different reaction. Called to Malacañang (the term often used for the executive branch) by Carandang to explain the video after her earlier support for PNoy, she remembers the secretary telling her, in speaking of the video, "I have not seen it and I don't care" (Paner 2013). Paner notes that Carandang's dismissive remark prompted her in subsequent interviews with the press to say, "If they don't care, then I do. I care." She observes that the video also marked the end of her relationship with PNoy: "Yeah, it's because of that we're not friends anymore. He took it very personally" (Paner 2013). Had PNoy himself listened to his own warm-up act during those rallies leading up to the election, he would have understood that Paner was merely doing what she promised tens of thousands of people around the country that she and others needed to do.

The ability to laugh at one's self is valued in the Philippines. Laughter at a good joke is fun, and even when at one's own expense, a joke is always worth telling or participating in. PNoy's purchase, so soon after the election, made him a sitting duck for public ribbing. Were an American president or British prime minister to buy a Porsche at age fifty shortly after assuming office, it is a safe bet that they would be ridiculed relentlessly in newspapers and on television. So for PNoy to just "not get" why others found this disturbing, ironic, or funny, even if it was a minor indulgence rather than a major sin, suggests that as the son of a martyr and a virtual saint, he lacks the capacity to laugh at himself, and possibly more dangerously, the capacity for self-reflection. Though Noynoy may not behave like a "trapo" politician, speeding through town in a noisy motorcade or living large in Malacañang, the fact remains that he is descended from one of the country's most powerful families, a family that melds political and economic power, and has wielded it to great effect for over a century. And if there's one class that cannot poke fun at themselves or brook criticism, it is powerful people from these families. Vice President Binay was able to joke about being a "black man" running for office inasmuch as he is the paterfamilias of a new political dynasty. Retired action movie star and former president Estrada behaved disgracefully with liquor and women and made no attempt to hide it. But those who descend from the "modern principalia" like PNoy have little if any capacity to see themselves or their actions in a comic light. The family must always protect its own interests, and if any individual in the family is attacked, then the entire weight of the dynasty must be brought to bear against any external force seen as hostile.

In the lead-up to the 2013 general election, Paner again shifted into social activist mode, this time mobilizing broader communities to create public performance events that resulted in two significant political victories and the beginning of what is shaping up as a war against political dynasties. The first target for what she refers to as her "advocacy" were the enormous tarpaulin banners created with public funds that routinely appear in the preelection period in which local politicians lay claim to every public construction project or expansion of health, education, or social services that took place during their term of office. Such banners trumpet their achievements and stretch across streets at festivals throughout the country, greeting people as if the local politician were the sole patron of the event. Furthermore, the size and ubiquitousness of these banners, typically made of woven plastic, means that in many *barangays* and congressional districts, much of the visual field in the public sphere is dominated by the smiling and sometimes menacing faces of local political incumbents. Typically the banners briefly list their achievements, linking them with the "gifts" they have bestowed on the local community using the community's own resources. Apart from the perverseness behind the exercise, the banners are just plain ugly, especially insofar as the same banner might appear on every single lamppost over a large area, whereas smaller, poster-sized images are endlessly replicated on fences and buildings or strung up on wires crossing the streets during fiestas. The local term for this visual blight is "epal," which plays on the word *mapapel,* Tagalog for an attention-grabber (Uy 2012; Rodriguez 2012; Yamsuan 2012). The term has come to indicate both the practice and the politician who engages in it. As Paner has observed, "Epals are those politicians who take credit for anything that they do, which is their duty to fulfil in the first place" (Arceo-Dumlao 2012).

Adopting her Juana Change character, Paner and Carlos Celdran teamed up to offer the public an anti-epal tour of Quezon City in Metro Manila, an area she termed the "epal Capital of the Philippines" (Rodriguez 2012). The duo offered a motorcade tour of the area from a flatbed truck starting at 6:30 a.m., essentially using "shame them and name them" (ibid.) tactics to entertain the audiences who came along for the show, while advocating for change. The larger audience was the general public, who saw brief clips of the tour on television. Paner and Vera are masters at manipulating the media and Paner especially has a gifted understanding of how to offer up a larger public performance that contains within it short segments that stand on their own and are ideally suited for television news, a skill she perfected over a career producing television commercials, a profession she left behind in 2013. This campaign launched a national anti-epal movement as well as the quick passage of a bill sponsored by key legislators in the Philippine Congress in October 2012 prohibiting the use of epals, using language that was both clear and comprehensive. Prohibited acts included:

> (a) Affixing, or causing to be affixed, the name, or image of any public official to a signage announcing a proposed or on-going public works project; and (b) Installing, or causing to be installed, signage announcing the maintenance, rehabilitation, and construction of public works crediting individual public officer, or bearing his or her image, for the maintenance, rehabilitation, and construction of such public works. (Senate of the Philippines, Senate Bill 1967)

Perhaps even more miraculously, anyone engaging in these practices faced serious penalties: disqualification from running for office for a minimum of six months, essentially ending their candidacy in any current election. The country's electoral commission, Comelec, joined forces with the movement, and in a nation that was one of the first to take up the mobile phone in mass numbers, a phone app was introduced that allowed users to take photos of offending epals and post them on the Anti-Epal Movement's Facebook and Twitter accounts. They are also able to pass them on directly to various government agencies through their respective Twitter accounts (Montecillo 2012).[22] Epals all over Metro Manila came down and virtually overnight ended the single most visible political practice that has dominated the public sphere for as long as I have been coming to the Philippines. The success of this campaign represents a significant opening in the political consciousness of Filipinos; epals provided a daily reminder of the subservience of the lower order to their political masters, notably the "trapo" politicians with recognized family names, from the class who "brought you" virtually all things that improve one's quality of life. By starting a process that has unchained those family names from public service and construction projects, Paner and Celdran have created an opening for individuals to consider the fact that they themselves are the ones whose money and labor is responsible for those public projects that better their lives.

The following year the country was rocked by a headline-grabbing corruption scandal after a series of exposés in the *Philippine Daily Inquirer,* revealing that as much as a billion pesos (in excess of US$22 million) had been redirected from the national Priority Development Assistance Fund to a number of prominent politicians through some bogus foundations and nongovernmental organizations. The mastermind behind the operation was businesswoman Janet Lim-Napoles, around whom a major media circus coalesced as she faced a range of charges that included kidnapping her cousin and former personal assistant after suspecting him of double-dealing. Napoles became the poster child for bad governance as she redirected government funds to congressional representatives and senators while herself pocketing a percentage through a range of legal entities. Once again, Paner demonstrated her command over the tools of the media, this time dressing up as the hangdog-faced Napoles, appearing before a Senate hearing on a Freedom of Information (FOI) bill that would prevent such abuses. Playfully impersonating Napoles as a representative of the "Right to Know" coalition, she articulated her fears about what would happen to her if the bill became law:

> They say I am the best example of FOI. If I truly am, what will happen if this is passed? I'm in jail forever? I don't like that. If it's not passed, am I free? Isn't it exciting? There's opportunity for big change. (Macaraig 2013)[23]

But what apparently elicited the strongest response from the assembled senators was her assertion—again as a fictional character—that she was able to provide the names of those among them who benefited from the scheme but were choosing not to, prompting two senators to make an immediate point of denying any wrongdoing (Corpuz 2013). Senator Grace Poe, a neophyte senator, asserted, "Hindi pa po namin natitikman ang pork" (We have not yet tasted pork), a comment that prompted unrestrained laughter from the audience (ibid.). Paner had again stolen the show, but in so doing had ensured that her appearance as the fictional Napoles would be broadcast on television and distributed through social media, keeping the anti-pork message in the public eye through a classically deadpan comic performance. Paner's further involvement in the anti-pork movement included appearing as a pig-in-a-barrel at the so-called Million People March in Manila's Luneta Park on August 26, 2013, the largest public protest in many years, and her presence in a range of original, theatrical costumes at subsequent rallies sponsored by a broad coalition of organizations.

In 2013 Paner left what had been a lucrative career in advertising for an uncertain future, observing, "Juana Change has changed me, what can I do? The advocacy has changed me" (2013). Her body has also changed:

> Whenever I go out and attack people for their excesses, I cannot ignore my own excesses. And people are saying, "How can you tell us to get rid of our excesses when you can't even get rid of your own?" And they're right . . . because what is personal is political. . . . So I really have to be the model for change. And in Filipino we call it *tangakatawanan. Katawan* is body. *Katawagan* is to embody. . . . So I have to embody change, be the body that will show change. (Paner 2013)

That year also saw the release of the feature-length *Juana C. The Movie,* a political and social satire in which Paner plays the role of a young woman from a rural village who receives a scholarship to study at a prestigious, private university in Manila and who uncovers the brazen hypocrisy and corruption of the powerful while also discovering that her ample figure is not without male admirers. Her determination to hold Noynoy accountable for his actions resulted in her total withdrawal of support in mid-2014, when she began to actively seek his impeachment because of his continued support of the executive discretionary fund, the Disbursement Acceleration Program (DAP) (Sauler 2014), even after the Supreme Court had ruled it partly unconstitutional.

The last straw for Paner may well have been Noynoy's suggestion, by midyear, that he was considering proposing an amendment to the constitution that would permit him to run for a second six-year term. By late 2014, Noynoy's popularity had fallen considerably from its earlier highs, and with only two years of his presidency remaining, he likely has legitimate fears that acting too boldly against the powerful could have the result that he himself would face legal prosecution by a hostile future government, in order to exact revenge over his adminstration's earlier anticorruption drive (Heydarian 2014). As one observer insightfully put it:

> In a country where there are no genuine political parties, and patronage politics determines day-to-day operations of the state, Aquino faced the

> Herculean task of building support for his reform agenda. In the process, he may have succumbed to Machiavellian logic: leveraging DAP funds to expedite his good governance initiatives. (Heydarian 2014)

Here it bears noting that the Liberal Party is also the party of Gina Reyes in Marinduque, the patrician Mar Roxas, and Noynoy himself. Like all of the country's leading political parties, it is held together by patronage, not policies. As long as the system in place cannot allow for viable political parties with actual platforms and some degree of internal unity, it would appear that Aquino's brief experiment with cleaning up the Philippines could well be doomed to failure. Returning to the story of the 2013 taxi ride that I invoked at the start of the chapter, the driver, annoyed by the road closures prompted by a campaign rally to ensure dynastic succession, asked me pointedly, "Do you have political dynasties in Australia?" I paused and answered that no, I could not think of one. In the silence that followed I heard a penny drop. Paner, like other Manileños I know, believes that "the conscience of Filipinos are changing" and that the only appropriate response is to "just keep on hammering and hammering and hammering away." As Paner (2013) puts it, "If epal is really the low-hanging fruit, we want to go to the root and political dynasties are the root problem."

We have seen how even in situations where people have very little, they create places for happiness through participating in mass performance events that connect them with others and give their lives meaning. Politicians as diverse and as similar as Imelda Marcos, Carmencita Reyes, and Noynoy Aquino have all used performance as the means through which to gather communities together. The former First Lady did it through her cultural policies and infrastructure program, which identified representative regional performance forms and brought them to the center to represent a *bayan* strong in its internal diversity. Reyes, like many politicians, not only supported a local community-based performance practice but also altered it to the point where it bears her personal stamp, making changes to the Boac *sinakulo* unlikely or even impossible until after her death. Noynoy, though lacking the flair for the dramatic possessed by Mrs. Marcos and Mrs. Reyes, owed his victory to the hard, backbreaking work of smaller, progressive groups that came together to support his "Rock the Vote" rallies, which featured song and dance, followed by the "warm-up act" of Juana Change. The speeches of politicians at these rallies were extraordinarily brief, with much more time given over to song, including a sing-along with the famed Apo Hiking Society who performed at the campaign rally in the shadow of the EDSA memorial. At this rally, thousands emotionally joined together in singing "Handog ng Pilipino sa Mundo," the tribute to the spirit of the EDSA Revolution. If the "gift that Filipinos gave to the world" in 1986 was the model of a bloodless revolution that brought down a tyrant, where the gift ceases to be one worth giving is in the follow-through. Fundamentally nothing has changed in terms of who owns and runs the Philippines. Corruption is still the bogeyman, as it has always been. The underlying problem is, as Paner asserts, political dynasties. And although the established dynasties have brought ruin to the country, new dynasties continue to emerge, as is the case with the Binay family, with the patriarch quietly, from his current post as vice president, setting the groundwork to win the top job in 2016. Because of the structural elements that virtually require dynastic politics, even eliminating entire families Pol Pot style would be pointless because another family with a less distinguished pedigree would be waiting in the wings to step into the void. These dynasties have tapped into the impulse toward the performative that is so deeply rooted in the culture and have used it for their own ends, but it may ultimately be only through performance that ordinary people can fight back and lay claim to their country.

Until and even beyond the day the family dynasties end, community-based performance events, particularly those associated with Holy Week and local religious and civic festivals in all of their limitless variety, will continue to be at the center of the lives of the poor, the struggling middle class, those who return to their hometowns and barrios, and those who plant the traditions of their homeland in foreign soil. Writing of the difficulty and indeed the impossibility of assembling a kind of Filipino genealogy of culture where a series of interlocking "texts" enable the cultural critic and historian to confidently offer a master text, J. Neil Garcia asserts that:

> If national identity is a performativity, then we might say that being a Filipino is not what one is, but what one does. There is no simple and singular performance of Filipino-ness, for it is a norm that can never be fully inhabited, only cited repetitively in a lifelong process of actualization. There is thus no essentially Filipino subjectivity, only its performative production as the effect of acts and discourses that do not simply characterize but actually constitute it. (Garcia 2003, 12)

The ways in which repeated performative acts constitute a Filipino subjectivity, that it is in the doing that the self is constructed, has been a key theme in this book. The flexible framework set out for *bayan* at the end of the previous chapter offers a model that can account for the virtually endless ways in which communities of performers can come together to self-define and activate the bonds of a shared subjectivity while grounding those encounters in place, nation, the cultural imaginary, and as a people. This book has also demonstrated how community-based performance events fulfill human needs that, though cultural in expression and offered as *panata,* are situated inside the body, where in their tight focus and shared communal expression, participants are made happy in the doing of the action. When a dance or festival performance is over, participants return to the quotidian, to the rhythms and temporalities of daily life; yet what sustains the individual, and perhaps what makes Filipinos happier than they might otherwise be, is the body-memory of being in this altered space and time and of the collective creation of that shared moment in time when we stand outside of time, at one with the crowd, but singular in our awareness, a singularity that moves us to participate again and again. And somewhere in that repetition is the doing that is being a Filipino.

Notes

Introduction

1. The earlier slogan, "Pilipinas, Kay Ganda!" (The Philippines, How Beautiful!) announced amid great fanfare in November 2010, was pulled after just a few days, presumably for ripping off the icon used by the Polish government to promote their own country, down to the color, font, and design, though in news accounts the slogan itself was criticized. Supporters hoped that "Kay Ganda" would eventually become identified with the Philippines as "Aloha" is associated with Hawai'i (Oiga 2010).

2. See Sissela Bok (2010) for a comprehensive, albeit Eurocentric account of the history of concepts relating to happiness.

3. Reynaldo Alejandro and Amanda Abad Santos-Gana cite three historical sources attesting to this propensity, starting with Antonio Pigafetta, Magellan's Italian chronicler, who in his *Primo viaggio interno al mondo (The First Voyage Around the World),* described "the rhythmic use of gongs in ritual dances performed by priestesses in the Cebu region" (2002, 69). A generation later, "Early missionaries of the Recollect Order reported that each year the natives held festive celebrations during which joyful dances were performed," and in the sixteenth century "Pedro Chirino gives an account of the music and dance of the natives during a religious festivity" (71). Additional evidence to support this point will be set out in chapter 4.

4. On decline, see Clifford Geertz's (1980) account of the Balinese theatre state. On extinction, see Jarod Diamond's chapter on the fate of Easter Islanders (2004, chapter 2), which shows how by devoting their physical and environmental resources toward building massive monoliths they ultimately condemned themselves to death.

5. *Sinakulo* is also spelled as *senakulo* and *cenakulo,* the latter presumably from the Spanish and Latin word *cenacle,* the site of the Last Supper. Throughout this book, I follow the spelling used by Nicanor Tiongson in the *CCP Encyclopedia of Philippine Art* (1994a). The *morion,* examined at length in chapter 3, is a Holy Week penitential practice primarily enacted by men, in which they dress up as Roman soldiers while wearing masks capped by a distinctive, crested helmet.

6. Filipino, which largely follows standard (i.e., Manila and lowland Luzon) Tagalog, is the constitutionally designated national language. For political reasons presumably related to the hegemony of Tagalog-speaking culture, this common language is referred to as Filipino rather than Tagalog. However, inasmuch as language is an expression of a particular culture, of which there are many in the Philippines, I will term the language "Tagalog" except when an author (as with Enriquez here) uses the category "Filipino language."

7. As Enriquez observes of this trinity of core "values": "*Hiya* got bandied about as 'shame' or 'embarassment.' *Utang na loób* got to be known as 'reciprocity.' But no one really got carried

away except when *pakikisama* was elevated to the status of **the** value and passed off as a Filipino 'goal, purpose and objective'" (Enriquez 1989, 55). *Pakikisama* suggests the quality of getting along well with others, but in its elevation as "the" preeminent Filipino value it has been held up by some as the singular quality that holds the nation back, the suggestion being that by excessively trying to get along, Filipinos are conflict-adverse and can never solve pressing problems. See Pe-Pua (2000) on the legacy of Enriquez and Sikolohiyang Pilipino.

8. In my early attempts to learn Tagalog by translating children's stories into English, I frequently encountered adjectives used to describe feelings for which there were no adequate translations. On such occasions my teacher showed me the facial expressions associated with these states because we could find no common expression through words or phrases.

9. A *barangay* is also an administrative and political unit, the smallest branch of local government.

10. Woods uses the spelling of the word found in Spanish sources. As Woods notes, the assertion that the *barangay* is the single, predominant mode of local political and social organization has its origins in a single source, *Las costumbres de los indios Tagalos de Filipinas*, written by Franciscan friar Juan de Plasencia in 1589 (Woods 2005, 2).

11. The Filipino *pasyon,* or the Passion of Christ, as Ileto argues, is more than simply the biblical story of Christ from his betrayal in the Garden of Gethsemane to his crucifixion and resurrection. It is an historical reality, a narrative trope, and a set of physical places in which Filipinos have connected their own struggle for independence with the power of Christ's sacrifice.

12. I have written elsewhere about transgendered performance created for a largely Korean audience (Peterson 2011) as well as the famous "dancing inmates" of Cebu (Peterson 2012).

13. Founded in 1967 by Ceclie-Guidote Alvarez, PETA is the oldest continuously operating theatre of this kind in Asia. Its work has been much documented. See especially van Erven (1992, 2001).

Chapter 1. Three Tagalog *Sinakulos*

1. According to Asian Development Bank figures, in 2011, 25.6 percent of the population lived below the poverty line. As of 2010, 18.4 percent lived on less than US$1.25 a day, the global measure of extreme poverty. Per capita gross national income in 2011 was US$2,210, slightly below that of Mongolia and fully half of that of Thailand (see ADB Basic Statistics 2013, http://www.adb.org/publications/basic-statistics-2013). Remittances from overseas Filipino workers contribute enormously to national and per capita income and were responsible for most of the country's economic growth in 2012 and 2013.

2. The U.S. State Department's "Philippines 2013 International Religious Freedom Report" estimates that 80–85 percent of the country are Roman Catholics (http://www.state.gov/documents/organization/222373.pdf).

3. As Fenella Cannell (2006) observes of the reading of the *pasyon* in the Bicol region, it is more accurate to characterize the delivery of the text as sung or chanted rather than "read." This style is found throughout the Tagalog-speaking region as well.

4. The *principales* were members of the privileged ruling class—known collectively as the *principalia*—under the Spanish colonial regime.

5. Scholarship on the *sinakulo* includes the foundational work of Nicanor Tiongson. See especially his entries in the *Cultural Center of the Philippines Encyclopedia of Philippine Art*, vol. 7 (1994e, 1994f), as well as his comprehensive book *Sinakulo* (1999b). Ricardo Trimillos

(1992) examines the performative qualities in the recitation of the *pasyon*, considering both the context for presentation and its aesthetic features. Sir Anril Pineda Tiatco and Amihan Bonifacio-Ramolete (2008) provide a detailed account of the practices at the country's most internationally renowned Holy Week site in San Fernando, Pampanga, and anthropologist Nicholas Barker's unpublished account (1997) of his earlier fieldwork at the same site was until recently available online. See also Tiatco's (2010) consideration of the *sinakulo* in Cutud. Reynaldo Ileto's *Pasyon and Revolution* (2006) provides a larger, foundational frame for the *pasyon*, while Fenella Cannell's chapter on the *pasyon* in *The Anthropology of Christianity* (2006) largely focused on the Bicol region, is compelling, detailed, and full of near-forensic insight.

6. Mandaluyong City Web site, Profile of *barangay* Barangka Ibaba, http://www.mandaluyong.gov.ph/govt/bgys.aspx?id=004 (accessed February 5, 2014).

7. Golgotha is another name for Calvary, the dome-shaped hill on which Christ is believed to have been crucified.

8. At one point I heard "Spanish Eyes," a popular song in the United States in the mid-1960s, and one I remember playing while learning the organ. Because of shared musical referents, it is not unusual for me to know the lyrics of virtually every tune played in a religious procession, particularly in the provinces.

9. To make it clear that I am using the term *hudyo* as a role category and not to signify Jewish people or the Jewish religion, *hudyo* will appear in lowercase. This is also consistent with Nicanor Tiongson's practice in his writings on *sinakulo*.

10. Held on the Thursday after Trinity Sunday, the Corpus Christi Festival celebrates the Eucharist, the transubstantiation of bread and wine into the body and blood of Christ. Coinciding with the longest days of the year in the Northern Hemisphere, in continental Europe and Britain the festival featured the staging of epic plays depicting the history of salvation until the mid-sixteenth century. In form, structure, and content, and in its civic and community-based ethos, the Boac *sinakulo* more closely resembles these plays than contemporary passion plays, which focus more narrowly on the betrayal, Crucifixion, and Resurrection of Christ.

11. Reyes (2007) asserts that she wrote the script with Carunungan, citing her facility in Tagalog as proof of her contributions. Although her key role in this collaboration cannot be independently corroborated, it is clear that she probably provided the dramatic structure for each night's *sinakulo* by selecting the content.

12. The same kind of booming, hypermasculine style of delivery is used in a recorded call to Mass that echoes throughout the center of the mountain town of Baguio from speakers outside the Baguio Cathedral.

13. Mojares uses the word *linambay*, the Cebuano word commonly used for the *komedya* form.

14. Rosario Cruz-Lucero provides a detailed account of the delight taken by residents in a *barangay* in Antique Province over the destruction of an effigy of Judas that explodes in a burst of firecrackers (Cruz-Lucero 2007, 73–102).

15. Although I am appropriating Augusto Boal's term here, I take it some distance from its original use in his Forum Theatre practice described in *Theatre of the Oppressed* (1993). Here I mean to suggest the process of moving from the position of the spectator to becoming an active participant embedded in the action, experiencing the event in many of the same ways an actor would.

16. As is true of most of the country, flagellation or mortification of the flesh is not a widespread practice in Marinduque. On Good Friday in 2007, when I witnessed a group of young

men on the streets of Boac self-flagellating, one informant told me that the appropriate place for such activity was the graveyard and not the streets.

17. After the death of Herod the Great, the kingdom of Judea (a Roman client state) was divided among Herod's three sons. Herod Antipas (20 BC–ca. 39 AD) ruled over Galilee (which included Nazareth) and Perea. This is the Herod often depicted in film as enslaved by sensual passions. Among the best known are Frank Thring in *King of Kings* (1961), Jose Ferrer in *The Greatest Story Ever Told* (1965), and Christopher Plummer in *Jesus of Nazareth* (1977). The Gospel of Luke (23:7–15) says that after Jesus was arrested in the Garden of Gethsemane he was brought before Herod as well as Pilate inasmuch as Herod was the ruler of Jesus' homeland of Nazareth and he was in Jerusalem at that time.

18. Although in conversation many Filipinos use the words "gay" and *bakla* as synonyms, *bakla* is a complex gender category that does not translate directly into "gay" as it is understood in the West. For more information, see Neil Garcia (1996, 2003) and Manalansan (2003).

19. According to Reyes (2007), Celso Carunungan added this subplot to the script in the late 1970s to "make it more interesting" and add "the human touch."

20. According to Matthew 27:19, Pilate's wife, who is not named in the Bible, sent a message urging her husband not to condemn Jesus: "When he [Pilate] was set down on the judgment seat, his wife sent unto him, saying, Have thou nothing to do with that just man: for I have suffered many things this day in a dream because of him." This and all subsequent Biblical passages are from the King James version, available at http://www.kingjamesbible online.org/.

21. In the "Sinakulo" entry in the *CCP Encyclopedia of Art*, Tiongson observes that Santos' *sinakulo* "staged its first scene on Smokey Mountain and then marched to Mendiola, where the 13 Christs with huge masks were accused of seven sins against urban law by the three Pilates who represent the establishment. After the Christs were condemned to carry the cross, the procession, which also featured seven large murals interpreting Christ's Seven Last Words according to contemporary social realities, moved on to Quiapo where the crucifixion was held" (Tiongson 1994e, 124). Mendiola, located just outside Malacañang Palace, was the site of a 1987 massacre where thirteen farmers were killed by government security forces while protesting the lack of action on land reform promised by the Aquino government.

22. Tickets to the CCP show cost 400 pesos (US$9.20), well beyond the financial reach of the urban poor.

23. More commonly known as Dimas in the Philippines.

Chapter 2. The Body of Christ

1. Indeed, the same headline was used for the same story by Singapore's Asia One online, http://news.asiaone.com/News/Latest%2BNews/Asia/Story/A1Story20100402-208143.html.

2. For an account of the social dimension of the crucifixion practice at Kapitangan, see Bräunlein (2009).

3. Though it may be difficult for many outside of Australia to fathom, there was no appreciable negative reaction domestically to Savran's actions. On the national broadcaster's Web page associated with this show, Savran, who has garnered numerous national awards for his television documentaries, has his actions set out in a lighthearted manner. See http://www .abc.net.au/tv/racerelations/.

4. Though Beltran's use of the designation "the inarticulate" in the title of his book might appear dated today, it needs to be seen as a response to a call put out by the influential Filipino historian, Renato Constantino, in 1970 to reconstruct a "history of the inarticulate" (see Scott 1982, 8).

5. On the Web site of OMF International (formerly the Overseas Mission Fellowship), a prominent international organization with a long history of furthering Christianity in Asia, Folk Catholicism is identified as the dominant religion in the Philippines, which they define as "a socio-religious system that blends traditional animistic beliefs and practices with Roman Catholicism." See http://omf.org/asia/philippines/ph-country-profile/.

6. Building on Enriquez's concepts, Pe-Pau argues that "looking at *utang na loób* more closely in the context of Filipino culture, it actually means 'gratitude/solidarity' and is not necessarily a burden as the word 'debt' connotes" (Pe-Pau 2000, 55).

7. The "Gospels" are the foundational books of the New Testament that focus on the life of Christ: Matthew, Mark, Luke, and John.

8. The "two Marys" are Mary the Blessed Virgin and Mary Magdalene. A third Mary, "Mary, the mother of James," also known as "Mary of Cleophas," is depicted along with the other two at the foot of the cross. This "third Mary" was also present at the holy sepulchre (Christ's tomb) on Easter morning and, along with Mary Magdalene, was one of the first to witness his Resurrection.

9. In drugstores, most skin-care products for women contain skin lighteners, whereas on the streets of Metro Manila enormous billboards featuring tall, slender models with translucent white skin and aquiline features look down on a population that is largely differently complected and built. The construction of "mestizo" beauty is largely built around this look, which does not necessarily require Spanish blood insofar as many Chinese have features that fit within this frame of beauty.

10. Consider the many iconic images of Saint Sebastian in which his beauty and youth are essential features of his tragic representation. Unlike the images of other saints enduring terrible torments, Saint Sebastian's beauty rather than his suffering is foregrounded in most representations of the saint from the fifteenth century onward.

11. One of the country's most internationally acclaimed film directors, Mendoza received the award for best director at the 2009 Cannes Film Festival for his film *Kinatay*. Mendoza grew up in the *barangay* and was present for the 2010 *sinakulo*, of which he filmed significant segments.

12. I also witnessed Al Gatmaitan's Christ on alternating nights and he too projected a similar quality of earnestness.

13. The convention of capitalizing "He," "Him," and "His" in reference to Christ appears in the original.

14. Generally spelled *katoto*, this Tagalog word denotes an intimate friend or disciple, going a step beyond an ordinary *kaibigan*.

15. McCormack (2007, 28) notes that though the film was lauded for its linguistic authenticity, the film's Romans speak Latin rather than the dialect of Greek that was the colony's official language at the time of Christ.

16. Mel Gibson himself was the original holder of the "Sexiest Man Alive" title when *People* magazine started the practice in 1985. Jude Law won in 2004, beating out Caviezel, who though beautiful, was evidently not quite as sexy.

17. Though this description may seem similar to public behavior in rituals where a sacrificial victim is pursued through the streets by a mob, there is no evidence of such a practice among the Tagalog people in pre-Christian times.

Chapter 3. *Panata,* Politics, and the *Morions* of Marinduque

1. A "tricycle" consists of a relatively small–cubic centimeter motorcycle attached to a sidecar. The sidecar, depending on its size, can seat up to eight (two in the front, six in a back section), with another place for riding pillion-style behind the driver.

2. The apocrypha are books not included in the standard Bible accepted by the Church. The story of Longinus is found in the Gospel of Nicodemus, a book of doubtful authenticity that includes the "Acts of Pilate," an account of the events associated with the Crucifixion reputedly based on writings by Pontius Pilate.

3. Bernini's sculpture of Longinus is prominently situated outside St. Peter's Basilica in Rome, reflecting his then-accepted position in the pantheon of unofficial saints.

4. The period in which Father Santiago served as parish priest of Mogpog is not entirely clear. Whereas virtually all written sources suggest that he served from the 1870s into the 1880s and possibly beyond, in 2011 the Diocese of Boac announced that recently discovered documents show that his appointment to the post was in 1855, and that he took it up the following year (see http://dioceseofboac.org/?p=1506). It is unusual for a priest to have served for so long in that capacity in a single location, but if Santiago did, that might partly explain why the tradition took such strong hold in Mogpog.

5. In Marinduque, some of my informants referred to the soldier as Longhino rather than the Romanized Longinus.

6. Though this may be true of the other towns in Boac, it is beyond the scope of this research to provide an overview of the practice elsewhere.

7. Danny Mandia, a few years Madrigal's senior, believes that the taunt referred to the fact that during his childhood many of the *morions* were people who worked in the fields planting rice, thus imparting a class basis to the taunt.

8. Teruya Adachi's 1994 account of the *morion* at the Boac festival, based on fieldwork conducted nearly a decade earlier, demonstrates how much the "tradition" has changed over the past generation. Many of the practices he describes from this earlier period were confirmed by my informants, notably Mandia.

9. Though Nicholson marks that distinction by using the term *Moryonan* when describing practices in Mogpog and *morion* when considering how they function elsewhere, I use the term *morion* for the practice throughout the island, insofar as that is how most Marinduqueños and those from outside the region understand the term.

10. This and all subsequent quotes by Carmencita Reyes were taken from a 2007 interview with the provincial governor.

11. In just one of many examples of dynastic politics, Diosdado Macapagal's daughter from his second marriage, Gloria Macapagal-Arroyo, served as president of the Philippines from 2001 to 2010.

12. The Batasang Pambansa replaced the bicameral Congress, which was dissolved when Marcos declared martial law in 1972.

13. Reyes does not translate the Tagalog phrase literally, which would render the meaning closer to "Christ is a God," and not "Christ is the true God," as she states. Tellingly, her "translation" comes closer to the actual view that many in the Tagalog region have of Christ, that he is not merely an intermediary, but rather the "true God."

14. Also known as Minorcan outside the Philippines and the Spanish-speaking world.

15. In the end, Father Diego de Saura was not beatified. Essential to making the case for beatification was demonstrating that he had been martyred. According to Reyes, she "argued that Father Diego de Saura could not have been martyred there because the Moros were never able to come to shore because of the Virgin." Reyes is referring to the Virgin of Biglang Awa, venerated in Boac for scaring away marauding Moors by appearing miraculously at the site of the Boac Cathedral.

16. Imelda Romualdez famously lost the pageant competition in 1953, although after a private meeting with the mayor, Arsenio Lacson, was awarded the title, "Muse of Manila." She met her future husband, then-congressman Ferdinand Marcos, the following year and they were married after a courtship of just a few months.

17. As Beltran quite correctly observes, "The Filipino countryside during the summer months hardly symbolizes the new life that the Resurrection pledges" (1987, 77).

18. This is the total count from extracts of the 1882 edition of the *pasyon* found in Nicholson (2011).

19. Nicanor Tiongson, in the "Moriones" entry in the *CCP Encyclopedia of Philippine Art*, credits Carunungan with authorship.

20. Tanduay is an inexpensive domestic rum. When conducting fieldwork in Marinduque during Holy Week 2013, informants in a seaside *barangay* revealed that a candidate for local representative had been by the previous day with Tanduay for the men of the village. I was given to believe that this, along with vote-buying, was a common practice.

21. At the time of a protracted dispute over the legality of permitting Regina "Gina" Reyes, Carmencita's daughter, as a naturalized American citizen, to take up an elected post as congresswoman from Marinduque, Obligacion's home burned down under suspicious circumstances. Sources in Marinduque tell me that at the time of the incident Obligacion was living in Manila after receiving death threats. His blog, Marinduque Rising, followed the contested election carefully, routinely posting links to news articles and legal documents connected with the dispute (see http://marinduquegov.blogspot.sg/).

22. Reyes lost that election to Jose Antonio N. ("Bong") Carrion, but was returned as provincial governor in 2010 and again in 2013.

23. Alberto Lim served briefly as secretary of tourism from 2010 to 2011, and was widely regarded as a failure in this role, in spite of his "knighthood."

24. A very expensive and large truck with four doors, the Toyota Hi-Ace is a rare sight on the island. In my many trips there I have never seen another one.

Chapter 4. Dancing Natives, Dancing Nation

1. The company's complete name today is the Bayanihan Philippine National Folk Dance Company.

2. The correct spelling is Fischer-Dieskau.

3. This lowland Philippine dance form has long been a crowd-pleaser and will be examined later in this chapter.

4. Though in the 2004 book from which this passage is drawn Santos would appear to be the author, much of the same text appears in the 1987 book on the company in an essay credited to Leticia Perez de Guzman (see Lardizabal et al., 78). The latter publication borrowed freely from the earlier work and all of the writing appears to be the company's communal property, which makes attribution, even when it appears, difficult to ascertain.

5. Angus Maddison's (1983) weighted calculations for 1950, which include British colonies, place per capita income in the Philippines ahead of all nations in East and Southeast Asia except Japan, Malaysia/Singapore, and Hong Kong.

6. This quote appears on the Bayanihan Company's Web site (http://www.bayanihan nationaldanceco.ph/reviews/08review.html). The original source could not be located.

7. Writing in 1943, Carlos P. Romulo, aide-de-camp to General Douglas MacArthur and part of the Philippine government-in-exile, observes that "the Filipino is as yet an unknown quantity to the world. It is easy to misrepresent an unknown quantity. A known one cannot be misrepresented" (Romulo 1943, 80).

8. In his historical essay in the "Philippine Dance" volume of the *Encyclopedia of Philippine Art,* Basilio Esteban "Steve" Villaruz (1994b, 6:18–27) identifies the following troupes that along with Bayanihan have continued the work of Reyes: the Baranggay Folk Dance Troupe, the Leyte Kalipayan Dance Company, the Ramon Obusan Folkloric Dance Group, as well as a number of university and school-based ensembles. He also notes that the Philippine Folk Dance Society "protects and extends Reyes-Aquino's efforts not only through their research but through annual workshops" (6:21). Also cited is choreographer Leonor Orosa-Goquingco (Filipinescas Dance Company), who used native themes and styles in her work, as well as the folk and indigenous-inflected dance in the repertory of Ballet Philippines (formerly CCP Dance Company). The Integrated Performing Arts Guild (IPAG) at the Mindanao State University Iligan Institute of Technology, under the leadership of Steven P. Fernandez, has a long history of sensitively and successfully working with Muslim dance traditions from the south and also a history of international tours. Dance scholar and choreographer Ligaya Fernando-Amilbangsa is well known for her work with *pangalay,* a Muslim dance form. Readers interested in an account of the genealogy of folk dance should consult Theodore Gonzalves' impeccably researched and deeply historicized rendering of this story (2010).

9. The name Francisca Reyes-Tolentino appears when referring to some of her earlier work. Reyes' first husband, professor Ramon P. Tolentino Jr. (d. 1939), was at the time of their marriage the assistant director of the Department of Physical Education and the two worked together closely. In 1947 she remarried and adopted her second husband's surname, Aquino, while retaining her own family name.

10. For insights into Bocobo's contributions to the invention of Philippine folkloric forms see Gonzalves (2010, 37–44, loc. 553–656).

11. Among her influential publications are *Philippine Folk Dances and Games* (1935), *Philippine National Dances* (1946), the six-volume *Philippine Folk Dances* (1953–79), published by the Bureau of Philippine Public Schools, *Fundamental Dance Steps and Music* (1948, 1979), and *Playground Demonstration* (1951). While a complete set of these works is unlikely to exist anywhere, the University of Hawaiʻi library has all of the books by Reyes listed in the Work Cited section.

12. While physical education had been incorporated into the school curriculum since early in the twentieth century, partly a legacy from the American Thomasites and the YMCA movement, from 1950 it became a formal requirement, and also included dance as a standard subject.

13. This quest is invoked by Santos in her book, which starts with the phrase, "In the beginning was the search for the essence of the Filipino soul" (Santos 2004, 1).

14. *Kikay* is a Tagalog word used for a fashionable and sassy young (or youthful) woman. Joaquin is probably using it here playfully and as a term of endearment insofar as Reyes was sixteen years his senior. National Dance artist Leonor Orosa-Goquingco founded the Filipinescas

Dance Company. The company toured extensively internationally in the 1960s and 1970s and her signature work, *Filipinescas: Philippine Life, Legend and Lore in Dance,* is described by Villaruz as "a stylized merger of the ballet and the folk dance with regional dances, tales, and traditions" (1994b, 25). In the larger field of dance in the Philippines she was a towering figure.

15. In the Philippines, "pagan" is the designation most often used when referring to pre-Christian Filipinos or tribes that were Christianized after Spanish colonization. In its domestic usage, the term refers to indigenous spiritual belief systems and practices, many of which continue to have a significant place in people's daily lives. The term does not appear to have the same negative connotations it has in the West.

16. Among the largely Manila-based dance elite, virtually everyone who writes on dance or uses folk material with which to create new dances is referred to as a "scholar" of dance. I suspect that the reason it so important for dancers and those who write about it to position themselves in this manner extends back to Reyes and her foundational stamp on the field. Her practice, reinforced by the dance researchers at PWU, Bayanihan, and the many choreographers and companies that have followed, suggests that once one has had an "authentic" encounter, it is up to the genius of the artist to pass it along through their own mysterious, largely unarticulated internal process.

17. The indigenous suite featuring a compendium of ritual dances from the Bagobo, Subanon, and T'boli people of Mindanao has largely disappeared from the current repertory.

18. The *kulintang* is a percussive instrument from the Muslim south of the country consisting of metal gongs set out on wooden racks, whereas the *gandigans* are the larger, hanging gongs.

19. Loie Fuller (1862–1928) was a devotee of the Art Nouveau movement, and a pioneer of modern dance. Her work featured moments of spectacular visual display, heightened by flowing costumes and swaths of fabric. A *vinta* is a traditional boat found in the Sulu Archipelago and Zamboanga Peninsula, and a *vinta* dance captures the movements of being on this boat as a narrative dance tells the story of the migration by boat to the region.

20. In her "message" on the company's Web site, founder Helena Benitez observes: "But Bayanihan could not have gone from folklore into creative growth without a very critical supportive element: Research. Bayanihan never stopped its research into Philippine folk culture," http://www.bayanihannationaldanceco.ph/helenazbenitez.html#foundersvision (accessed January 2, 2012).

21. Villaruz also uses "ethnic dance" in the same way in his essay, "Philippine Ethnic Dances," on the National Commission for Culture and the Arts Web site, http://www.ncca.gov.ph/about-culture-and-arts/articles-on-c-n-a/article.php?igm=1&i=122 (accessed December 18, 2014).

22. Another source, the online Tagalog Dictionary, translates the term from Tagalog as "folk dance," http://www.tagalog-dictionary.com/index.htm.

23. The term "Igorot" encompasses numerous ethnic/cultural groups, generally those from the Ifugao, Bontoc, Kalinga, Apayo, Ibaloy, and Kankanaey tribes.

24. Jose Fermin (2004) provides a fascinating account of how the Igorot were received at this colonial exposition. See also Scott (1992, 7) for an even earlier example when Bontoc warriors were displayed in the Madrid Zoological Gardens at the Exposition of the Philippine Islands in 1887.

25. The online video promoting the company's 2009 season began with the vigorous dancing of male warriors in the *Kayasig,* described as "a hunting dance" that simulates "warfare movements." The Web site has been changed and no longer shows clips of current work.

26. When I conducted research in Benguet Province during the time of an Adivay festival hosted by the local provincial government in 2007, this dance was presented at three separate dance festivals.

27. In Sally Ness' analysis of the dance *Igorot,* choreographed in 1987 by Agnes Locsin for the Ballet Philippines, she notes how that pan-Cordilleran dance seeks to assert "a positive, respectful appreciation of the cultural communities represented by the Igorot label via an idealized depiction of the material and ritual culture of these groups." *Igorot,* observes Ness, "Can most immediately be read as an attempt to recuperate a colonial stereotype" (Ness 1997, 71).

28. For an analysis of a *canao* sponsored by the provincial government of Benguet, see Peterson (2010).

29. Capuyan suggests that a more apt translation is "Let us see who gets tired" (1994, 25).

30. The dance scholar/practitioner most associated with *pangalay* is Ligaya Ferdinando-Amilbangsa. Hers is the most significant and rigorous dance scholarship on a *katutubo* dance form.

31. A version of the *pamansak* from Mindanao State University can be found at http://www.youtube.com/watch?v=3dKZtdRBSVM. It is interesting to contrast this performance with those presented as authentic at PCNs in North America. See especially http://www.youtube.com/watch?v=mCukpjb1De4.

32. The claim that these dances in the Bayanihan repertory are "royal" appears to go back to the conditions under which they were first presented to PWU dance researchers Lucrecia Reyes Urtala, Henrietta Hofer, and Manuel Cordova who, when visiting Mindanao in the mid-1950s, saw the *singkil* performed by Princess Tarhata of the Alonto clan, and in Davado City they witnessed a presentation of "authentic Muslim dances" at a regional college (de Guzman 1987, 82). While in Dinaing, Cotobato, de Guzman (1987, 82) describes a dance reserved "only for the royal family" presented to them by the daughter of the mayor, Odin Sinuat. It bears noting that the Sinuats and Alontos are two of the region's most prominent clans, and any claims to royal lineage are questionable. Indeed, the region's newly prominent families had much to gain by suggesting that they were the inheritors and preservers of a rich, cultural tradition passed on intergenerationally.

33. "Moro National Liberation Front" entry, *Encyclopedia Britannica* online, http://www.britannica.com. This figure is also cited by Moro National Liberation Front leader Nur Misuari (Steinberg 1994, 342).

34. The Tagalog spelling of "Pilipino" is used here rather than the more commonly used "Filipino."

35. Known in its generic form as *langka,* this martial-arts-inflected movement style is similar to Indonesian and Malay *pencak silat.*

Chapter 5. Time and Transcendence at Ati-atihan

I am grateful to my former colleague Stuart Grant at Monash University for conceptualizing, organizing, and convening the 2010 conference, "Time, Transcendence, and Performance," which exposed me to frameworks used by phenomenologists and philosophers of performance that have enriched my scholarship.

1. I will follow the practice of using Tagalized *karo* from the Spanish word *carro* to denote a float or cart of which the centerpiece is a holy image, statue, or relic. These wheeled carts are pushed through the streets in a religious procession and are typically tiered and made of wood,

but may be covered with stainless steel. At Ati-atihan, *karos* are also lavishly decorated with cut flowers.

2. Though there is no historical evidence of this event, anthropologist F. Landa Jocano (1968) found a similar account of this displacement of peoples in the oral tradition of the highland-dwelling Sulod peoples of central Panay. He also cites the work of H. O. Beyer (1921), who provides similar details about the transactions between migrant Borneans and the island's indigenous inhabitants. The *CCP Encyclopedia of Philippine Art* "Aklanan" entry cites the *Maragtas*, a "historical-fictional account by Pero Monteclaro," written in 1907, noting the lack of verifiable documentation setting out the widespread belief that Bornean *datus* (chiefs) "purchased Panay from the Aeta" (Tiongson 1994a, 1:65).

3. Tirazona uses the word "Aeta," known locally as "Ati." As Aeta and Ati both reflect a collectivity, the word "Aetas" is technically incorrect, though clearly in use nevertheless.

4. The theatrical presentation of the *Barter of Panay*, which has been presented for fifty or more years, essentially recounts this same story, suggesting that the legend had currency long before Benny Tirazona put the specifics down on paper for distribution by the Ati-atihan Management Board.

5. A senior informant who grew up in the nearby town of Numancia notes that there they believe the blackface tradition commemorates how villagers survived a Moro raid by painting their faces black and hiding (Aguirre 2010). In a similar vein, Alejandro Roces observes that in the nearby coast town of Ibajoy, residents believe the town was saved from the Moro by the intercession of the Santo Niño and that the festival's practices date from this event (Roces 1980, 241). The Philippine Airlines Web site, on its page devoted to Kalibo, repeats this narrative: "Besides commemorating the lively thanksgiving festivities between Negrito and Malay settlers, citizens pay homage to their patron saint—the Santo Niño, who miraculously saved the town from pirates" (Philippine Airlines 2010).

6. The most famous effigy of *Hesus Nazareno* is the "Black Nazarene" in the Minor Basilica of the Black Nazarene, also known as the Quiapo Church, in Metro Manila. Significantly, this icon shows Christ bearing the cross toward Calvary, not as the crucified one. Thus it records the act of carrying a burden, inviting a similar act of *panata*, motivated by *damay*.

7. In 2012 Gomez was crowned "Miss Tourism International" at an international pageant in Kuala Lumpur.

8. My own informal poll while living in Manila revealed that a majority of informants thought Cebuanos were the "hottest" people in the Philippines.

9. By suggesting that *pakikisama* is more accurately "fellowship or camaraderie," Bautista is referring back to the framework made famous by Lynch (1962), which reduced it to "smooth interpersonal relations." In its wide circulation since that time, this sociological concept has been seen as a negative value, one holding the country back.

Chapter 6. Street Dance and a *Bayan*-Centered Framework

1. If one were to tally up the number of individuals who participate as dancers, including those who shuffle a few well-worn steps in the countless festivals that take place in every village, town, city, and region in the country, one would end up with a number in the tens of millions. According to the official guidelines of the 2010 Aliwan Fiesta, the national festival for competitive street dancing, groups are to consist of "a minimum of 60 and a maximum of 100 dancers and a maximum of 60 musicians."

2. The terms "fiesta" and "festival" are used interchangeably in the Philippines, although the Spanish term is sometimes used specifically for festivals offering a more party-like atmosphere, as is the case with the Aliwan Fiesta. The Spanish used the term "fiesta" to denote religious celebrations linked to the liturgical calendar or devoted to the local patron saint. Today the word "fiesta" has a broader social application. For instance, economy class on Philippine Airlines is referred to as "Fiesta Class," offering up the promise of "more fun in the Philippines!"

3. The largest, most comprehensive list is probably on the Department of Tourism's Web site, where hundreds of festivals are listed by month and date, accompanied by a short description (see http://www.tourism.gov.ph/sitepages/FestivitiesList.aspx?monthCode=1).

4. See also Resil Mojares's essay, "Cathechisms of the Body" (Mojares 2002, 183–184).

5. Valdemar Smith, writing about conversion of the indigenous peoples of Central America, observes, "The fiesta system, as the basis of Indian social organization, was . . . politically useful to Spanish Society. It provided Indians with personal satisfactions, as well as being a source of religious belief and of harmless social competition. More important, it was an institution that produced leaders, interests, and organizations that were strictly local, turning Indian villages in on themselves rather than out toward one another" (Smith 1977, 11).

6. For instance, although many festivals are devoted to the Santo Niño, only a few are distinctive ones that are nationally famous and might attract tourists because of their scale or unique characteristics.

7. The title of National Artist in a particular branch of the performing arts, instituted during the Marcos era, was in 2003 elevated to an Order, the highest state honor.

8. The complete story of the ways in which dance was placed into the service of the state as it moved toward totalitarianism under martial law is yet to be written. The ways in which citizens might have actively resisted dance or dancing would be fascinating to consider as well.

9. While the 2010 Aliwan Feista guidelines state that "each performance shall be limited to five minutes excluding the entrance and exit," in 2013 the Aliwan publicist, Susan Isoreno-Arcega, suggested it had been increased to six minutes. The 2013 winning routine from the Dinagyang Festival clocked in at nearly seven minutes, suggesting that the time limit may not always be strictly enforced.

10. Sally Ann Ness (1995) writes of how this shift away from ritual dancing in Cebu's Sinulog and toward street spectacle occurred in the early 1980s.

11. I also carried out fieldwork at Aliwan in 2005 and 2010. Some of the venues associated with this event have changed and are likely to continue changing from year to year.

12. These criteria for the 2013 Aliwan Fiesta were supplied by Susan Isorena-Arcega.

13. As we saw in Marinduque, here the category of flamboyant characters is again played by *bakla*, or men who identify as women. Among the topics that might well be investigated further in street dancing are the roles undertaken in these presentations by local *bakla*, who seem to consistently enact the most extravagant characters, those marked as female, or those possessing supernatural powers.

14. Though the execution of the dance is similar to a Chinese Lion Dance, this legend, observes Susan Isorena-Arcega, is unrelated to the Chinese tradition.

15. That "Reyna ng Aliwan" is translated into English as "Miss Aliwan" reflects a common practice. Beauty pageants literally produce "Queens," and in the Filipino version, the name of the event typically reflects this. Yet when rendered into English the less regal "Miss Aliwan" is used.

16. The ways in which Cebu sets itself apart as a more civilized, graceful region is fascinating. As noted in the previous chapter, the exoticization of Cebu is projected externally and seems eagerly embraced by Tagalog people.

17. Tiongson observes that the practice of a festival queen goes back at least as far as 1907, when an American Queen and a Filipino Queen presided over the first Manila carnival (Tiongson 2003, 167).

18. The largely English-competent Manila audience seems to eagerly anticipate verbal blunders from contestants, sniggering and repeating them immediately after they are uttered.

19. The thread on the meaning of *grabe* on Google Answers speaks to the nuances of this word as it is currently being used. See http://answers.yahoo.com/question/index?qid=2007 1017161923AArZx80 (accessed February 12, 2014).

20. During election years, funds are often used for other purposes and indeed this was the reason given for the absence of a contingent from Sinulog in 2013.

21. Flogen's nearly five thousand friends on his very active Facebook page speak to his sizable fan base.

Chapter 7. Juana Change

1. PETA developed this genre of plays that informed and educated audiences through performance.

2. PETA's Women's Theatre Program created and produced two "informances," *Tumaway Kay Libby Manaoag*, and *Libby Manaoag Files: Ang Paghahanap sa Puwertas Prinsesas*, which toured the country from 1998 to 2002.

3. For an account of the group's work during the period of martial law, see Pambid (2010) and Vera (2010).

4. Key PETA members frequently presented workshops at international conferences and undertook residencies. Singaporean theatre workers trained in PETA techniques were placed in "detention" by the government in 1986 for their socially conscious plays, one of which was critical of the treatment of domestic workers (maids) from the Philippines (Peterson 2001). *Iloilo*, the 2013 Singapore film that won the Caméra d'or (for best first feature) at Cannes, also focused on this theme.

5. *Juana C. The Movie*, written by Paner and Rody Vera and directed by Jade Castro, was released in the Philippines in 2013.

6. Local warlords have increasingly relied on heavily armed private armies in the years since World War II to maintain their influence when money alone is not enough.

7. His father, Mariano Marcos, a trained lawyer and educator, also served as the elected congressional representative for the second district of Ilocos Norte.

8. The conflation of the former First Lady with a particular kind of deep, inner beauty, continues to be reflected in her own rhetoric. As she opined in the 2003 documentary, *Imelda: Power, Myth, Illusion*, "Unfortunately people think of beauty as a luxury. People think of beauty as frivolity. No. Extravagance. Beauty is a discipline. Beauty is art, is harmony. In the ideological sense, in the theological sense beauty is god and love made real. The ultimate reach in this world is beauty."

9. Other significant PETA plays from this period that addressed the current political situation unflinchingly were *Panunuluyan* (The Search for an Inn, 1979) and *Pilipinas Circa 1907* (The Philippines during the 1900s, 1982). For a fuller account of activist theatre during this period see Fernandez (1995b), Barrios (2013), and Atienza (2010).

10. Lyrics from GMA News Web site, http://www.gmanetwork.com/news/story/194992/showbiz/sing-along-with-noel-cabangon-s-ako-y-isang-mabuting-pilipino (accessed February 3, 2015). English translation mine.

11. Lyrics from Lyrics Mode, http://www.lyricsmode.com/lyrics/a/alamid/handog_ng_pilipino_sa_mundo.html (accessed February 3, 2015). English translation mine.

12. A 1988 survey conducted by the Institute of Popular Democracy observes that: "Out of 200 House Representatives, 130 belong to the so-called 'traditional political families,' while another 39 are relatives of these families. *Only 31 Congressmen have no electoral record prior to 1971* and are not related to these old dominant families. . . . Of the 24 elected senators, there are a few non-traditional figures but the cast is largely made up of *members of prominent pre-1972 political families*" (cited in Anderson 1988, 27).

13. Tagalog lyrics from the Wikipedia entry on "Bayan Ko," http://en.wikipedia.org/wiki/Bayan_Ko (accessed February 3, 2015). English translation mine.

14. The marriage of Kris Aquino and James Yap was annulled shortly after the 2010 election.

15. The view that Villar was conducting a "traditional campaign" was widely held. There is nothing particularly secretive about running a "traditional campaign." Money is given out quite publicly to residents and/or *barangay* captains for their support.

16. The so-called Hyatt 10 consisted of seven members of then-president Gloria Macapagal-Arroyo's cabinet. Along with three bureau chiefs, they announced their resignation from the government on July 8, 2005, after the president refused to resign over charges of electoral fraud in the 2004 presidential election.

17. For the Juana Change video, see https://www.youtube.com/watch?v=piYRN9–3P4I (accessed February 3, 2015). English translation mine.

18. The ticket was composed of presidential candidate Benigno "Noynoy" Aquino II and vice-presidential candidate Manuel "Mar" Araneta Roxas II. Thus the campaign became popularly known as the "Noy-Mar" campaign.

19. Transcription and English translation is mine, from a video shot at the event.

20. There are numerous clips with raw footage of the Hacienda Luisita massacre on YouTube, and a documentary on the massacre in Tagalog by the Ecumenical Institute for Labor Education and Research can be found at http://www.youtube.com/watch?v=9Ab1ux2DiHw (accessed January 23, 2014).

21. For the "Porsche Video" with English subtitles, see http://www.youtube.com/watch?v=2Rsx4ZVllGM (accessed February 3, 2015).

22. The Anti-Epal App that permits users to pass on photos of offending epals to the electoral commission is available at https://play.google.com/store/apps/details?id=com.kwaninitiatives.instapatrol&feature=search_result#?t=W251bGwsMSwyLDEsImNvbS5rd2FuaW5pdGlhdGl2ZXMuaW5zdGFwYXRyb2wiXQ.

23. The article translates it from its original delivery in Tagalog: "Ako daw ang best example sa FOI. Kung ako na nga, ano mangyayari pag napasa? Kulong ako forever? Ayaw. Pag di napasa, malaya ba ako? Exciting, di ba, ang saya? May oportunidad for big change."

Works Cited

ABC Television. n.d. John Safran's Race Relations, Episode 8 Promotional Video. http://www.youtube.com/watch?v=i9kxChKsAVo. Accessed March 14, 2013.

Adachi, Teruya. 1994. "The Morion as Stranger." In *Cultures and Texts: Representations of Philippine Society,* edited by Raul Pertierra and Eduardo F. Ugarte, 18–45. Quezon City: University of the Philippines Press.

Agamben, Giorgio. 2002. "The Time That Is Left." *Epoché* 7, no. 1: 1–14.

Aguirre, Lia. 2010. Personal interview, Navitas, Aklan, Philippines, January 19.

Alcedo, Patrick. 2007. "Sacred Camp: Transgendering Faith in a Philippine Festival." *Journal of Southeast Asian Studies* 38, no. 1: 107–132.

Alejandro, Reynaldo G. 1978. *Philippine Dance: Mainstream and Crosscurrents.* Quezon City, Philippines: Vera-Reyes, Inc.

Alejandro, Reynaldo Gamboa, and Amanda Abad Santos-Gana. 2002. *Sayaw: Philippine Dances.* Manila: National Bookstore and Anvil Publishing.

Aligan, Rodel. 2001. *Pasyon.* Manila: University of Santo Tomas Publishing.

Anderson, Benjamin. 1988. "Cacique Democracy in the Philippines: Origins and Dreams." *New Left Review* 169 (May/June): 3–31.

———. 1991. *Imagined Communities: Reflections on the Origin and Spread of Nationalism.* Rev. ed. London: Verso.

Angeles, Nolan. 2010. Personal interview, Mandalyuong City, Philippines, March 29.

Aquino, Tricia. 2012. "OMG! Philippines Is the World's Most 'Emotional' Country, Poll Says." Interaksyon Web site. http://www.interaksyon.com/article/48582/omg—philippines-is-the-worlds-most-emotional-country-poll-says. Accessed December 23, 2014.

Arceo-Dumlao. 2012. "Juana Change, Cultural Activist Celdran Lead Anti-Epal Campaign." *Philippines Daily Inquirer* Online, September 30. http://newsinfo.inquirer.net/280282/juana-change-cultural-activist-celdran-lead-anti-epal-campaign. Accessed January 5, 2015.

Arrizón, Alicia. 2006. *Queering Mestizaje: Transculturation and Performance.* Ann Arbor: University of Michigan Press.

Asuncion, Dindo L. 2004. *Marinduque: The Heart of the Philippines.* Marinduque: Provincial Government of Marinduque.

Atienza, Glecy C. 2010. "Spectacle! The Power of Protest Drama During Martial Law." *Kritika Kultura* 14: 120–141.

Bagamaspad, Anavic, and Zenaida Hamada-Pawid. 1985. *People's History of Benguet*. Baguio: Baguio Printing and Publishing.

Bagong Bayani Foundation. n.d. "Bagong Bayani Awards." http://www.bbfi.com.ph/bagong-bayani-awards/. Accessed January 2, 2014.

Baguio City. 1960. *Knowing Our Own Culture: Ifugao, Benguet, Bontoc, Kalinga, Apayao Customs and Beliefs*. Baguio City: Curriculum Workshop, Area B: Customs, Traditions and Beliefs.

Balance, Christine Bacareza. 2008. "Notorious Kin: Filipino America Re-imagines Andrew Cunann." *Journal of Asian American Studies* 11, no. 1: 87–106.

Barba, Eugenio. 1991. "Theatre Anthropology." In Eugenio Barba and Nicola Savarese, *A Dictionary of Theatre Anthropology: The Secret Art of the Performer*, translated by Richard Fowler, 8–22. London: Routledge.

Barker, Nicholas. 1997. "The Revival of Religious Self-Flagellation in Lowland Christian Philippines." http://www2.hawaii.edu/~millado/flagellationfolder/flagellation.html. Accessed November 20, 2006.

Barrios, Joi. 2013. "Theaters of Vigil and Vigilance: A Playwright's Notes on Theater and Human Rights in the Philippines." In *Imagining Human Rights in Twenty-First Century Theatre: Global Perspectives*, edited by Brenda Werth, Florian Nikolas Becker, and Paola Hernández, 195–208. New York: Palgrave Macmillan.

Bautista, Julius J. 2010. *Figuring Catholicism: An Ethnohistory of the Santo Niño de Cebu*. Quezon City, Philippines: Ateneo de Manila University Press.

Bayanihan Philippine Dance Company. 1961. Program of the 1961–1962 U.S. Tour. New York: Columbia Artists Management.

Bayanihan Philippine National Folk Dance Company Web site. 2015. Reviews, 1958–1959. http://www.bayanihannationaldanceco.ph/reviews/08review.html. Accessed January 5, 2015.

Bello, Walden. 2001. *The Future in the Balance: Essays on Globalization and Resistance*. Quezon City: University of the Philippines Press.

Beltran, Benigno P. 1987. *The Christology of the Inarticulate: An Inquiry into the Filipino Understanding of Jesus the Christ*. Manila: Divine Word Publications.

Benitez, Helena Z. 1987. "It's the Magic," In Lardizabal, Guillermo, Santos, and Feleo, eds., *Bayanihan*, 6–7.

Beyer, H. O. 1921. "The Philippines before Magellan." *Asia* 21, no. 10: 864.

Bhabha, Homi K. 1994. *The Location of Culture*. London: Routledge.

Boac, Diocese of. 2011. "Historical Updates." September 12. http://dioceseofboac.org/?p=1506 Accessed December 9, 2012.

Boal, Augusto. 1993. *Theatre of the Oppressed*. New York: Theatre Communications Group.

Bok, Sissela. 2010. *Exploring Happiness*. New Haven, CT: Yale University Press.

Bräunlein, Peter J. 2009. "Negotiating Charisma: The Social Dimensions of Philippine Crucifixion Rituals." *Asian Journal of Social Science* 37: 892–917.

Callois, Roger. 1961. *Man, Play and Games*, translated by Meyer Barash. New York: Free Press of Glencoe.

Cal Performances. 2010. Program Notes performance at Zellerbach Hall, September 24. http://www.calperfs.berkeley.edu/learn/program_notes/2010/pn_bayanihan.pdf. Accessed January 2, 2014.

Cannell, Fenella. 1999. *Power and Intimacy in the Christian Philippines.* Cambridge: Cambridge University Press.

———. 2006. "Reading as Gift and Writing as Theft." In Fenella Cannell, ed., *The Anthropology of Christianity,* 134–162. Durham, NC: Duke University Press.

Capuyan, Stephen, project director. 1994. *Cordillera Ethnic Dances: A Manual for Teachers.* National Commission for Culture and the Arts. La Trinidad: ALA Printing Press.

Casey, Edward. 1996. "How to Get from Space to Place in a Fairly Short Stretch of Times: Phenomenological Prolegomena." In *Senses of Place,* edited by Steven Feld and Keith Basso, 13–52. Santa Fe, NM: School of American Research Press.

———. 2000. *Remembering: A Phenomenological Study.* 2nd ed. Bloomington: Indiana University Press, 1987.

Castro, Christi-Anne. 2011. *Musical Renderings of the Philippine Nation.* Oxford: Oxford University Press.

Catholic Encyclopedia New Advent Website. 2015a. "Sacraments" entry. http://www.newadvent.org/cathen/13295a.htm. Accessed July 14, 2015.

———. 2015b. "Way of the Cross" entry. http://www.newadvent.org/cathen/15569a.htm. Accessed July 14, 2015.

Catholic Online. 2014. "St. Longinus 1st Century Martyr." http://www.catholic.org/saints/saint.php?saint_id=11. Accessed February 4, 2014.

Celdran, Carlos. 2013. Intramuros Walking Tour. April 5.

Cheng, Willard. 2011. "Palace Ignores Juana Change 'Porsche' Video." ABS-CBN News Online. http://www.abs-cbnnews.com/nation/02/02/11/palace-ignores-juana-change-porsche-video. Accessed January 23, 2014.

Chi Viet Giang. 2010. "Don't Worry, Be Happy!" *Deutsche Welle,* September 25.

Click the City.com. n.d. "45 Years Sinakulo in Barangka, Mandaluyong." http://www.clickthecity.com/events/details.php?id=7347. Accessed February 27, 2014.

Clifton, Jon. 2012. "Singapore Ranks as Least Emotional Country in the World." Gallup Poll Web site. http://www.gallup.com/poll/158882/singapore-ranks-least-emotional-country-world.aspx. Accessed December 23, 2014.

Corpuz, Niña. 2013. "Juana Change Steals Show during FOI Hearing." ABS-CBN News Online, September 4. http://www.abs-cbnnews.com/focus/09/04/13/juana-change-steals-show-during-foi-hearing. Accessed January 5, 2015.

Cortez, Alexander. 2010. Personal interview, Quezon City, Philippines, June 2.

CPC News. 2008. "Now on Its 19th Year: *Martir sa Golgota* Not a Simple 'Sinakulo.'" March 22. http://cbcpnews.net/?q=node/1470. Accessed April 3, 2008.

Cruz, Ellis. 2009. "Kalibo Ati-atihan Festival Historical and Religious Background." Unpublished paper distributed by Kalibo Ati-atihan Management Board, Kalibo, Aklan.

Cruz-Lucero, Rosario. 2007. *Ang Bayan sa Labas ng Maynila: The Nation Beyond Manila.* Quezon City, Philippines: Ateneo de Manila University Press.

Csikszentmihalyi, Mihaly. 1992. *Flow: The Psychology of Happiness.* London: Rider.

Csordas, Thomas J. 1990. "Embodiment as a Paradigm of Anthropology." *Ethos* 18, no. 1 (March): 5–47.

Cunanan, Marian. 2007. Personal interview, Lupa, Marinduque, Philippines, April 5.

Day, Tony. 2002. *Fluid Iron: State Formation in Southeast Asia.* Honolulu: University of Hawai'i Press.

de Guzman, Leticia Perez. 1987. "The Bayanihan Story." In Lardizabal, Guillermo, Santos, and Feleo, eds., *Bayanihan,* 77–94.

de la Cruz, Roman A. 2001. *For the Child King: An Image and a Song.* Kalibo, Philippines: Macar Enterprises.

de Quiros, Conrado. 2010. "There's the Rub." *Philippine Daily Inquirer* Online, May 16. http://opinion.inquirer.net/inquireropinion/columns/view/20100516-270436/Quite-another-story. Accessed January 24, 2014.

———. 2012. "Fun." *Philippine Daily Inquirer* Online, January 10. http://opinion.inquirer.net/20905/fun. Accessed February 8, 2014.

Delmendo, Sharon. 2004. *The Star Entangled Banner: One Hundred Years of America in the Philippines.* New Brunswick, NJ: Rutgers University Press.

Diamond, Catherine. 2012. *Communities of the Imagination: Contemporary Southeast Asian Theatres.* Honolulu: University of Hawai'i Press.

Diamond, Jarod. 2004. *Collapse: How Societies Choose to Fail or Succeed.* New York: Penguin Books.

Diaz, Ramona S., director. 2003. *Imelda: Power, Myth, Illusion.* DVD of documentary film. Unitle Pictures, Inc.

Dollete, Monsignor Jose. 2009. Public sermon. Pastrana Park, Kalibo, Philippines, January 18.

Duran-Seco, Liza Kaye. 2009. "DJ Yap Woman's Lenten 'Panata' Comes Full Circle." *Philippine Daily Inquirer,* April 8. http://newsinfo.inquirer.net/inquirerheadlines/metro/view/20090408-198630/Womans-Lenten-panata-comes-full-circle. Accessed December 23, 2014.

Enriquez, Virgilio G. 1986. "Kapwa: A Core Concept in Filipino Social Psychology." In *Philippine World-View,* edited by Enriquez, 6–19. Pasir Panjang, Singapore: Southeast Asian Studies Program, Institute of Southeast Asian Studies.

———. 1989. *Indigenous Psychology and National Consciousness.* Tokyo: Institute for the Study of Languages and Cultures of Asia and Africa.

Fermin, Jose D. 2004. *1904 World's Fair: The Filipino Experience.* Quezon City: University of the Philippines Press.

Fernandez, Doreen G. 1995a. "The Philippine Komedya: Tradition and Revitalisation." In *Traditional Theatre in Southeast Asia,* edited by Chua Soo Pong, 55–72. Singapore: UNiPress for SPAFA, National University of Singapore.

———. 1995b. "The Playbill after 1983: Philippine Theatre after Martial Law." *Asian Theatre Journal* 12, no. 1 (Spring): 104–118.

———. 1996. *Palabas: Essays on Philippine Theater History.* Quezon City, Philippines: Ateneo de Manila University Press.

Fernando-Amilbangsa, Ligaya. 1983. *Pangalay: Traditional Dances and Related Folk Artistic Expressions.* Manila: Filipinas Foundation.

Finin, Gerald. 2005. *The Making of the Igorot: Contours of Cordillera Consciousness.* Quezon City, Philippines: Ateneo de Manila University Press.

Fisher, Jennifer. 2006. "Bayanihan Philippine National Dance Company." *Orange County Register* Online, October 3. http://www.ocregister.com/articles/company-4669-dance-bayanihan.html. Accessed July 17, 2015.

Forbes, John, principal author. 2010. *Arangkada Philippines 2010: A Business Perspective.* Makati City: American Chamber of Commerce.

Foster, Susan Leigh. 2011. *Choreographing Empathy: Kinesthesia in Performance.* New York: Routledge.

Gaerlan, Barbara S. 1999. "In the Court of the Sultan: Orientalism, Nationalism, and Modernity in Philippine and Filipino American Dance." *Journal of Asian American Studies* 2, no. 3: 251–287.

Garcia, J. Neil C. 1996. *Philippine Gay Culture: The Last 30 Years.* Quezon City: University of the Philippines Press.

———. 2003. *Performing the Self: Occasional Prose.* Quezon City: University of the Philippines Press.

Geertz, Clifford. 1980. *Negara: The Theatre State in Nineteenth-Century Bali.* Princeton, NJ: Princeton University Press.

———. 2000. *Available Light: Anthropological Reflections on Philosophical Topics.* Princeton, NJ: Princeton University Press.

Gómez Rivera, Guillermo. n.d. "Why Bayanihan Goes beyond Folklore." http://www.bayanihannationaldanceco.ph/mestizajearticle.html. Accessed January 2, 2014.

Gonzales, Danilo. 2010. Personal interview, Kalibo, Aklan, Philippines, January 18.

Gonzalves, Theodore S. 2005. "The Day the Dancers Stayed: Expressive Forms of Culture in the United States," *Kritika Kultura* 6: 25–44. http://kritikakultura.ateneo.net/issue/no-6. Accessed February 7, 2014.

———. 2010. *The Day the Dancers Stayed: Performing in the Filipino/American Diaspora.* Kindle version. Philadelphia: Temple University Press.

Guillen, Josefina B., ed. 1999–2004. *Sayaw: Dances of the Philippine Islands.* Vols. 1–6. Pasay City, Philippines: Philippine Folk Dance Society.

Guillermo, Lourdes E. 1987. "A Tribute to the Filipino Soul." In Bayanihan Company, *The Bayanihan Experience,* 8–9. Manila: Bayanihan Folk Arts Center.

Heydarian, Richard Javad. 2014. "NoyNoy Stumbles: How Aquino Lost His Way." *Foreign Affairs* Online, October 15. http://www.foreignaffairs.com/articles/142214/richard-javad-heydarian/noynoy-stumbles. Accessed December 16, 2014.

Ilagan, Bonifacio P. 2010. "Crossing Borders: Philippine Activist Theater and Martial Law." *Kritika Kultura* 14: 111–119.

Ileto, Reynaldo Clemeña. 1979. *Pasyon and Revolution: Popular Movements in the Philippines, 1840–1910.* Quezon City, Philippines: Ateneo de Manila University Press.

Invest Philippines. 2010a. "Arangkada Philippines 2010: A Business Perspective." http://www.investphilippines.info/arangkada/. Accessed January 8, 2014.

———. 2010b. "Background (Creative Industries)." http://www.investphilippines.info/arangkada/seven-winners/creative-industries/background-ci/. Accessed January 5, 2015.

Isorena-Arcega, Susan. 2012. *Aliwan: The Festival of Champions.* Manila: Manila Broadcasting Company.

———. 2013. Personal interview, Manila, Philippines, March 11.

Janbog, Chybelle Joy. 2009. Personal interview, Kalibo, Aklan, Philippines, January 15.

Jardin, Nestor. 2009. "Street Dance Festivals: Contemporary Expressions of Local Culture. Paper presented at the University of the Philippines Asian Institute of Tourism Conference on Tourism and Hospitality, October 16.

———. 2010. Personal interview, Manila, Philippines, May 19.

Joaquin, Nick. 1980. "Introduction." In Leonor Orosa Goquingco, *A Great Heritage: The Dances of the Emerald Isles,* 8–9. Quezon City, Philippines: Ben-Lor.

Jocano, F. Landa. 1968. *Sulod Society: A Study in the Kinship System and Social Organization of a Mountain People of Central Panay.* Reprint, Quezon City: University of the Philippines Press, 2008.

———. 2001. *Filipino Worldview: Ethnography of Local Knowledge.* Manila: PUNLAD Research House.

Kalibo Ati-atihan Web site. 2013. Official rules. http://www.kaliboatiatihan.ph/Kalibo-Atiatihan-Activities-2012/rules-and-regulation-of-the-2013-ati-atihan-contest.html. Accessed January 23, 2013.

Kramer, Paul. 2006. *The Blood of Government: Race, Empire, the United States and the Philippines.* Chapel Hill: University of North Carolina Press.

Lardizabal, Jose, Lourdes E. Guillermo, Isabel Santos, and Anita Feleo, eds. 1987. *Bayanihan.* Manila: Bayanihan Folk Arts Center.

Legion of the Marinduque Morions, Inc. 2014. Web site. http://legion09012008.blogspot.nl/. Accessed February 4, 2014.

Levinas, Emmanuel. 1969. *Totality and Infinity: An Essay on Exteriority,* translated by Alphonso Lingis. Pittsburgh: Duquesne University Press.

Lilles, Joven M. 2005. Personal interview, Boac, Marinduque, Philippines, March 25.

Locsin, Agnes. 2008. "Ethnicity and the Choreographer." *Dagmay: Literary Journal of the Davao Writers Guild,* February 17. http://dagmay.kom.ph/2008/02/17/ethnicity-and-the-choreographer/. Accessed January 5, 2015.

Lonely Planet Web site. 2012. "Introducing Philippines." http://www.lonelyplanet.com/philippines. Accessed February 15, 2014.

Lopez, Mellie Leandicho. 2006. *A Handbook of Philippine Folklore.* Quezon City: University of the Philippines Press.

Lynch, Frank. 1962. *Four Readings on Philippine Values.* Quezon City, Phillipines: Ateneo de Manila University Press.

Macaraig, Ayee. 2013. "Ridiculous for FOI not to Pass under Aquino." September 4. http://www.rappler.com/nation/38104-senate-first-foi-hearing-16th-congress. Accessed January 24, 2014.

Macuja-Elizalde, Lisa. 2012. "Looking Back at 10 Years of Aliwan Fiesta." *Philstar* Online, April 2. http://www.philstar.com/arts-and-culture/792995/looking-back-10-years-aliwan-fiesta. Accessed February 12, 2014.

Maddison, Angus. 1983. "A Comparison of Levels of GDP Per Capita in Developed and Developing Countries, 1700–1980." *Journal of Economic History* 43, no. 1 (March): 27–41.

Madrigal, Allen. 2005. Personal interview, Manila, Philippines, April 16.

Malakunas, Karl. 2010. "Filipinos Mark Easter with Whippings." *Sydney Morning Herald,* April 2. http://news.smh.com.au/breaking-news-world/filipinos-mark-easter-with-whippings-20100402-rjcd.html. Accessed July 17, 2015.

Malanes, Maurice. 2000. "Igorot Dances in Their Pure Form" *Philippines Daily Inquirer,* October 3. http://news.google.com/newspapers?nid=2479&dat=20001003&id=tFg1AAAAIBAJ&sjid=gSUMAAAAIBAJ&pg=1712,31962902. Accessed February 17, 2014.

Malitao, Rufino "J. R." Jr. 2007. Personal interview, Boac, Marinduque, Philippines, April 5.

Manalansan, Martin F. IV. 2003. *Global Divas: Filipino Gay Men in the Diaspora.* Durham, NC: Duke University Press.

Mandaluyong City Web site. n.d. "The Sinakulo in Mandaluyong City." http://www.mandaluyong.gov.ph/updates/news/index.aspx?id=154. Accessed March 26, 2010.

Mandia, Danilo Ledesma. 2002. "Moryon: Panata sa Likod ng Maskara." MA thesis, University of the Philippines, Diliman, Quezon City.

———. 2005. Personal interview, Quezon City, Philippines, March 19.

Marche, Alfred. 1970. *Luzon and Palawan,* translated by Carmen Ojede and Jovita Castro. Manila: Filipiniana Book Guild.

Martin, John. 1959a. "Dance: Bayanihan." *New York Times,* October 18.

———. 1959b. "Dance: Filipino Troupe." *New York Times,* October 14.

McCormack, Jim. 2007. "'His Blood Be on Us': Trauma, Transcendence and Masculinity in *The Passion of the Christ.*" *Déjà Vu: antiTHESIS* 17: 23–38.

Merleau-Ponty, Maurice. 1962. *Phenomenology of Perception,* translated by Colin Smith. London: Routledge and Kegan Paul. 2005 Taylor and Francis e-Library edition.

Miranda, Father Dionisio M., SVD. 1989. *Loob: The Filipino Within: A Preliminary Investigation into a Pre-theological Moral Anthropology.* Manila: Divine Word Publications.

Mittelstrass, Jürgen. 2001. "On the Philosophy of Time." *European Review* 9, no. 1: 19- 9.

Mojares, Resil B. 1985. *Theatre in Society, Society in Theatre; Social History of a Cebuano Village, 1840–1940.* Quezon City, Philippines: Ateneo de Manila University Press.

———. 2002. *Waiting for Mariang Makiling: Essays in Philippine Cultural History.* Quezon City, Philippines: Ateneo de Manila University Press.

Montecillo, Paolo. 2012. "Anti-Epal Movement Gets Big Boost from New App." *Philippine Daily Inquirer,* September 18. http://technology.inquirer.net/16704/anti-epal-theres-an-app-for-that. Accessed January 24, 2014.

Montesa, Grino-Caoyonan. 2012. "Retraining Course for IC Choreographers Eyed." *Iloilo News Today,* April 18. http://iloilonewstoday.com/index.php/component/content/article/98-local-news/8861-retraining-course-for-ic-choreographers-eyed. Accessed April 25, 2012.

Moreno, Migui. 2010. Personal interview, Manila, Philippines, June 4.

Morgan, David. 1999. *Visual Piety: A History and Theory of Popular Religious Images.* Berkeley: University of California Press.

Ness, Sally Ann. 1995. "When Seeing Is Believing: The Changing Role of Visuality in a Philippine Dance." *Anthropological Quarterly* 68, no. 1 (January): 1–13.

———. 1997. "Originality in the Postcolony: Choreographing the Neoethnic Body of Philippine Ballet." *Cultural Anthropology* 12, no. 1: 64–108.

———. 2003. *Where Asia Smiles: An Ethnography of Philippine Tourism.* Philadelphia: University of Pennsylvania Press.

Nicholson, Trish. 2011. *Masks of the Moryons: Easter Week in Mogpog.* Kindle edition. Oxted, Surrey: Collca.

Obligacion, Eli. 2002. "The Moriones Festival and Lenten Ritual: Strengthening the Marinduqueño's Cultural Identity." In *Mask: The Other Face of Humanity,* edited by Djoko Moerdiyanto and Rudi Corens, 48–54. Quezon City, Philippines: Rex Bookstore, Inc.

———. 2007. Personal interview, Amoingon, Marinduque, Philippines, April 7.

———. 2013. Personal interview, Boac, Marinduque, Philippines, April 2.

Oiga, Jacky Lynne. 2010. "Pilipinas Kay Ganda." *Manilla Bulletin* Online, November 16. http://www.mb.com.ph/node/287929/pilipina. Accessed November 20, 2010.

Orbista, Carmelo "Nonoy." 2009. Personal interview, Navitas, Aklan, Philippines, January 14.

Orosa-Goquingco, Leonor. 1980. *A Great Heritage: The Dances of the Emerald Isles.* Quezon City, Philippines: Ben-Lor.

Pambid, Manuel D. 2010. "Paano nga ba ang Peta Play: O and nga ba ang isang Play na Matatawag na Petang-PETA." *Kritika Kultura* 15: 195–225.

Paner, Mae. 2010. Personal interview, Makati, Philippines, May 27.

———. 2011. "Pikon talo." *Abante Tonite* Online, May 25. http://www.abante-tonite.com/issue/may2511/edit_juana.htm. Accessed February 14, 2014.

———. 2013. Personal interview, Makati, Philippines, April 3.

Pastor Roces, Marian. 2010. Personal interview, Makati, Philippines, May 27.

Patricio, Joseph Michael. 2010. Personal interview, Amsterdam, December 1.

Pe-Pua, Rogelia. 2000. "Sikolohiyang Pilipino (Filipino Psychology): A Legacy of Virgilio G. Enriquez." *Asian Journal of Social Psychology* 3: 49–71.

Pendon, Lydia C. 2013. "Dinagyang Fest Wins 5th Aliwan Award." *Iloilo Sun Star* Web site, April 15. http://www.sunstar.com.ph/iloilo/local-news/2013/04/15/dinagyang-fest-wins-5th-aliwan-award-277713. Accessed July 17, 2015.

Pertierra, Raul. 1988. *Religion, Politics and Rationality in a Philippine Community.* Quezon City, Philippines: Ateneo de Manila University Press.

———. 2002. *The Work of Culture.* Manila: De La Salle University Press.

Peterson, William. 2001. *Theatre and the Politics of Culture in Contemporary Singapore.* Middletown, CT: Wesleyan University Press.

———. 2010. "Performing Indigeneity in the Cordillera: Dance, Identity and Politics in the Highlands of Luzon." *Asian Theatre Journal* 27, no. 2: 246–268.

———. 2011. "Amazing Show in Manila: 'Fantasy-Production' and Filipino Labor in a Transnational, Transcultural, Transgendered Theatre Enterprise." *Theatre Journal* 63: 587–605.

———. 2012. "The Disciplined Body: Dancing Inmates in Cebu's Provincial Detention and Rehabilitation Centre." *About Performance* 11: 41–62.

Phelan, John Leddy. 1959. *The Hispanization of the Philippines: Spanish Aims and Filipino Responses, 1565–1700.* Madison: University of Wisconsin Press.

Philippine Airlines. 2010. "Kalibo, Aklan." http://www.philippineairlines.com/destinations/the_philippines/kalibo.jsp. Accessed January 10, 2014.
Philippine Daily Inquirer. 2010. "RP Marks Good Friday with Tradition, Rituals." April 2. http://globalnation.inquirer.net/news/breakingnews/view/20100402-262039/RP-marks-Good-Friday-with-tradition-rituals. Accessed February 5, 2014.
———. 2012. "Place for Fun." Editorial, January 9. http://opinion.inquirer.net/20843/place-for-fun. Accessed February 3, 2014.
———. 2013. "Filipino Devotees Reenact Crucifixion of Christ." March 29. http://newsinfo.inquirer.net/381571/filipino-devotees-reenact-crucifixion-of-christ. Accessed February 4, 2014.
Philippine Entertainment Portal. 2009. "*Martir Sa Golgota* by the Manila Mobile Theater." April 8. http://www.pep.ph/guide/3693/Martir-sa-Golgota-to-be-presented-April-8-9. Accessed February 4, 2014.
Philippines, Government of. 2006. "Gloria Macapagal-Arroyo, Sixth State of the Nation Address." July 24. Official Gazette online. http://www.gov.ph/2006/07/24/gloria-macapagal-arroyo-sixth-state-of-the-nation-address-july-24-2006/. Accessed January 2, 2014.
Philippines Civil Service Commission. 1989. Republic Act No. 6713. "Code of Conduct and Ethical Standards for Public Officials and Employees." http://excell.csc.gov.ph/cscweb/RA6713.html. Accessed January 23, 2014.
Rafael, Vicente. 1998. *Contracting Colonialism: Translation and Christian Conversion in Tagalog Society under Early Spanish Rule.* Quezon City, Philippines: Ateneo de Manila University Press.
———. 2000. *White Love and Other Events in Filipino History.* Durham, NC: Duke University Press.
Reyes, Carmencita. 2007. Personal interview, Lupa, Marinduque, Philippines, April 5.
Reyes-Aquino, Francisca. 1952. *Rhythmic Activities.* Manila: N.p.
———. 1953. *Philippine Folk Dances.* Vol. 1. Quezon City, Philippines: Kayumanggi Press.
———. 1957. *Fundamental Dance Steps and Music.* Rev. ed. Manila: Department of Education.
———. 1966. *Philippine Folk Dances and Songs.* Manila: Bureau of Printing for Department of Education, Republic of the Philippines.
———. 1976. *Philippine Folk Dances.* Vol. 6. Manila: N.p.
Reyes-Tolentino, Francisca. 1946. *Philippine National Dances.* New York: Silver Burdett Co.
Richter, Linda. 1980. "The Political Uses of Tourism: A Philippine Case Study." *Journal of Developing Areas* 14, no. 2: 237–257.
———. 1989. *The Politics of Tourism in Asia.* Honolulu: University of Hawaiʻi Press.
Ringrose, David. 1973. "The Impact of a New Capital City: Madrid, Toledo, and New Castile, 1560–1660." *Journal of Economic History* 33, no. 4 (December): 761–791.
Roces, Alejandro R. 1980. *Fiesta.* Hong Kong: Vera-Reyes Inc. Philippines and Toppan Printing.
Rodel, Paul A. 2002. *Culture and Customs of the Philippines.* Westport, CT: Greenwood Press.

Rodriguez, Jon Carlos. 2012. "Juana Change Takes Anti-Epal Drive to the Streets." ABS-CBN News Online, September 7. http://www.abs-cbnnews.com/-depth/09/07/12/juana-change-takes-anti-epal-drive-streets. Accessed January 24, 2014.

Romulo, Carlos P. 1943. *Mother America: A Living Story of Democracy.* Garden City, NY: Doubleday.

Ross, Scott, and Shannon Woodland. n.d. "Jim Caviezel Talks about Playing Christ in 'The Passion.'" The 700 Club. Christian Broadcasting Network Web site. http://www.cbn.com/700club/features/ScottRoss-Jim_Caviezel_1.aspx. Accessed August 19, 2011.

San Juan, Epifanio Jr. 1970. "Prolegomena to Philippine Poetics." *Comparative Literature Studies* 7, no. 2 (June): 179–194.

———. 1996. *The Philippine Temptation: Dialectics of Philippines-U.S. Literary Relations.* Philadelphia: Temple University Press.

———. 2000. *After Postcolonialism: Remapping Philippines–United States Confrontations.* Lanham, MD: Rowman and Littlefield.

———. 2001. "Interrogating Transmigrancy, Remapping Diaspora: The Globalization of Laboring Filipinos/as." *Discourse* 23, no. 3: 52–74.

San Pablo Burns, Lucy Mae. 2013. *Puro Arte: Filipinos on the Stages of Empire.* New York: New York University Press.

Santa Maria, Ofelia T. 2009. "Aussie Documentarian Crucified in Bulacan." *Philippines Online Chronicles,* April 13. http://ec2-50-18-45-155.us-west-1.compute.amazonaws.com/breaking-news/local/1149-aussie-documentarian-crucified-in-bulacan-.html. Accessed November 3, 2013.

Santos, Isabel. 2004. *Bayanihan: A Memory of Six Continents.* Manila: Anvil.

Sauler, Erika. 2014. "'Juana Change' Drops Yellow Color, Joins Call for Aquino's Impeachment." *Philippine Daily Inquirer* Online, July 28. http://newsinfo.inquirer.net/624260/juana-change-drops-yellow-color-joins-call-for-aquinos-impeachment. Accessed December 16, 2014.

Schulman, Michael. 2013. "Bling Ring." *New Yorker,* May 13. http://www.newyorker.com/talk/2013/05/13/130513ta_talk_schulman. Accessed February 4, 2014.

Scott, William Henry. 1982. *Cracks in the Parchment Curtain and Other Essays in Philippine History.* Quezon City, Philippines: New Day Publishers.

———. 1992. *Looking for the Prehispanic Filipino and Other Essays in Philippine History.* Quezon City, Philippines: New Day Publishers.

———. 1994a. *Barangay: Sixteenth-Century Philippine Culture and Society.* Quezon City, Philippines: Ateneo de Manila University Press.

———. 1994b. "Igorot Responses to Spanish Aims: 1576–1896." In *Resistance and Revolution in the Cordillera,* edited by Delfin Tolentino Jr., 1–32. Baguio City: University of the Philippines College Baguio.

Seligman, Adam B., and Robert P. Weller. 2012. *Rethinking Pluralism: Ritual, Experience, and Ambiguity.* Oxford: Oxford University Press.

Seligman, Adam B., Robert P. Weller, Michael J. Puett, and Bennett Simon, eds. 2008. *Ritual and Its Consequences: An Essay on the Limits of Sincerity.* New York: Oxford University Press.

Senate of the Philippines. Fifteenth Congress of the Republic. 2012. Senate Bill 1967. http://www.senate.gov.ph/lisdata/96148089!.pdf. Accessed January 24, 2014.

Shirley, Steven. 2004. *Guided by God: The Legacy of the Catholic Church in Philippine Politics*. Singapore: Marshall Cavendish International.
Simbulan, Dante C. 2005. *The Modern Principalia: The Historical Evolution of the Philippine Ruling Oligarchy*. Quezon City: University of the Philippines Press.
Sisante, Jam. 2011. "PNoy Buys Himself a Porsche." *GMA News* Online. http://www.gmanetwork.com/news/story/210469/news/nation/pnoy-buys-himself-a-porsche. Accessed January 23, 2014.
Smith, Valdemar R. 1977. *The Fiesta System and Economic Change*. New York: Columbia University Press.
Sorillo, Russel. 2010. Personal interview, Manila, Philippines, April 29.
Squires, Pamela. 2012. "Dance Troupe Bayanihan of the Philippines Should Focus More on Folklore Than History." *Washington Post*, November 4. http://www.washingtonpost.com/lifestyle/style/dance-troupe-bayanihan-of-the-philippines-should-focus-more-on-folklore-than-history/2012/11/04/27dea32c-26b6-11e2-ac64-5d52a2c5953e_story.html. Accessed January 2, 2014.
Steinberg, David Joel. 1994. *The Philippines: A Singular and a Plural Place*. Boulder, CO: Westview Press.
Storey, John. 2003. *Inventing Popular Culture*. Oxford: Blackwell.
Symons, Emma-Kate. 2009. "Safran 'Crucifixion' Offends Villagers." *Australian*, April 13. http://www.theaustralian.com.au/news/safran-crucifixion-offends-villagers/story-e6frg6n6-1225697029213. Accessed December 23, 2013.
Tadiar, Neferti Xina M. 2004. *Fantasy-Production: Sexual Economies and Other Philippine Consequences for the New World Order*. Quezon City, Philippines: Ateneo de Manila University Press.
Tan, Michael. 2007. "Pasma, Part 1." *Philippine Daily Inquirer*, August 8. http://opinion.inquirer.net/inquireropinion/columns/view/20070808-81222/%E2%80%98Pasma%E2%80%99. Accessed February 13, 2014.
Taussig, Michael. 1993. *Mimesis and Alterity*. New York: Routledge.
Taylor, Diana. 2003. *The Archive and the Repertoire: Performing Cultural Memory in the Americas*. Durham, NC: Duke University Press.
Tiatco, Sir Anril Pineda. 2010. "*Libad nang Apung Iru* and *Pamaka king Krus*: Performances of Ambivalence in Kapampangan Cultural Spectacles." *Drama Review* 54, no. 2 (T206) (Summer): 91–102.
Tiatco, Sir Anril Pineda, and Amihan Bonifacio-Ramolete. 2008. "Cutud's Ritual of Nailing on the Cross: Performance of Pain and Suffering." *Asian Theatre Journal* 25, no. 1 (Spring): 58–76.
Tiongson, Nicanor. 1983. "What Is Philippine Drama?" Paper presented as official country report at Asian Theatre Festival. Manila, August.
———. 1992. "Dulaan: An Essay on the Spanish Influence on Philippine Theatre." Manila: Special Publications Office, Cultural Center of the Philippines.
———, ed. 1994a. *CCP Encyclopedia of Philippine Art*. 10 vols. Manila: Cultural Center of the Philippines.
———. 1994b. "Lightning Plays." In Tiongson, *CCP Encyclopedia of Philippine Art*, Vol 7: 128.

———. 1994c. "Moriones." In Tiongson, CCP *Encyclopedia of Philippine Art*, Vol. 7: 95.
———. 1994d. "Philippine Theatre." In Tiongson, *CCP Encyclopedia of Philippine Art*, Vol. 7: 18–31.
———. 1994e. "Sinakulo." In Tiongson, *CCP Encyclopedia of Philippine Art*, Vol. 7: 122–128.
———. 1994f. "The Spanish Colonial Tradition." In Tiongson, *CCP Encyclopedia of Philippine Art*, Vol. 7: 44–53.
———. 1999a. *Komedya*. Quezon City: University of the Philippines Press.
———. 1999b. *Sinakulo*. Quezon City: University of the Philippines Press.
———. 2003. "Traditional Festivals of the Philippines." In *Traditional Festivals of ASEAN*, edited by Pham Duc Thanh, 165–181. Hanoi: ASEAN Committee on Culture and Information.
———. 2005. Personal interview, Quezon City, Philippines, April 20.
Tirazona, Benny. 2009a. "Kalibo Ati-atihan: The Peace Pact That Gave Birth to the Philippine Nation." Unpublished paper distributed by the Kalibo Ati-atihan Management Board.
———. 2009b. Personal interview, Kalibo, Aklan, Philippines, January 16.
Transparency International. 2004. "Global Corruption Report 2004." http://www.transparency.org/whatwedo/pub/global_corruption_report_2004_political_corruption. Accessed February 4, 2014.
Trimillos, Ricardo D. 1992. "Pasyon: Lenten Observance of the Philippines as Southeast Asian Theatre." *Essays on Southeast Asian Performing Arts: Local Manifestations and Cross-Cultural Implications,* edited by Kathy Foley, 5–22. Berkeley: Centers for South and Southeast Asia Studies.
Turner, Victor. 1982. *From Ritual to Theatre: The Human Seriousness of Play.* New York: PAJ Publications.
Uy, Jocelyn. 2012. "Anti-'epal' Move: Remember Their Faces, Forget Their Names on Poll Day." *Philippine Daily Inquirer,* September 12. http://newsinfo.inquirer.net/268604/shun-epal-politicians-on-election-day-comelec. Accessed January 24, 2014.
van Erven, Eugène. 1992. *The Playful Revolution: Theatre and Liberation in Asia.* Bloomington: Indiana University Press.
———. 2001. *Community Theatre: Global Perspectives.* London: Routledge.
Veloso, Lou. 2010. Personal interview, Manila, Philippines, April 29.
Vera, Rody. 2010. "Playwriting in the Time of Exigency." *Kritika Kultura* 14: 103–110.
———. 2011. "Who Is Juana Change." Juana Change Web site. http://juanachange.com/v0/Juana_Change.html. Accessed January 24, 2014.
Vergara, Benito M. Jr. 1995. *Displaying Filipinos: Photography and Colonialism in Early 20th Century Philippines.* Quezon City: University of the Philippines Press.
Vergara, Enrique "Ricky." 2013. Personal interview, Boac, Marinduque, Philippines, April 1.
Villaruz, Basilio Esteban "Steve." 1989. *Sayaw: An Essay on Philippine Dance.* Manila: Cultural Center of the Philippines.
———. 1994a. "The Ethnic Tradition." In Tiongson, *CCP Encyclopedia of Philippine Art,* Vol. 5: 28–35.
———. 1994b. "Historical Essay: Philippine Dance." In Tiongson, *CCP Encyclopedia of Philippine Art,* Vol. 5: 18–27.

———. 2006. *Treading Through: 45 Years of Philippine Dance*, Quezon City: University of Philippines Press.

Witcher, Tim. 2010. "Happy Bhutan Proposes a New Global Goal." Agence France Presse, September 21.

Wolters, O. W. 1999. *History, Culture, and Region in Southeast Asian Perspectives*. Rev. ed. Ithaca, NY: Southeast Asia Program Publications.

Woods, Damon L. 2005. "From Wilderness to Nation: the Evolution of Bayan." Colloquium paper. UCLA Center for Southeast Asian Studies. http://www.escholarship.org/uc/item/24m1q0f9. Accessed February 27, 2014.

Yahoo! 2013. Answers to "Why Did Kuya Kim Say 'Ang Buhay Aw Weather Weather Lang'?" http://answers.yahoo.com/question/index?qid=20090531014438AAae3jV. Accessed December 6, 2013.

Yamsuan, Cathy. 2012. "Anti-Epal Bill Reaches Senate Plenary Debates." *Philippine Daily Inquirer*, October 30. http://newsinfo.inquirer.net/298138/anti-epal-bill-reaches-senate-plenary-debates. Accessed January 24, 2014.

Ylanan, Regino, and Carmen Wilson Ylanan. 1974. *The History and Development of Physical Education and Sports in the Philippines*. 2nd ed., rev. and enl. Quezon City: University of the Philippines Press.

Zafra, Nicolas. 1967. *Philippine History through Selected Sources*. Quezon City, Philippines: Alemar-Phoenix Publishing House.

INDEX

Page numbers in boldface type refer to illustrations.

About the Author

William Peterson is a senior lecturer in Drama at Flinders University in Adelaide, Australia, and former director of the Centre for Theatre and Performance at Monash University in Melbourne. He served as foundational academic staff in Theatre Studies at the National University of Singapore, as a lecturer at the University of Waikato, and as associate professor at California State University, San Bernardino. He is the author of *Theatre and the Politics of Culture in Contemporary Singapore* (Wesleyan 2001), and has published widely on performance in the Philippines, Māori and Pākehā theatre in Aotearoa/New Zealand, intercultural theatre practice, and international theatre festivals. His current research focuses on community-based performance in the Philippines and cross-cultural interactions through performance at international expositions. A graduate of Georgetown University's School of Foreign Service, he holds an MA from San Diego State University and a PhD from the University of Texas at Austin, where he studied under the late Oscar Brockett.